8 FREEDOM HEROES

# 8 FREEDOM HEROES

## CHANGING THE WORLD WITH FAITH

BRENNAN R. HILL

ST. ANTHONY MESSENGER PRESS
Cincinnati, Ohio

Excerpts from *My Witness for the Church,* by Bernard Häring, copyright ©1992, reprinted with permission of Paulist Press. Excerpts from *The Moral Vision of Cesar Chavez,* by Frederick John Dalton, copyright ©2003, reprinted with permission of Orbis Books. Excerpts from *Sister Thea Bowman, Shooting Star: Selected Writings and Speeches,* Sister Celestine Cepress, ed., copyright ©1993, reprinted with permission of the author (www.fspa.org). Excerpts from *Long Walk to Freedom,* by Nelson Mandela, copyright ©1994, 1995, reprinted with permission of Little, Brown and Co. Excerpts from *The Struggle Is My Life,* by Nelson Mandela, copyright ©1986, reprinted with permission of Pathfinder Press. Excerpts from *Community & Growth: Our Pilgrimage Together,* by Jean Vanier, copyright ©1979, reprinted with permission of Paulist Press.

Scripture passages have been taken from *New Revised Standard Version Bible,* copyright ©1989 by the Division of Christian Education of the National Council of the Churches of Christ in the U.S.A., and used by permission. All rights reserved.

Cover illustrations by Julie Lonneman
Book design by Mark Sullivan

LIBRARY OF CONGRESS CATALOGING-IN-PUBLICATION DATA

Hill, Brennan.
8 freedom heroes : changing the world with faith / Brennan R. Hill.
p. cm.
Includes bibliographical references and index.
ISBN 978-0-86716-671-2 (pbk. : alk. paper) 1. Liberty—Religious aspects—Christianity. 2. Liberty. 3. Heroes—Biography. I. Title. II. Title: Eight freedom heroes.

BT810.3.H55 2007
270.8092'2—dc22

2007003481

ISBN 978-0-86716-671-2
Copyright ©2007, Brennan R. Hill. All rights reserved.
Published by St. Anthony Messenger Press
28 W. Liberty St.
Cincinnati, OH 45202
www.AmericanCatholic.org

Printed in the United States of America.

Printed on acid-free paper.

07 08 09 10 11   5 4 3 2 1

# CONTENTS

# DEDICATION

To my granddaughters, Marie, Natalie and Lauren. May they always
be free and dedicated to the liberation of others.

# ACKNOWLEDGMENTS

Special thanks to Katie Carroll for her excellent editing in the midst of such trying times; to Abby Colich for the fine job of checking the references; to Darleen Frickman for her able assistance; and to my wife, Marie, for her wonderful suggestions and proofreading.

# INTRODUCTION

This is my second book about "heroes," the first being *8 Spiritual Heroes: Their Search for God.* This direction began for me when I came to realize that many people today, especially the young, have few genuine heroes they can look up to and imitate. Instead, they have celebrities and sports stars, and few of them serve as good role models. With this in mind, I began to teach courses and conduct programs on people that I considered to be genuine heroes, individuals who could provide inspiration and motivation to people in their search for their own mission in life.

In my first book on heroes I chose to examine the individuals in terms of their search for God. I wanted to give a detailed account of the diverse searches that went on in the lives of such people as Mohandas Gandhi, Dorothy Day, Martin Luther King, Jr., Pierre Teilhard de Chardin, Oscar Romero, Edith Stein, Daniel Berrigan and Mother Teresa.

As I explored their searches for God, I found myself engaged in what I call a "biographical theology," a lived theology that comes out of experience and events. Like liberation theology, this is not so much a scholarly or ecclesiastical theology "from above," but rather a "theology from below," that is born in the hearts of individuals. It is a theology that arises out of the human search for ultimacy and meaning. It is a theology that evolves from truth to truth as we live out our lives and search for our true selves, our mission in life and the meaning of the world around us.

In this book I continue with my "biographical theology" and turn to eight new heroes. I focus on their search for freedom—their own personal freedom and their amazing efforts to free others. Freedom is, of course, unique to us as human beings. We are the only creatures on earth who can make choices, make or break promises and determine our own futures and the futures of others. It is an extraordinary power to choose from innumerable possibilities, and the exercise of freedom has been the source of incredible creativity, as well as horrible cruelty and destruction. It has driven the great saints to serve others, and the worst sinners to the holocausts of history.

The great theologian of grace, Piet Fransen, once described authentic freedom as the spontaneous creativity to realize one's own truth. It is the possibility of saying "yes" to the best that is within us, or, as Thomas Merton put it, the choice to be one's true self. From the achievement of personal freedom springs the desire to see to it that our sisters and brothers achieve the freedom they need to develop, unfold and write their own histories. True freedom thus begins with the self, and then moves to the social self and our common mission to free others.

More recently, we have used the language of liberation, and we have seen movements among many groups to free themselves from oppression and gain just human rights. Whether they are people of color, women, gays and lesbians, homeless, illegal immigrants, poor or the millions of refugees around the world, there are many seeking liberation from oppression and injustice. Although each person is created to be free, millions experience unbearable limits to their freedom and are deprived of their basic human rights.

The following are eight stories of outstanding heroes for freedom: people who freed themselves and then set out to free others. They are a diverse group indeed, with regard to gender, race, nationality and cultural background. Together they can teach us much about the mystery of human freedom and they can serve as role models for our own search for freedom, as well as our own dedication to free others.

There is Harriet Tubman, an escaped slave, who dedicated herself to freeing her people from the bonds of slavery, from the wounds of war and from poverty and homelessness. We will encounter Susan B. Anthony, a prim and proper Easterner, who traveled far and wide, even through winters in the mountains, advocating freedom for women's rights, especially the right to vote. We will meet Father Bernard Häring who, in the trenches of World War II, became convinced that human freedom was at the foundation of a moral life and then went on to change the direction of Catholic moral theology and promote renewal in the church. We will discuss the life of a black Catholic nun, Sister Thea Bowman, who spent her years—even the time when she was dying—helping people realize the great culture of African Americans, freeing many from racial prejudice. We will meet Corrie ten Boom, a Dutch woman, survivor of German concentration camps, and one who lost loved ones in these camps. Once released, she spent the rest of her life preaching the gospel of the power of love and forgiveness and revealing from personal experience the destructive power of hatred. We will walk with Cesar Chavez, who spent much of his life leading the freedom movement for migrant workers, conducting strikes, boycotts and painful fasts for their healthcare, better wages, retirement funds, decent housing, good education and fields clear of deadly pesticides. We will study Jean Vanier, who gave up a comfortable life as a professor to live with and serve the mentally disabled. In his efforts to free the disabled from abandonment and abuse, he established homes all over the world where they could live in dignity, surrounded by a loving community. And finally, we will study the life of Nelson Mandela, who spent one-third of his life in jail as punishment for his efforts to free his people in South Africa from apartheid. Once released, he came out of prison healthy and dignified, still committed to bring freedom to his people, ultimately as their president.

It is my hope that your encounter with these heroes will help you, as it has helped me, discover the things from which you need to be freed, as well as come to a better understanding of your own personal calling to free others.

## CHAPTER ONE

## Bernard Häring: Freedom to Be Faithful

It was February 1942. Stalingrad, described as the "battle of the century," was ending with a disastrous defeat for the German forces. The entire German Sixth Army (over three hundred thousand men) had been surrounded. The soldiers who did not die in the battle to control the city were dying from starvation or from the bitter cold in the streets they claimed for Germany. Food, fuel and medical supplies dwindled. Soldiers ate the cavalry's horses to stay alive and abandoned the heavy machinery. Ultimately, the Russians took ninety thousand prisoners. Only a few thousand of those would ever return to their homeland alive. Many surrendered only to be shot (the Russian losses in the battle were equally staggering and prompted revenge). Countless others died of typhoid or were sent to labor in Siberia.

In the midst of all this carnage, a young German priest-medic, Bernard Häring, led a number of his fellow soldiers (many of them wounded), out of the death ring around Stalingrad. Aided by sympathetic Russian peasants, Bernard was able to take his men to an evacuation hospital where they could be treated. He was later captured by the Russians, only to be saved by some heroic Polish citizens who helped him return safely to Germany.

Bernard returned to his Redemptorist community to resume his teaching and writing. He continued his efforts on a work that would revolutionize Catholic moral theology, *The Law of Christ.* Häring had become convinced that Catholic morality had become too clerical, too focused on legalism, obedience and sin. In his new work he returned to the Gospels and early Christian sources and centered on the power of Jesus' love. His work would bring about a sea change in moral theology that would focus on Jesus working in the lives of all of God's people— lay, religious and clerical—as they followed their consciences to make free and responsible choices. He would go on to teach many years in Rome, becoming one of the shapers of the Second Vatican Council, and then would spend the rest of his life spreading the exciting news of church renewal around the world.

## The Early Years

Bernard was born on November 10, 1912, the eleventh of twelve children. He says that he grew up as country boy "under the sun of my family's love."[1] His mother was a wise homemaker; his father was a successful farmer. His parents were deeply in love and had what Bernard calls a "partnership marriage"[2]—rather atypical at that time, particularly in Germany. His mother was known for her extraordinary hospitality, often inviting beggars in for a meal and encouraging the children to bring the infirm or elderly in for some food and care. She was a peaceful woman who disciplined the children herself, to limit the ill-effects of her husband's short temper and inclination toward physical punishment. But Bernard's father was also known for his kindness and often spent his free time writing letters for neighbors who could not do so for themselves.

Bernard describes his parents' faith as "the air we breathed."[3] Both were devout Catholics who read Scripture in the evenings, said the rosary and told stories about holy people. Their devotion, according to Bernard, was always deep and heartfelt, free from the sense of duty and obligation that so typified German Catholicism at that time.

When Bernard was a child, the start of World War I disrupted the family. Two of his older brothers went to war; one was killed and the other returned home seriously ill from lupus. After the war, Bernard followed his father's interest in politics. Widespread unemployment was giving Communism a strong foothold in Germany, and Bernard began studying Communism so that he could speak against it at rallies. He displayed courage in such confrontations, as well as when he wrote a play that warned against the dangers of Communism and its threat to religion.

Hitler came to power in Germany in 1933, when Bernard was twenty-one. Free radios were distributed to all families so that they could listen to the Führer's speeches, but Bernard's father refused to accept the radio "as long as this criminal screams on it."[4] He was later sent to a work camp for leading local farmers in resisting an SS land takeover. Bernard's mother also had the courage to rebel against the Nazis: She refused the Golden Mother's Cross, awarded to women who had large families for the Reich. She said that she had "not borne and raised my children for National Socialism."[5]

Bernard was not much of a student at first, showing much more enthusiasm for his farmwork. By age twelve, though, he had decided to become a missionary and began to take his studies more seriously. Soon he was first in his class and chosen to be valedictorian, but his speech against Nazism was not popular with his teachers, many of whom were dedicated to Hitler.

Inspired by missionaries like Francis Xavier and Matteo Ricci, Bernard looked into joining the Jesuits after graduation. Finding that the Jesuits trained their most gifted students to be professors rather than missionaries, Bernard applied instead to the Redemptorists, who assured him that he would be sent to the missions. He went to the seminary and began studying the language and culture of Brazil.

Few of Bernard's fellow seminary students supported Hitler; those who did were sent home. Most were shocked and angered when Hitler invaded Austria, and disappointed by the lack of resistance offered by many of the Austrian bishops. Soon the seminary began to provide sanctuary to bishops and others hunted by the Nazis. Häring was pleased to know that he had joined an order that valued the freedom to dissent from abusive authority.

The one subject that Bernard tried to avoid in the seminary was moral theology. Moral theology of the time was "the science of sin," closely linked with the legalism of canon law. Bernard preferred the newer approaches championed by scholars such as John Sailer, John Hirscher and Max Scheler. They used the Gospels, an emphasis on virtue and an understanding of psychology to underpin their moral writings.

Just after ordination, though, as Bernard prepared to leave for the missions in Brazil, he was told that the college needed a professor of moral theology. He protested to his superior that teaching such a sub-ject as boring as morality would be his last choice, but he eventually was persuaded by the promise that he would be trained to help change the field of Catholic moral theology. Bernard enrolled at Tübingen University to study for a doctorate and work on the rela-tionship between morality and religion. But just as he was to begin his studies, he was drafted into the German medical corps and sent to France in 1940.

### The War Years

Rather than disrupting his studies, Bernard's years on the front during World War II taught many lessons that would later help him reshape moral theology and also enable him to make significant contributions to the Second Vatican Council. One of the most important of these les-sons he learned during his years working as a medic with the German army was to never blindly obey any authority. He had witnessed first-hand how blind obedience to Hitler had led so many to horrible vio-lence and self-destruction. Conversely, he met many who followed their consciences, often at great risk, to offer love and compassion to others.

Bernard tells many stories of how freedom and courage prevailed over legalism. In his very first assignment to France, it was made clear to him that, under punishment of imprisonment, he would not be allowed to act as a priest. Yet, he soon encountered German officers who were willing to risk severe punishment in order to allow him to celebrate Mass and engage in pastoral care of the soldiers and French citizens. When he was transferred to Poland, Bernard continued to celebrate Mass for his fellow soldiers along with Polish civilians. He was reported, put on trial and narrowly escaped punishment, but still continued his ministry. One of the most moving experiences of Häring's life was presiding at a Mass and penance service for the soldiers as they prepared to enter the horrors of the Russian campaign. When the fighting started, he found himself ministering to his own countrymen (both Catholic and Protestant), as well as to wounded or dying Russian soldiers.

In following his conscience and acting as priest not only for his own but also for the enemy, Häring had placed himself in double jeopardy. Nevertheless, as he ran from Russian tanks and dodged shells, he believed that he was carrying out Jesus' mission. Eventually, he was wounded and hospitalized. As soon as he recovered, Bernard asked to be returned to the Russian front. Even after contracting typhoid there, he remained to serve. The deep faith and gratitude he saw in the faces of the suffering and dying—regardless of belief or nationality—inspired him to carry on. Häring learned to respect the deep and fundamental goodness in human persons.

During Häring's dramatic rescue of many men from Stalingrad, he was impressed by the Russians who risked their own lives to help them. When asked why she took such risks, one mother said: "We have four sons in the Russian army, and each day we pray to our Father in heaven to bring them home healthy and safe. How could we pray to him if we had forgotten that your father and mother, your family and friends, are praying to the same Father for the same thing?"[6]

Häring knew that these people had had their churches torn down and had seen their loved ones sent off to the gulags for practicing their faith. But he saw that nothing could stop the faith and love in their hearts or prevent them from carrying on the Spirit of Christ. He wrote: "I often experienced the faith and Christian love that transcends all the ethnic divisions and the hatreds sown by nationalism, materialism, and the lust for power."[7]

Häring's personal experience with Nazism and Communism also taught him the destructiveness of a godless morality. No matter what ideal was being promulgated—the thousand-year reign of the Aryan super-race or the Bolshevik classless society—the common people were subjected to an absolute authority that demanded blind obedience. In such a system, the state becomes the ultimate good, rather than God, and responsibility is reduced to carrying out destructive duties. Rather than images of God, people are seen as followers of Hitler or comrades of Stalin. Bernard was resolved to spend his life leading people to the only true absolute—God.

During the war, Häring witnessed how the Spirit of Christ prevailed over the powers of evil. He learned that a morality that focused solely on law was impoverished and did not provide the impetus for heroism and self-sacrifice. He resolved to teach a Christian morality that was bold, daring and visionary; one that inspired people to be humbly attentive to the will of God in their lives. He knew that obedience to the will of God can, at times, call for noncompliance with authority—even outright dissent.

He later wrote: "Looking back, I see the difficult experiences of the war as a hard school for discovering the unique value of freedom of conscience…as well as a more mature approach to law, including church law."[8] He was resolved to develop a moral theology whose core concept "would not be obedience but responsibility, the courage to be responsible."[9]

## Returning Home

Bernard was a pastoral priest at heart, so when he returned to his home-land he continued ministering to people suffering from the horrors of war and defeat. During this work, he lived among the destitute and found himself saying Mass and preaching in dance halls and Protestant churches. Soon, he was asked by his superiors to return to Tübingen and finish his studies. There he attended lectures by famous Catholic scholars Karl Adam and Romano Guardini, and with his new interest in ecumenism, studied with Protestant moralists Helmut Thielicke and Friedrich Rückert. He also continued work on his doctoral dissertation on "The Sacred and the Good," an ecumenical study of the relationship of religion to morality. He finished this in 1947, but continued to see morality as connected with pastoral care and thus continued his work with war refugees.

Bernard taught in his own Redemptorist seminary for several years. A brief visit to Rome in 1948 helped convince him of the need for change in Christian moral theology. Visiting the lecture halls of Roman seminaries, he found professors speaking in Latin about minute legal questions around the sacraments and challenging any new theological position as though they were "matadors." Bernard asked himself over and over what had happened to the Good News of Jesus.

In 1953 Bernard was appointed to teach in an exciting new Redemptorist Academy in Rome, founded in part to change Catholic moral theology. Many of his students were veterans of the war who had seen the horrors of battle and were ready for a morality linked to real life. Häring taught two very popular courses: one on spiritual conver-sion as the basis of morality; the other on what Protestant and Orthodox Christians can teach Catholic moral theologians. Meanwhile he finished the work that would set aside the traditional manuals on morality and begin a revolution in Catholic morality. Published in 1954 as *The Law of Christ*, it went through three reprintings and was trans-lated into fourteen languages.

## The Reform of Moral Theology

Many Catholics can remember the "old days" of morality. It was a morality largely focused on the confessional, concerned with lists of sins, both mortal and venial. Confession was to be a review of one's sins: "mortal sins" like missing Mass, eating meat on Friday, or (seemingly) anything to do with sex; and then venial sins like disobeying, getting angry or stealing small items. Priests were usually the only ones trained in this "science of sin," which from the days of the Protestant Reformation was designed to sort out sins, give penances for them, and bring absolution and discipline to the faithful. Training in moral theology was designed to make good confessors, who would bring the laity moral instruction, chastisement and (we hope) mercy. Some confessors interpreted their time in the confessional as an opportunity to judge and to "give hell" to penitents, but fortunately others saw this as an opportunity for counseling, healing and spiritual formation.

Häring realized that Catholic moral theology had become rather legalistic, and had been cut off from Scripture, doctrinal theology, spirituality and liturgy. Generally the focus of such morality was narrowly on the sacrament of penance as a means of bringing the forgiveness needed to be worthy to receive Holy Communion. For many this morality resulted in a scrupulosity toward sin, a fear of hell, an isolated and extremely personal morality, and a preoccupation with obedience. Häring found himself in agreement with the spiritual writer Paul Claudel, who remarked: "Certainly we love Christ; but nothing in the world can move us to like moralism."[10]

## The Law of Christ

In *The Law of Christ*, Bernard Häring set to restore the person of Jesus Christ to the center of Christian morality and to establish his law of love as a way of life. Using the New Testament as his primary source, Häring described Christian morality as "in Christ," that is, freely choosing to allow the very life and Spirit of Jesus to flow through our daily activities, both personal and communal. Convinced that the faithful

Christian is somehow mystically united to Christ, Häring believed that morality should be a response to this intimate relationship through acts of love, compassion, sacrifice and service toward others. Rather than a minimalist keeping of commandments and laws, morality should be a call to conversion to the gospel way of life. Morality is concerned with spiritual growth, to which all Christians are called.

Häring had already laid out his vision in his dissertation, in which he pointed out that religion must go beyond obeying laws and performing rituals. In addition, religion should be experienced as a free, vital and intensifying response to a covenant relationship with God. Truly religious persons freely choose to allow God to act in and through them.

Häring proposed a moral theology that went far beyond training priests to deal with sin to calling all Christians to conversion and holiness. Christian morality is not a static set of laws, but rather a call to follow virtues and values concerned with both private and public matters and addressed to the changing needs of the times. Häring linked morality closely with spirituality and the search for holiness and shifted the emphasis from the Ten Commandments to the Beatitudes and Jesus' two commandments of love.

### Return to the Sources

Häring began his approach to morality with the good news of the Gospels: God extended a loving covenant with all people and manifested this by sending Jesus. "God so loved the world that he gave his only begotten Son..." (John 3:16). In turn, Jesus lived a life of intense love for others and then gave a new commandment "that as I have loved you, you also love one another" (John 15:12). Paul thus continually taught the early communities that it is the love of Christ that drives them. The apostle proclaims to the small community in Galatia: "It is now no longer I that live, but Christ lives in me" (Galatians 2:20). At first, Häring used Scripture as the traditional proof texts, but in later editions and in future work he learned to make use of current biblical studies.[11]

Bernard visited the ancient Christian sources to find the basis for morality. Jesus' invitation to imitate him is stressed in ancient Christian documents like the *Didache* (c. 75) and by many other ancient Christian writers, especially Clement of Alexandria (d. 216), who instructed the early disciples to be a loving community, reflecting Christ in the troubled world in which they live. This tradition was carried on by Augustine (d. 430), who centered morality in a faith and love driven by divine grace and guided by conscience.

Bernard also studied the history of moral theology. He pointed out that this authentic tradition of Christian morality was obscured in the Dark Ages (600–1200), with the appearance of the so-called "penitential books" that were composed to help confessors sort out the various kinds of sins. Fortunately, new life was given to Christian morality in the medieval period, when Bernard of Clairvaux and Thomas á Kempis once again linked morality with spiritual growth, as well as with the work of Thomas Aquinas (d. 1274), who closely related morality with Christian beliefs.

The modern decline of Christian morality began in the fourteenth century with the beginning of a legalistic approach to morality that focused on individual acts rather than on one's relationship with God. Christian morality was separated from Scripture, doctrine and spirituality, and was presented in "dictionaries" of morality that were used by priests. This approach was promoted by the Council of Trent, which defended confession against the Protestant reformers and decreed that the faithful must confess their sins according to number, species and circumstances. Häring observed a confession-centered morality, closely linked with canon law, and saw how manuals, composed in the sixteenth century, had emerged. These sterile manuals, he regretted to say, were still in use in seminaries, and had shown few changes since the days following the Reformation.

Bernard believed that the time had come for a renewal of Christian morality. He followed the foundational work of such scholars as John

Sailer, who developed an approach to morality that helped *all* Christians grow spiritually by following the Gospels. Bernard also was influenced by John Hirscher, who based his morality on a theology of the kingdom of God and who used modern psychology in his approach. At Tübingen, Häring was introduced to many scholars who had returned to Christ and the Scriptures as the basis of morality, and who emphasized the heart as well as the head, the power of grace and the importance of freedom and love in the responsible use of conscience.

**Morality as Response**

Bernard's vision of morality goes beyond the traditional need to "save one's soul," to a dynamic response to God, an encounter with the holy that transforms the whole person. For him, religion was not so much about laws and rituals as it was concerned with a personal and communal response to God's call to holiness. He often pointed to the tragic example of how the churches, concerned only with personal salvation, did not have the social conviction or the courage to stand up to strong dictators and their social and political ideologies during the recent war. Häring wanted moral theology to train Christians to be adults in their faith and actions, and to be engaged in changing their church and their world.

Indeed, Bernard wanted to move the focus in morality from "souls" to whole persons who live in community and who are shaped by the world and history in which they live. As such, persons are dynamic in themselves, and their moral choices are made amid unique and ever-changing circumstances. The shift in morality here is from legal minimalism to freedom and responsibility within an intimate relationship with God. Häring's moral theology, therefore, would be pastoral and serve as a guide for all Christians in their responses to both God and neighbor.

## True Freedom

Häring taught that true freedom originates in Jesus, whose whole life was a "total response to God's grace." The disciple exercises freedom identified with and in unity with this same Christ. Christian morality involves a dialogue with Christ, the neighbor and the world. It is a response in faith, a faith wherein "we freely entrust ourselves to God in a joyous, grateful and humble response to his self-revelation."[12] The disciple acts as one loved by God, as one who is a partner in a divine covenant.

Bernard believed that the true essence of freedom was the "power to do good."[13] Freedom exists in the depths of our personality, where we form our convictions and it is authentic when it proceeds from the true self, the self that carries the image of God. As Häring puts it: "[I]t is precisely when we entrust our whole being to God that we experience the joy and peace of having, at last, found our true selves."[14] Authentic freedom, then, is carrying out the freedom of Christ through the power of grace. This is the freedom that Jesus promised his disciples: "[T]he truth will make you free.... So if the Son makes you free, you will be free indeed" (John 8:32, 36). True freedom is surrendering to the guidance of the Spirit of the Lord. Bernard quotes the apostle Paul: "where the Spirit of the Lord is, there is freedom" (2 Corinthians 3:17).

For Bernard, authentic freedom cannot be controlled or predetermined by absolute authority. It responds to motivation, not command. "True freedom is always fresh and new, always a fresh beginning."[15] Fidelity to such a freedom listens to the situation and "responds creatively with utter freedom."[16] Such freedom must be exercised and nurtured or it will atrophy. If freedom is practiced only in failure, which is sin, it progressively becomes impotent and we become enslaved by our basest drives. True freedom, according to Häring, should liberate us from selfishness and from the "bondage of a...depersonalizing law."[17]

Genuine freedom, according to Häring, should liberate people from the external observance of laws and dogma, which results only in self-seeking, self-perfection and the desire to save only our own souls. Such freedom liberates us from the fears and lack of trust caused by a system of religion that is built on sanctions, laws and controls. It liberates us from oppressive structures, whether political or religious, and gives us the courage to confront and dissent from abusive authority that contradicts the freedom of the kingdom of God. The freedom of Christ also opens our lives to the love and service of others. Häring writes: "When, by faith, we respond with our hearts, our minds and all our energies to Christ, the great conversion and liberation has happened. We join Christ in his love for our fellow men and for ourselves, and in this we find the new freedom."[18]

## Conscience

In his earlier work, Häring viewed the conscience as the moral faculty or power to decide on what is morally good. Later he moved to see the conscience as the secret core and sanctuary of the human person, the deep-down place where God's voice echoes, the place in the heart where the law of God regarding love is written.[19]

The Christian conscience has a voice of its own, a voice that is aware of being personally linked with Christ and guided by his Spirit. For the Christian, the faith and the teachings of Jesus enlighten this conscience. Here the voice of Christ directs the inner yearnings of the heart toward love and goodness. It is the inner voice of the true self, the best self, the self intimately related to Christ. Such a vision of morality is neither external nor legalistic. Conscience here is more than external conformity to laws or obedience to authority. It acts, but it is from the whole person, mind, will, emotions, indeed from the heart.[20] It acts out of a faith that is not committed to a catalog of laws and doctrinal formulations, but a faith that is a profound friendship with Jesus Christ. It goes beyond the limited norms of a traditional morality to a moral spirituality where the Beatitudes and Jesus' laws of love are normative. With this view of conscience, Häring develops a creative and dynamic "pilgrim ethic," which is dedicated to social justice, nonviolence and discerning the "signs of the times."[21]

## Häring at Vatican II

In 1960 Pope John XXIII stunned the church by announcing that there would soon be a worldwide council (Vatican II), which would renew and reform Catholicism. Pope John said that he wanted to open the windows of the church and allow in fresh winds of the Spirit. He wanted the church to return to its gospel roots and to read the "signs of the times"[22] so that it could bring Christ to the modern world. Good Pope John also wanted to reach out to other churches and religions as brothers and sisters.

A conservative commission, headed by Cardinal Alfredo Ottaviani, was appointed to prepare the Council. Häring was excluded, largely because his *Law of Christ* called for a new self-awareness in the church, and he was considered by Ottaviani to be "one of the bad guys." Fortunately, Pope John intervened and insisted that Häring be on the commission because he would be in a position to be very influential in the planning and guiding of the Council. He was a progressive world-class theologian, whose many years of teaching in Rome had provided him with a thorough knowledge of the political system in the Vatican. His experience had taught him that the church is a people with Jesus at their center, that the church has a responsibility to listen to the signs of the times and minister to the world, and that love—a love that transcends national and religious differences—is the central Christian virtue. His fluency in Latin and five other languages enabled him to be a major consultant throughout the Council, as well as an effective spokesperson with the press.

Before the Council opened in 1962, the preparatory commission had developed traditional doctrinal documents, which it presumed would be approved and then the Council would end. To prevent this, Bernard prepared counterarguments to the documents, and gave them to three progressive cardinals, who saw to it that the preparatory commission's work was sent back to the drawing board. As for the commission's work on morality, Bernard was excluded until the very end.

Again, the pope appointed him, but he arrived only to see the documents finished. He could not believe how rigid these documents were and was stunned to see how reactionary the morality was, especially when reading sentences such as: "It is forbidden to say that love is essential for marriage."[23] For Häring, love was the very heart of marriage and the basis for its sacramentality.

## The Document on the Church

When the Second Vatican Council opened, Bernard was appointed to the theological commission that would guide the Council. Along with such outstanding theologians as Karl Rahner, he struggled to see the text on the church rewritten. He wanted it to look at the church as "the people of God," and as "a community of faith," and in that context to discuss the pope and the hierarchy. He would later write, "It appears to me that even today there are still some people who come to grief with 'the Church,' even leave the church, because by church they still understand mainly the Curia and the Vatican."[24]

Bernard strongly opposed those who still saw the church as a fortress possessing all truth, an institution with centralized and absolute authority. During the Council he wrote, "The Church is an organism whose concept of authority excludes lust for power. Ecclesiastical authority is a…service of love, a guarantee of sisterhood and brotherhood in humility." He believed that the church should not use such means as inquisition, temporal power or privileges. He advocated that the church put aside all juridical practices that are not animated by love.[25]

Bernard strongly supported the collaborative, collegial model of church authority. Throughout the Council, he encouraged many cardinals and bishops to make their voices for renewal heard and assisted many of these church leaders in their understanding of the documents. He gave many lectures to bishops' groups on the importance of biblical criticism, the need for the church to admit its mistakes, the importance of eliminating "all legal harshness and all dead formalism" and many other topics.

Bernard was also among those who fought for an active role for the laity in the church. In fact, he was given the personal responsibility to revise the Dogmatic Constitution on the Church to link the laity with Christ's priestly, prophetic and liberating mission. His revised text received unanimous approval.

## Religious Freedom

Bernard was also an advocate for religious freedom, the freedom which gives each person a right to practice his or her own religion without pressure from the state. Häring personally took on Cardinal Ottaviani on this issue and insisted that Jesuit John Courtney Murray, a longtime expert in this area who had been silenced by the Vatican, be allowed to speak to this issue. Murray's presentation and his subsequent work on the document brought on reactionary foot-dragging delays, but eventually ended in a positive vote. In the end, Murray would be one of the framers of this revolutionary document.

## The Church in the Modern World

Toward the end of the first session of the Council, Häring, along with many others, came to believe that the Council was focusing too much on the inner life and institutions of the church. Many of the cardinals and theologians felt that the Council needed a broader vision. Häring addressed the group: "Why this gigantic outpouring of energy on theories and speculations? What is at stake here is nothing less than our helping to shape history and the world, and hence we should above all focus on understanding this world and the 'signs of the times.'"[26]

Ultimately it was decided to produce what would become one of the key documents of Vatican II, the Pastoral Constitution on the Church in the Modern World. Bernard was chosen to be the coordination secretary for the committee that wrote this astounding document. It opens with the now-classic statement: "The joys and the hopes, the grief and the anxieties of men and women of today, especially the poor and oppressed of all types, are also the joys and the hopes, grief and anxieties of the disciples of Christ."[27] Häring insisted that Pope John's focus on the "signs of the times" remain central. Häring guided the committee to consider four themes, which had become paramount for him in his own pastoral work, especially during the war years: marriage and family, culture, politics and peace and justice.

Häring's views on marriage and the family were vigorously opposed by some cardinals and charges against him were brought to the pope. Häring held that love should be given primacy in any discussion about marriage, that the church's laws on marriage were too rigid, and that its view on birth control lacked compassion, kindness and sympathy.[28] He urged that ecumenism and religious freedom be honored in any discussion of mixed-religion marriages, and proposed that only the Catholic party should be required to make promises about the religious education of the children.[29] It was his conviction that church laws should be at the service of divine law, not put on a parallel level.

Häring was undaunted by the vigorous public criticism he received from conservative cardinals and the Holy Office for his views on marriage. When someone remarked to him that he must have suffered when he heard such criticism, he remarked: "No, I expected something like that…. It is not we who are important, but the work which each one should do humbly in his place."[30] He proceeded to broaden the committee's membership to include Bishop Hélder Câmara from Brazil and Bishop Karol Wojtyla from Poland (the latter would become Pope John Paul II). He did this to move away from the dominance of Western European culture and to begin to listen to the voices of other cultures in the world.[31] Only then could the church hope to deal with the many problems of a pluralistic world. Against fierce opposition, Bernard was able to keep the "signs of the times" in the document and also invited women into the discussions. He also faced strong opposition when he refused to condemn Communism, hoping that the Russian Orthodox leaders would be permitted by the Soviet leaders to attend the Council.

As one might suspect, Häring made sure the Second Vatican Council would consider the renewal of moral theology. The statement in the document on priestly formation on such renewal is from his hand. It reads: "Special care should be given to the perfecting of moral theology. Its scientific presentation should draw more fully on the teaching of holy Scripture and should throw light upon the exalted vocation of the faithful in Christ and their mission to bear fruit in love for the life of the world."[32]

Bernard was proud to have served at the Second Vatican Council. The church was now described as the "people of God," which fit his approach to morality, and church structures were reformed, which allowed for more consultation and collaboration. He was particularly pleased with the ecumenism of the Council, noting that "This is no longer a church defending its claim to full possession of all truths of salvation and all moral directives in opposition to other branches of Christianity."[33] The church now valued the spirituality of the Eastern churches and their use of consultative synods. He was pleased to have made contributions to ethics before the Council that opened the way for changes, and he was delighted that the Council had supported his renewal of moral theology. There was now a return to Bible-oriented ethics, rooted in ancient Christian sources and centered on "freedom in Christ." The Council's official approval of biblical criticism as a means for discovering the richness of the Scriptures greatly pleased Bernard.

After Vatican II, Häring updated his eighth edition of the *Law of Christ* in light of the Council. He soon realized, however, that with all the changes in theology, biblical criticism, the sciences and the new "signs of the times," he would have to produce a new work, *Free and Faithful in Christ*. In addition, he decided to spend all his vacations spreading the Council's message of renewal throughout Africa, Asia, Latin America, the United States and other parts of the world. Many thousands flocked to hear lectures and take courses he taught in plain language with a pastoral tone. Bernard had become the missionary he had always wanted to be, a missionary for the renewal of the church throughout the world.

## The Controversy Over Birth Control

The issue of birth control was addressed only in general at Vatican II, for Pope Paul VI reserved final study of these matters for a later commission. Eventually the pope expanded the commission to number seventy-five and to include lay scholars, marriage counselors, therapists and founders of family movements. Patty and Patrick Crowley, who started the Christian Family Movement in the United States, were members. At the heart of the debate was whether or not to enforce the Augustinian view (held by Pius XI) which held that every marital act must be open to procreation. Häring and many others held the view of Saint Alphonsus, that every marital act must express and promote marital love and loyalty, but not necessarily be open to procreation. In the end, only four theologians supported the traditional view against artificial birth control. One of them, Jesuit Father Zalba, said, "What then about the millions of souls which according to the norms we have damned to hell, if those norms were not valid?" To that, Patty Crowley answered, "Do you really believe that God has carried out all your orders?"[34]

The commission recommended that conscience be an individual's ultimate guide in considering the use of artificial birth control. In response, Pope Paul VI set up another commission of cardinals and bishops. Two-thirds of this commission went along with the decision of the first commission. (As an interesting note, Bishop Wojtyla was on the second commission and opposed the use of contraception, but did not show up for the final vote.[35])

At first it seemed that the pope was impressed with the findings of his two commissions. But then Ottaviani asked two conservative theologians to persuade the pope to hold the traditional line (Häring's attempts to see the pope were always thwarted). In the end, Pope Paul on his own, issued the bombshell encyclical *Humanae Vitae*, which along with a fine, progressive theology of marriage, forbade the use of contraception.

Five days before the publication of the encyclical, both *TIME* and *LIFE* contacted Bernard, who was lecturing in the United States. When asked how they got the document, they reported that it had cost them several thousand dollars. Shocked at the "selling" of the document by a Vatican official and stunned by its position, Häring withdrew to a house of prayer in California to pray over the matter. His phone rang constantly as theologians and priests called for advice on dealing with the rigid Vatican position.

Fearing that many would leave the church, yet reluctant to make a public statement, Häring remained silent. When Cardinal Felici in Rome proclaimed that anyone who did not accept the encyclical in obedience and faith should leave the church, Häring realized that he owed it to the people of God to express his views. After a night spent in prayer, he issued this statement:

> Whoever can be convinced that the absolute forbidding of artificial means of birth control as stated by *humanae vitae* is the correct interpretation of divine law must earnestly endeavor to live according to this conviction. Whoever, however, after serious reflection and prayer is convinced that in his or her case a prohibition could not be the will of God should in inner peace follow his/her conscience and not thereby feel her/himself to be a second-class Catholic.[36]

His statement was published in the *New York Times* the following day and later by many newspapers throughout the world. Bernard later said that this might have been the first time a pastoral theological statement had gained such media attention. He eventually wrote two books and several articles to clarify his position on this burning issue.

Now in great demand, Häring was asked to speak to representatives from the American and Canadian bishops' conferences and to gatherings in Europe. Eventually, he was called before the Vatican and was asked to explain his position on birth control and other moral issues. Häring, who had given a retreat to Pope Paul and members of the Curia, was known to love the church and its people. As he once said, "Even when I disagree with anyone, I do it with love and respect." At this point, the Vatican seemed unsure about what to do with this dissenting theologian.

Within a few years, though, the Holy Office had made up its mind. Officials there initiated a "doctrinal trial" against Bernard. Häring had seen many theologians endure similar persecution in Europe and the United States. In fact, many of the leading theologians of Vatican II, as well as many who attempted to carry on renewal after the Council, were banned from teaching, driven out of the church and treated, in Häring's opinion, "as lepers." Careers were destroyed and lives broken simply because these scholars proposed positions with which Rome disagreed.[37] Hans Küng, Edward Schillebeeckx, Charles Curran, Gustavo Gutiérrez, Leonardo Boff, Bob Nugent and Jeannine Gramick are just a few examples. Häring pointed out that there was indeed something like a "rule" that Catholic scholars who produce pioneering work will ultimately fall into the hands of the Holy Office.

The process against Häring began in the early 1970s when he was called into the Holy Office and dressed down for his views. But having been steeled through his experiences with the Nazis and the Soviets, Bernard was not easily intimidated. He challenged his accusers, and they backed off.

In 1975, a formal doctrinal trial was initiated against Häring and approved by Pope Paul VI. The specific issue there was Häring's work on medical ethics. His views, especially on contraception, were attacked in great detail. Charged with undermining the magisterium (teaching authority) of the pope, Häring fired back a series of long and detailed defenses of his work, often citing the error of the charges. The trial lasted four years, and Häring was constantly hounded, even as he waged a life-and-death battle with throat cancer. He reported many sleepless nights and lost considerable weight as a result of the experience.

In 1980 the Congregation of Studies in the Vatican again publicly attacked Bernard for his views on sexual ethics. Though still very ill, he again rose to his own defense and successfully quieted his attackers. Indeed, Bernard paid a steep price for his defense of the free and responsible use of conscience in moral matters.

It is an indication of Bernard's courage and strength that he not only survived the trial, but felt that it "had a liberating effect on me."[38] He says that it was the most creative period of his life. The possibility of death at any moment had freed him from being vulnerable to external pressures. The attacks from the Vatican actually strengthened him and freed him from being cowardly or untruthful in order to save his career. During this period, he also finished *Free and Faithful in Christ*. This new work updated his earlier scholarship in the light of Vatican II and the new "signs of the times."

### The Curran Affair

Many of Häring's students have been attacked and sidelined by the Vatican, but the most celebrated is Father Charles Curran. Curran became a professor of moral theology at The Catholic University of America soon after the Second Vatican Council. Efforts to fire him early on for his liberal views were averted by a strike by the faculty and students. In 1968 he signed a declaration about *Humanae Vitae* and became a spokesperson for the use of conscience with regard to the use of birth control. Curran was seemingly given a pass for the time, but in 1979 a doctrinal trial was opened against him and lasted until 1986. His careful but progressive views on such matters as contraception, masturbation, premarital sex and homosexuality were condemned, and he was asked to recant. Curran, like Häring before him, claimed that his dissent was not in doctrinal matters, but in matters on which the Vatican did not claim infallibility, and that he was carrying out his responsibility as a scholar and exercising his right to academic freedom.

In 1986, Curran was called before Cardinal Josef Ratzinger (now Pope Benedict XVI), the head of the Doctrinal Congregation, for a "colloquium." Curran was accompanied by his former professor, Häring, and by several high-ranking priests from the United States. When Ratzinger appeared, he announced that a decision had already been made. When Curran's defenders asked "Why, then, the colloquium?" they were told that there was a small possibility of changing the decision. Häring made a carefully worded plea for his former student and compromises were suggested. Despite Häring's efforts, Curran soon was told that his position was terminated and that he could no longer teach or write as a Catholic theologian. Father Curran now teaches at Southern Methodist University, but is still an exemplary priest and scholar with a talent for reaching out to the poor. He still makes major contributions to Catholic moral theology. Many believe that he was singled out and condemned in order to put a "chill" into Catholic sexual ethics. If so, the goal has been effectively achieved, for few Catholic scholars have since ventured into such treacherous waters as sexual morality.

**Häring and John Paul II**
Bernard first met Karol Wojtyla when the latter was a bishop at the Second Vatican Council. Häring describes him as genial, gregarious and devoutly dedicated, with an outstanding gift for languages. When Wojtyla was elected pope, Bernard was happy for the church as well as for the Polish people who had been so good to him during the war. As the years passed, Häring admired how John Paul II reached out to the poor and the oppressed, and was also impressed by his outreach to Jews, Protestants, Anglicans, Orthodox and those of other religious traditions.

In 1988 the pope gave an address to moralists in Rome that took rigid positions on sexual morality. This deeply disturbed Bernard, and he wrote that he could hardly believe that this was the same man that he had known at the Council. Saddened, Bernard wrote a letter to the pope, objecting to his setting a moral norm for the use of contraception that allowed for no exceptions, and gave no consideration to personal or social circumstances. Häring further objected to the pope, saying that this norm comes from the hand of God and is confirmed by divine revelation. The pope had said further that to call this into question is refusing to give God obedience, and that to appeal to conscience in this matter is to reject the Catholic concept of the magisterium and conscience.[39] Bernard pointed out that such intransigent views bring crisis, distress and polarization into the church. Häring pleaded, as an old man near the grave, that the pope extend compassion and mercy to the many good Christians who are grievously hurt and even alienated by such rigorism. Receiving no answer, Häring wrote several articles on the matter and went public with his critique.

In 1993 John Paul II published a full encyclical on morality, and Häring would be caught up in a controversy once more. In *The Splendor of Truth*, the pope expressed his alarm at the collapse of the objective moral order and opposed the contemporary emphasis on freedom and conscience. The pope went on to teach that there are certain actions that are evil in themselves, regardless of intention, circumstances or consequences. He based his arguments on revelation and on natural law, which he maintained is of divine origin and is accessible to everyone. As for conscience, its role is "to discover and act on truths which are already present, not to create values and duties of its own."[40]

Bernard answered the encyclical. He began by pointing out that reading it made him very discouraged and brought on a severe health reaction. He observed that the purpose of the document seemed to be "to endorse total assent and submission to all utterances of the pope, and above all on one crucial point: that the use of any artificial means for regulating birth is intrinsically evil and sinful, without exception…."[41] Häring expressed his distress over the way these teachings call for obedience and allow for no dissent, without consideration of the effect all this will have on the faithful. He was amazed that the Vatican made exceptions in regard to killing in matters of self-defense, the death penalty and war, but allowed for no exceptions in the matter of contraception. Moreover, Bernard was alarmed at the absolute trust the pope expressed in his own wisdom coupled by the distrust the document displays toward theologians who disagree. He criticized the pope for supporting such moral theologians as Carlo Caffara, who considered contraception "murder." He opposed the pope for making dissent a punishable church crime, for attempting to take total control over theologians who teach, for controlling the appointment of bishops and for requiring a confession of faith that includes assent to papal teaching in non-doctrinal matters.[42]

Häring pointed out how the vast majority of married people and most moral theologians are unable to agree with the absolute ban on contraception. He directly challenged the pope: "Let us ask our Pope: are you sure your confidence in your supreme human, professional and religious competence in matters of moral theology and particularly sexual ethics is truly justified?"[43] Häring closed his remarks by calling for an end to the "structures of distrust" in the church, which wound so many of its members and prevent effective ecumenism.

### Häring's Final Testimony

The year before he died, Bernard published *My Hope for the Church*, the last of his ninety books, which has been called "his last will and testament for the church he loved and served so whole-heartedly."[44] Here Bernard shows himself to be truly a man of love, courage and freedom in expressing his hopes for the church of the twenty-first century. He deals with a number of key issues: the future of moral theology, the need for new church structures, the role of women in the church, celibacy, ministry to the divorced, peace and justice and ecology.

### The Future of Moral Theology

In describing his vision for the future of moral theology, Häring first expresses alarm at the efforts on the part of John Paul II and the Vatican to restore the old order of morality, where absolute norms and a call for blind obedience are stressed. From his youth Bernard had challenged the legalistic approach to morality. When he wrote his *Law of Christ*, he had hoped to help bring about a shift from an emphasis on law to an emphasis on love, but admits that at that time he had to pass over many points out of deference to church leaders. He says: "I did not have the courage to look all the questions in the eye and give them an unflinching answer."[45] As time passed, he was prepared to deal with many of these questions head-on.

Even early on Häring had moved the audience of moral theology beyond the clergy to include the laity. Now he had a deeper awareness of the "people of God," and knew that moral theology has to be addressed to "the Christian in the present, the Christian in the world and the church, the 'grown up Christian.'" Morality has to deal with real life in a flexible and caring fashion, and the moralist has to be both listener and teacher, aware that there is wisdom in the people, especially in the poor and oppressed. The Catholic moralist must also be ecumenical and be in dialogue with scholars from other churches and other religions.

**New Church Structures**

Bernard expresses distress at the renewed emphasis on the centralization of authority in the church. To him this indicates a lack of trust that the Spirit of God works in and through everyone. He believes that such centralization comes from the drive to control and to make others conform by use of threat and punishment. Häring strongly opposes the Vatican's inquisitional style of imposing authority. He maintains that not only does it stifle scholarship and cause suffering among the members, but it also serves to alienate other churches rather than promote unity.

Häring advocates that the church, long dominated by European culture, give much more autonomy to the churches in Africa, Asia, Latin America and other parts of the world and allow the church to benefit from the variety of these many cultures. His hope for the future of the church is in a renewed subsidiarity wherein the local bishops and their people will be listened to and take part in decision-making. He calls for a return to the way the community of disciples began, as brothers and sisters open to the Holy Spirit together. Bernard writes: "The Church as a whole must be a prophetic voice, a messenger of liberating truth, a place of frank and free exchange of opinion."[46] All methods of forced conformity through brutal measures must cease.

Häring also calls for a downsizing of papal authority. The pope should be, above all, a witness to faith in Jesus Christ and also a pastor who promotes unity amid difference. He should enter dialogue humbly and openly with other leaders and his own people. Bernard felt the pope should be elected through a global process and for a limited term. Moreover, a retirement provision should be established for any pope whose health prevented him from carrying out his responsibilities.

Bernard points out that at the Second Vatican Council two versions of the church and the world clashed, and that a new synthesis of these views took place. He feels that the pope and other church leaders have since tried to destroy this synthesis and restore the church to the way it was before the Council. It is his hope that this reactionary movement would soon end and that an exciting new era in church renewal would open.

### The Role of Women in the Church

Bernard points out that one of the prominent "signs of the times" is the recognition of the equality of women. In this area he believes that the Catholic church has a great deal of catching up to do. At the same time he points out many encouraging trends: that there are many qualified women serving as theologians, religion teachers and catechists in the church today. While Bernard is cautious about when to implement women's ordination, he considers the pope's "definitive" and "infallible" decision on this matter to be "untimely, unnecessary and unhelpful."[47] Häring does not see this declaration to be infallible since it has neither been determined by a Council nor "received" by the people of

God. In a rather startling remark, Bernard writes, "It would be splendid if the pope were to realize and humbly acknowledge his error before he leaves us."[48]

Häring points out that the majority of theologians, particularly exegetes, have resolutely concluded that holy Scripture and sound theology fail to support misgivings about the ordination of women. He calls the traditional arguments against the ordination of women faulty and shameful, often based on the belief that women are inferior and too subservient to aspire to such an "eminent" position as priesthood.[49] He cites that polls in different countries have revealed that only a minority considered ordaining women impossible. Bernard points out that women now run parishes, baptize, preach, lead penance services and attend to the spiritual needs of the sick and dying. He observes that during the war he saw sisters bringing forgiveness to dying soldiers and that "there was indeed a sacramental moment much more profound than those confessions heard by harsh and ritualistic priests."[50] He observes that the crucial point now seems to be whether women can preside at the Eucharist. Häring thinks that this question can be answered by realizing that it is the Holy Spirit who transforms the bread and wine, and that either women or men can invoke the Spirit.

## Celibacy

Bernard valued his own commitment to celibacy, but at the same time says that the suffering he experienced watching those who wanted to be excused from celibacy was worse than what he experienced from his own severe illnesses. He had seen many men who had left the priesthood excommunicated from the church they loved and served, and unable to marry validly. Instead of responding with love and compassion, the church had continued to surround celibacy with a "barbed-wire fence."[51] Häring had pursued this with Pope Paul VI, who knew that John XXIII on his deathbed was saddened by this problem, and had advised Paul to give dispensations. Häring regretted that at the time he was not bold enough to recommend that priests receiving dispensations be permitted to continue in ministry. Instead, they were defrocked, and not allowed to perform even ministries permitted to the laity.

Bernard thought it tragic that John Paul II early on refused such dispensations, declaring that any priest who left and married would be excommunicated. Only after a number of years, due to the pressure of mounting requests and interventions from religious superiors, did dispensations begin to come through once more. Bernard felt the rigid enforcing of sanctions had cost the church many good disciples and their wives.

Häring examined the history of celibacy, not enforced until the Middle Ages. He said that in a past church culture where sex was looked upon as degrading and where there was a strong attraction to the social prestige of the clergy, celibacy was somewhat viable. Today, where there is a positive appreciation for sex and where the clerical life does not hold the prestige it once had, few are attracted to celibacy. Bernard believed that here the church is out of touch with the times and should reconsider its position. He believed that optional celibacy and permission for those priests who have left and married to return to the ministry should be part of the church's future. The communities' rights to pastoral care and the availability of Eucharist demand such changes. Häring was blunt: "Jesus' testament should never be sacrificed to a purely human law, however venerable."[52]

## Ministry to the Divorced

Bernard believed that the church should study the teaching about marriage and divorce in the Eastern churches. The Eastern tradition does not share Rome's contractual view of the sacrament of marriage, but rather sees the marital union as a bond of love and life, which can die. Häring observed, "[W]e could no longer demand that couples persist in the bond of matrimony once it was definitely clear that a concrete marriage not only wasn't serving the spiritual welfare and healthy human relations of the couple, but was actually destroying them."[53]

Bernard pointed out that for the first thousand years the church took a pastoral and flexible approach to divorce and remarriage. It was in the medieval period that the church began to take a hard line and legislate that those marrying after divorce were banned from the sacraments until they did harsh penance. Of course, this was all in a different cultural era, when divorce generally was not acceptable and when those who did divorce could be reabsorbed into the extended family.

Bernard pointed to the different culture of today, when there are new social and economic pressures on marriages, when greater longevity extends the length of marriage, and when divorcees are often isolated from their extended families. He held that with the changing times, new insights into the Scriptures and tradition and modern ecumenical exchange, the time has come for changes. Bernard vehemently opposed the present ban of the remarried from Eucharist unless they abstain from intercourse. He agreed with therapists who observe that such conditions put second marriages in jeopardy. Bernard strongly calls for a much more compassionate and pastoral approach to those who experience the trauma of divorce.

### Peace and Justice

The centerpiece of Bernard's notion of salvation is not washing original sin from souls, but rather "saving the world as a whole from the disastrous chain of violence and counter-violence."[54] He sees the church's future mission to be calling individuals and communities to nonviolence and reconciling love.

Naturally, Bernard saw peace as integrally connected with the recognition of human rights throughout the world and with the saving of the earth. On the latter he writes, "It is a crime that cries out to heaven, a crime against the Creator and all of humanity, when a bare fifth of the human race, namely the inhabitants of the Northern Hemisphere, seize four-fifths of the most valuable raw materials and then spew out nearly four-fifths of the pollution on our planet and destroy its ecological balance."[55] He called upon the church to be a stronger advocate for promoting nonviolence, peace and justice, and care for the earth and its resources.

### Free and Faithful

Bernard Häring died July 3, 1998, in his monastery in Germany. Charles Curran has called Häring "the foremost Catholic moral theologian in the twentieth century and a leading advocate for the Church."[56] Even more fundamentally, Bernard was a missionary, following the calling that he had as a youth. He brought the gospel of Jesus' freedom to the battlefield, to lecture halls, to the Second Vatican Council and to his many readers and listeners all over the world. His main mission was to bring Jesus' message of love and freedom to the "trenches"—both in war and in everyday life. He had his sufferings: witnessing the horrors of war, losing his loved ones, enduring war wounds, suffering from cancer, his humiliating and aggravating doctrinal trials in Rome. But through it all he stood tall, courageous and loving. Above all, Bernard always remained "free and faithful in Christ."

C  H  A  P  T  E  R      T  W  O

## *Cesar Chavez: Freedom for Farmworkers*

It was a warm California day in April 1993. Over fifty thousand people gathered in Delano for the last march with their leader, Cesar Chavez. He had died in his sleep at age sixty-six, at a farmhouse close to his birthplace near Yuma, Arizona. He had just spent several grueling days in court defending the United Farm Workers (UFW) for one of their strikes against the growers. Those marching with the plain pine coffin were a diverse group: politicians, labor leaders, bishops, sisters and priests, celebrities, but mostly "chavistas," migrant farmworkers.

Many had shared other such marches with Cesar before, including the three-hundred-mile march from Delano to Sacramento to push for labor legislation. They recalled how he kept up the pace even though he had a bad back and painful blisters. No doubt there were memories of this small, quiet man showing up at their houses to ask if they would join the union. There were memories of the countless strikes, which he led against the growers. There were high moments of excitement when contracts were signed; the low times of defeat when strikes failed; the painful times when some were beaten, cursed and jailed. They recalled how Cesar was at one point stripped and handcuffed to others. There were the tragic moments when some from their community were brutally killed during the strikes. They recalled how Cesar spoke at the funerals, condemning the injustice, but always urging nonviolence as the answer.

There were the more than fifty boycotts that Cesar organized; the many times he appeared in court to defend his people; his constant struggle to gain higher wages for his people; his tireless efforts to gain healthcare, retirement funds, fields safe from pesticides, good schools and decent shelter. There were Cesar's many long fasts, when he sought to purify himself, show them how to bear suffering and urge them to resist violence.

At the funeral, Cardinal Roger Mahony, archbishop of Los Angeles, declared that Cesar was indeed "a prophet for the world's farm workers." After the Mass, he was buried in La Paz, the UFW headquarters in Keene, California.

**Idyllic Years on the Farm**

Cesario Librado Chavez was born in 1927 in Arizona, but his roots went back to Mexico. His grandfather and namesake Cesario had moved from Mexico and settled there in the Gila Valley in the Arizona Territory, hoping to homestead there after a federal dam was built to provide irrigation. Later on, Cesar always was proud that his family lived there before Arizona was even a state, and thought it ironic that they were often told to "go 'back' to Mexico."[1] Papy Chayo, as his grandfather was called, built a large mission-style hacienda in the valley and settled down with his wife, Dorotea, raising fifteen children together. Cesar's father, Librado, was the only sibling who remained home tending the farm, and when he was in his late thirties he married Juana Estrada.

The couple at first lived in the large family hacienda, but soon Librado wanted his own place. He set up his home behind a grocery store he bought, also running a garage and a pool hall, and continuing to work on his father's farm. Little Cesario was born in the home attached to the grocery. Eventually his father wanted to acquire forty acres of his own and slaved stumping the land, only to have it swindled out from under him. When the Great Depression hit, Librado lost his business and had to move his family back into the large adobe hacienda where his mother, now a widow, lived.

Little Cesario had a happy childhood on his grandparents' farm. He helped with the work, weeding, cultivating, tending the horses and chickens, playing in the fields and climbing trees. The family had plenty of food, fresh vegetables, fruit and chicken. There was no electricity and they had to take water from a nearby ditch, which was common in rural life. Cesario was a cheerful child and enjoyed the freedom to play and enjoy family life on the farm.

School was a chore for the little Cesario, especially because he was treated as a second-class citizen. The teachers shortened his name to Cesar and paddled him if he spoke Spanish or pronounced English with a Spanish accent. He was most confused when he was not allowed to say that he was a Mexican, and when it was insisted that he was an American.

At one point, a severe drought hit the area, preventing the family from putting in a crop. The tax bill and the interest on it kept accumulating, and finally in 1937 it came due. The family was unable to pay and was forced off the land that Librado had farmed for thirty years. One morning a huge bulldozer roared into their farm and leveled the lovely trees and pushed down the corrals. The family members piled their pots and pans, clothes and bedding into their old Studebaker, left the graves of the grandparents and their baby sister, Helen, behind and drove off homeless.

Cesar always remembered that moment. He was ten years old.

I realized something was happening because my mother was crying, but I didn't really realize the import of it at the time. When we left the farm, our whole life was upset, turned upside down. We had been part of a very stable community, and we were about to become migratory workers. We had been uprooted…. If we had stayed there, possibly I would have been a grower. God writes in exceedingly crooked lines.[2]

**Migrant Days**

As the family drove off in their old car loaded with all their possessions, the father tried to cheer everyone up by telling them that they were going to California, a great farming area where there was always a need for many workers to pick the fruits and vegetables. They would work hard and one day buy another farm of their own. The family made their first stop in the fertile Imperial Valley, and Librado approached the labor contractor and asked him for work. They were hired to start the next day in the lettuce fields and were then led to a long, dilapidated shed with a rusty sink and a series of sagging beds with thin, dirty mattresses. This would be their new home for now, and in the future they would at times be forced to live in tents or even in their car. As one migrant put it, "We travel a lot, but we don't see nothun."[3] Migrants might travel for a thousand miles yet be confronted with the same metal shacks and piled-up garbage.

Very early the next morning, the family rose, splashed cold water on their faces, visited a foul outhouse, had a breakfast of fried cornmeal and headed off into the fields. Very small children were left in the shade of a tree, and everyone else was expected to work all day in the burning sun, stooping over to cut the lettuce, picking up batches and putting them in boxes and then carrying the heavy boxes and loading them on trucks. When thirsty, a worker could buy a cola from the grower or have a drink of tepid water from a barrel with a common dipper. Some workers carried flasks of "moonshine," which they swigged to dull their senses. Sometimes there was an outhouse for a bathroom break, but often the workers were forced to relieve themselves right in the fields. Pregnant women often worked the crops; some actually gave birth while on the job in the fields.

The family worked their way through the carrot harvests near Brawley and then migrated to the rich San Joaquin Valley and the grape harvests near Fresno. Carrot-picking might bring in two dollars a day for the family, but in the grape fields they might make twenty dollars among them. But the payoff was not always there. On one occasion the contractor kept stalling them for their money, and after weeks of working, they went to collect their pay only to find that the contractor had left. They were left destitute, and when they complained to the owner he didn't understand Spanish and just shrugged them off. On another occasion, the mother watched the family under a tree while the father was picked up in a truck to pick peas. He worked all day for fifty cents, but had to pay fifty cents for the truck ride. Librado went to work each day, hoping that things would get better, but they never did. He saw new crews or workers coming every day, and from the start they were usually lied to and cheated. All the workers knew well that if they made a fuss, the owner would call the police and have them arrested. They also feared getting blacklisted, preventing them from being hired on other farms. The Chavez family quickly grew to distrust the "Anglos."

In the late fall the family began to work in the cotton fields, where some money could be made if they picked three to four hundred pounds of cotton per day. They worked very hard, trying to get just enough money to get through the winter. Young Cesar found that he had lost the freedom he had on the farm, and now didn't even have any time or place to play.

During the winter the family lived in a tarpaper-and-wood cabin alongside rows and rows of other cabins. Life was miserable in the cold, damp cabins and there was not enough food. Outside, the cabins were surrounded by a quagmire of ditches and ponds, so they had to walk in ankle-deep mud to get to the communal faucets and outhouses. The family was usually overcharged for rent in these shacks. They were also gouged at company stores, and forced to live on credit that had to be "worked off" at a later time.

For years Cesar bitterly missed the ranch of his childhood and thought that being forced to leave it was the start of a sense of rebellion in him. While most migrants had been born into servitude and saw no way out, Cesar had known freedom and was quite clear about what he was missing. Cesar observed, "We were poor, but we had liberty. The migrant is poor, and he has no freedom."[4]

## Experiences of Prejudice

As a migrant, Cesar experienced racial prejudice from which he had been protected while living on the farm. When he shined shoes to make some extra money, he found that he was not allowed to enter the Anglo side of town. The diners had signs that read "White Trade Only," or "No Dogs or Mexicans," and he vividly recalled an incident when he went into a diner and ordered a hamburger, only to be laughed at and told: "We don't sell to Mexicans." It was always painful for Cesar to tell the story of the time when his father stopped the car along a long, dry, desert stretch of road to fill his thermos with coffee at a gas station. He was refused and told to "get out." Cesar would comment: "[W]hat really hurts most of all is to see someone you love rejected like that."[5] Cesar remembered that in those days the Mexicans (and blacks and Filipinos) were treated as people from the other side of the tracks. He felt that his culture and language were under attack everywhere he went.

Cesar recalled an incident when he was first moved to speak out against discrimination. When he was a teenager, he and his family went into a diner to get some food. The young waitress seated them but was soon told by her boss to throw them out. When she protested, her boss threatened to fire her and she came over to the table in tears. The family got up to go, but Cesar hung back and confronted the boss. "Why do you have to treat people like that? A man who behaves like you do is not even a human being!" It was Cesar's first time speaking up, and he said that the waitress had given him the courage because she had treated him like a person.[6]

The Chavez family continued to follow the crops. There was the cotton to be picked and hauled in heavy bundles; the olives that were so small it seemed one could never fill a bucket; the apricots and grapes that required great skill to pick selectively. But the worst seemed to be the work done bent over double with infamous short-handled hoes, thinning crops like cantaloupe. This work was backbreaking, and the pay was twelve cents an hour for an adult and eight cents for a child. These tools outraged Cesar. He once remarked: "When I see crews bent double, working those goddamn hoes...I get mad. There is no need for such cruelty. I never want to see that again, not until I can do something about it."[7]

## Poor Education

Cesar's education during his days as a migrant worker was sporadic and poor. Even though children were not allowed to work in the fields, this was not strictly enforced, and the families needed the work of the youngsters for their income. Cesar attended local schools (about thirty-seven of them throughout the family's travels), where he went largely unnoticed. Migrant children were often forced sit on benches in the back of the classroom, were subject to racial slurs and punished for speaking Spanish. In school Cesar felt as though he didn't exist; he finally dropped out in the eighth grade, discouraged and sullen.

## The First Encounter With a Union

When Cesar was twelve, the family was picking prunes and apricots in the Santa Clara Valley along with thousands of other migrants. When an Anglo from the Congress of Industrial Organizations (CIO) showed up and began discussing the possibility of a strike for higher wages, Cesar's father picked up on the idea with enthusiasm and new hope. The strikers were jubilant the first day of the strike, hoping to pressure the grower, but their hopes were dashed when they saw that they were replaced by other workers. The strikers, for the most part, gave up and went back to work, and the Chavez family had to move on and seek work elsewhere. For the next few years, Librado was willing to join other union attempts to get better wages, but always saw such efforts destroyed by the power of the growers.

## World War II

During the early years of the war, work was sporadic for the Chavez family. To be near the vegetable- and fruit-packing center in San Jose, they moved into a shabby barrio called "Sal Si Puedes" (in English, "Get out if you can"). There were lots of opportunities there for young men to get into crime, and Cesar's parents worried about their sons. Cesar continued to do backbreaking beet-thinning, which he later described as "crucifying." Finally, he had it with that work and at seventeen decided to join the navy before he got drafted.

Cesar disliked the strict regimen of navy life, and often felt that he was treated like a piece of equipment. Racial prejudice followed him into the service. Blacks and Filipinos were given kitchen jobs or were painters, while Mexican-Americans were only allowed to serve as deck-hands. Cesar found the food terrible, and for a farm boy the roaring sea and screaming B-29 Super Fortress bombers were indeed frightening. Cesar would look back on his two years in the navy as the worst years of his life.

It was during this period while on leave and attending the movies with a couple of friends that Cesar had an occasion to rebel. The theaters provided a segregated section for Mexicans, blacks and Filipinos. Cesar suddenly decided to sit in the white area. The manager told him to move, and when Cesar refused the police were called; he was arrested and taken to jail. The police weren't sure how to charge him, so he was threatened with "life imprisonment," lectured and sent home. He later reflected: "It was the first time I had challenged rules so brazenly, but in our own way my family had been challenging the growers for some time. That was part of life."[8]

## Building a New Life

Cesar was honorably discharged from the navy in 1946, and as a fit nineteen-year-old he hoped now to make his mark in the postwar boom. He returned to the vineyards in Delano only to find that things really had not changed for the farmworkers. The barracks were in worse shape than before, and all attempts to strike for better wages and conditions were crushed by bringing in *braceros,* workers who had been brought in from Mexico during the war and given permission to work in California by both governments.

Cesar watched these injustices with frustration and anger and shared with his girlfriend, Helen, his desire to do something for these workers, who were being treated as "mindless, soulless animals."[9] In 1948 Cesar married Helen and they spent their honeymoon exploring the old Spanish missions in Sonoma. The strong adobe buildings reminded Cesar of the hacienda his grandfather had built and the good times of his childhood living there. The spirit of the Franciscans that still lingered over these missions drew him to the simplicity and poverty of Francis as well as to the security and freedom that the friars had given the Native Americans in these missions.

Refreshed and filled with love and hope for the future, the young couple returned to share a small house with Cesar's family, who were leasing a sharecropper's strawberry patch. They all worked seven days a week trying to make ends meet, but to little avail. With their expenses, they were each making about twenty-three cents an hour. Nevertheless, the family struggled on.

Cesar and his brother Richard decided to look for work as lumberjacks in the forests of northern California. The two young men worked there for some time and even built a cabin for themselves. Eventually, however, they were drawn back to be with their loved ones. They returned just as the family quit sharecropping and moved back into a crowded slum at the edge of town. Cesar took a job in a lumberyard and continued to work in the fruit orchards. He was now the father of three, and Helen was expecting another child.

### A New Awakening

Cesar says that his education really began when he met Father Donald McDonnell, a young priest who came to Sal Si Puedes to serve the Mexican-Americans. Father McDonnell started saying Mass in a broken-down shack and quickly became close friends with Cesar. The two repaired and painted the "church," and Cesar drove the young priest around to say Mass in labor camps and prisons. McDonnell was knowledgeable about the economics of work and helped Cesar realize the great divide between the wealthy growers and the poor farmers who did most of the work. The young priest took Cesar to some local strikes and encouraged him to read, a habit which Cesar maintained the rest of his life. Cesar read the labor encyclicals, books about Saint Francis and Mohandas Gandhi, and many books on the history of the farm labor movement. He learned how workers were repeatedly defeated by the often violent strikebreaking tactics of the growers, who were backed by banks, utilities, large corporations and the state and federal governments.

**A Stranger Arrives**

Someone who would dramatically affect Cesar's life was about to enter the picture. One evening in 1952, when Cesar returned dirty and sweaty from working in the apricot groves, his wife told him that a "gringo" (white person) had been there looking for him. Cesar placed little trust in gringos and told his wife not to tell the man where he was. Several days later the man showed up when Cesar was at home and introduced himself as Fred Ross of the Community Service Organization (CSO). Ross explained that a chapter of his organization was helping Mexican-Americans in Los Angeles and wanted to set up a chapter in Cesar's area. Ross wanted to call a meeting with Cesar and some of his friends.

Cesar was suspicious of Ross and decided to shake him up a bit. He invited some of the *pachucos* ("cool" Mexican dudes with baggy suits) he knew to gather for a meeting and told them that at a given signal they should scare Ross. When the group gathered, Ross spoke with passion about the plight of the farmworkers and condemned the oppressive policies of the politicians and police. He said that the poor had to gain power and had to struggle for their rights. Cesar was stunned by Ross's knowledge and sincerity, and seeing that his buddies were itching to cause trouble had to wave them off. Cesar walked Ross to his car and agreed to accompany him to other meetings. He was amazed at how effectively Ross could organize groups and influence legislators and corporate owners. It was a new beginning for young Cesar.

## Work With the CSO

Night after night Cesar would come home from the fields, drop his lunch pail, change his shirt and head out to a meeting in a house, a garage or a hall to watch Ross tell people how to get organized and fight for their rights. The CSO was a project set up by a hard-nosed, brilliant organizer in Chicago named Saul Alinsky. Alinsky ran training sessions on organization and strategies for poor people to obtain their legal rights. Fred Ross was a student of Alinsky's and a man who dedicated his life to social justice for the underdog.

Probably no one noticed the small Mexican in the back of the room, with his coal-black hair slicked down and his sharp eagle's nose, but he was there, taking in everything. Ross spotted the potential in Cesar and wrote this in his notes early on: "Chavez has real push. Understanding. Loyalty and Enthusiasm. Grassroots leadership quality." "I've met the man among men."[10]

Cesar did so well in organizing the Mexican-Americans in Sal Si Puedes that he was put on salary with the CSO and assigned to work in San Jose. He began to organize meetings himself, although hesitantly. Shy by nature and not used to being a leader, he would circle the meeting place several times trying to get up the nerve to go in. Initially he would sit quietly in the back of the room as the people gathered. Only when someone would say, "Where the hell's the guy supposed to be running this deal?" would he then step forward.[11]

Cesar's sincerity and dedication soon began to win over his listeners, and he gained confidence. When the CSO sent him to Oakland to organize a chapter, he moved his family there. Day and night Cesar walked the slums talking to the Mexicans who were in trouble with the police, were unemployed or needed healthcare. He registered them to vote and showed them how to organize and take action for their rights.

Chavez was always more comfortable in the rural areas than in the cities, so he was pleased when he was moved to the San Joaquin Valley to serve the farmworkers. This was his home, and he was on the wavelength of the people here. He could listen patiently to their problems, and felt close to their causes.

Cesar received much opposition to his efforts to organize the workers. This was the McCarthy Era of the early 1950s, and it was easy to accuse anyone organizing workers of being a Communist. Cesar insisted that his views were founded in the social teachings of the Catholic church and that he was in no way associated with the Communists. But the charges kept coming at him, and at one point FBI agents were sent to investigate him.

Cesar spent ten years working with the CSO and became one of the leaders who helped the organization become a force for change throughout California. The organization continued to grow, held conventions and became a growing social force. Hundreds of thousands of Mexican-Americans were registered to vote; tens of thousands were assisted in gaining citizenship. The poor of the barrios were becoming a force to be reckoned with in city halls and other government centers. Cesar was learning the importance of power. He once observed, "I always have had, and I guess I will always have, a firm belief that if you muster enough power, you can move things."[12]

Of course, Cesar's heart remained with the farmworkers and he led a campaign in Oxnard, organizing the field-workers to gain better wages and conditions. Had his hands not been tied by his position in the CSO, Chavez could have at that point actually organized a union for farmworkers. Moreover, he had learned a valuable lesson: "that the growers weren't invincible."[13]

Cesar knew in his heart that his true calling was to free his own people, the farmworkers, from the oppressive situation they were in. When the CSO refused to let him form a union for the workers, he knew it was time for him to resign and give himself entirely to what would later be called "La Causa" ("The Cause"). In 1962 Cesar handed in his notice, moved his family to Delano, and gave himself full-time to organizing farmworkers.

## The History of Farmworkers

Chavez was a student of the history of the farm labor movement in California—a history of oppression, brutality and violence. In the early part of the nineteenth century, local Native Americans were used as near-slaves. They were paid one-half of what other farmworkers received, and when they protested they were often beaten or killed. By the 1860s most of the natives useful for work in California had either been massacred or had died off. The next group used were the Chinese, who had been brought over to build the Southern Pacific Railroad and were available for other work once it was finished. The thrifty and hard-working Chinese were resented by the small-acreage farmers and job-less folks from the gold rush, and therefore barred by the Exclusion Act of 1882. The Japanese were the next to be hired to work the farms. Their hard work and ability to cultivate extremely poor land for themselves eventually brought them resentment; their land was confiscated by the Alien Land Law of 1913. The Japanese were replaced by people from India and by immigrant Europeans. Many of the Europeans were able to gain a foothold and buy land. They would become the forebears of the present-day owners of large tracts of land and major growers.

The Mexicans entered the farm labor market as cheap labor after the Mexican Revolution in 1910. They competed with the Filipinos, who were brought in during the Great Depression, and many of the Mexicans were deported after 1931, when hordes of displaced workers flooded into California from the dust bowl.

By the time of World War II, the Chinese had moved to the cities, the Japanese were in detention camps, the Europeans owned land and the Anglos were either in the service or the factories. There was a farm labor shortage, so the Bracero Program was developed, whereby numerous desperate Mexicans were brought across the border and "allowed" to work for substandard wages. The availability of the *braceros* prevented American farmworkers from striking or making any effective demands on the growers. The Bracero Program was stopped in 1964, but its workers were replaced by "green-carders," immigrants who were allowed into the States to work on the farms. Finally, there were those who came into the country illegally to find work in the fields.

The cycle of oppression, protest and repression had often been repeated. Powerless workers were brought in for low pay and intolerable working conditions. In time each group attempted to rise up, but was quickly put down, and a new group brought in to replace them. Strikes were broken by growers and by the police who worked for them. Violence erupted, heads were split, sometimes strikers were killed and there were mass arrests. Each time the strike was broken, there was a shortage of workers and the next group was brought in. The workers were continuously rendered powerless and expected to simply accept their lot in life. They had no power against agribusiness, which had government, banking and the law on its side.

### Cesar's New Life

As Cesar began his new work, giving up a regular paycheck was both frightening and freeing for him. Still, he was convinced that to serve his people he would have to be free of the fear of insecurity. He said, "If we're afraid of that, then we might as well just forget it…. You and I have got to liberate ourselves."[14] Cesar believed that he could not change anything if he had to hold on to a good job and a good way of life, trapped in affluence and avoiding sacrifice. So he turned down several job offers with the Peace Corps and the AFL-CIO and let it all go. He said that he even though he was scared at first, he soon saw that things were still going all right. Cesar came to realize that "the moon was still there and the sky and the flowers. I began to laugh. I really began to feel free. It was one of my biggest triumphs in terms of finding myself and of being able to discipline myself."[15]

Cesar moved his family to a small rented house in Delano, and used the garage in the back for an office. Delano would put him near his brother Richard and his sister-in-law Rita, and also close to some of the largest growers in California. Richard agreed to work as a carpenter to help support the group and even mortgaged his home to loan Cesar some money. Cesar's wife, Helen, worked in the fields to make money, while Cesar was free to tour the farms, often babysitting his younger children in his car. He would have to cover an area five hundred miles long and eighty miles wide. Soon the group was joined by Dolores Huerta, an energetic mother of seven, Jim Drake, Gilbert Padilla and Cesar's cousin Manuel Chavez, all of whom would become major players in the movement.

Cesar began to appreciate the poverty in which they lived and saw that it gave them power. He said, "We also found out that while it's not beautiful to be poor if you have no choice...it's beautiful to give up material things that take up your time, for the sake of time to help your fellow human beings. I think that has a lot of beauty in it."[16] At times he actually found himself having to beg for gas money and food, but found that also to be a blessing. "We got some of our best members by asking for food. The people who give you their food give you their hearts."[17]

**Starting a Union**

Chavez realized from his study and experience that strikes failed not only because they were not well organized, but more importantly because they were not backed up by a permanent union that lasted after the strike to help the workers organize. So he set out to establish a stable farmworkers' union that would serve the needs of the workers, be an advocate for their causes and plan ongoing actions for change.

Cesar knew from firsthand experience the oppression from which the migrants had to be freed. Most of them worked in a kind of daily slavery like farm animals. Migrants had an infant mortality rate 25 percent higher than the national standard, a 300-percent-higher accident rate, and a life expectancy of only forty-nine years. The extreme irony was that the very people who pick food in abundance often had little to eat themselves. Most thought that it was their fate to suffer and be hungry and were generally filled with a sense of powerlessness and futility. The farmworkers needed a leader to show them that there were reasons for hope and possibilities for a new future.

The list of the farmworkers' needs was long. The migrants needed decent living conditions, fair wages, healthcare, clean water and adequate toilet facilities at home and in the fields. They needed good schools and day care for their children. They needed their own stores and gas stations, where they wouldn't be gouged with high prices; a credit union where they could save their money and secure low-interest loans; a hiring hall where employment would be done legally and fairly; and a pension plan for their retirement years. If migrants were to live freely and with human dignity, there was indeed much work to do.

The opposition would be formidable. There were no federal or state laws allowing farmworkers to engage in collective bargaining. The wealthy growers were running billion-dollar businesses with huge investments in irrigation, fertilizers, machines and pesticides.

Into this struggle of the "poorest of the poor against the strongest of the strong" walked a small, quiet Mexican-American man with an eighth-grade education.[18] He knew full well the seriousness of the situation, was aware of the eighty-five years of failing attempts to gain ground for the farmworker, and understood the gigantic advantages of the opposition. Nonetheless, Cesar was prepared and determined to give his life to free his people. As he put it: "When we are really honest with ourselves we must admit that our lives are all that really belong to us. So, it is how we use our lives that determines what kind of persons we are. It is my deepest belief that only by giving our lives do we find life."[19]

Cesar began slowly and methodically. First he took a three-week tour of the farm areas of the state, stopping to talk with the foremen and the workers. In the evenings he would go around to the barrios and stop in the stores and the bars to talk with the workers and distribute his flyers. In Delano, he went door-to-door calmly explaining the advantages of organizing to Mexican immigrants. He called his organization the National Farm Workers' Association, rather than a "union," because he knew that the word *union* would frighten the workers and anger the growers.

Next Cesar began an eleven-month campaign to cover eighty-seven communities in order to recruit new members. He received various responses. Some people were inspired, some indifferent, others just saw him as another "Commie trouble-maker," a "dumb Mex," or even a "nut." Often Cesar had to deal with deep prejudices against his people. He encountered those who thought that Mexicans were actually created for stooping to work in the fields—many were short and had dark skin to endure the sun. Many growers viewed the Mexicans as trash who had no culture and deserved to be herded around like animals.

As farmworkers became interested in the association, they were asked to pay $3.50 per month in dues, a sizeable commitment for people who made ninety cents an hour. Many couldn't pay, but the willingness of some to give from what little they had inspired Cesar with hope. He later wrote: "Sometimes, fathers and mothers would take money out of their food budgets just because they believed that farm workers could and must build their own union. I remember thinking then that with spirit like that…we had to win. No force on earth could stop us."[20] Initially this money went to support the association, as well as establish a credit union and offer burial insurance for the members.

Cesar and his aides built the National Farm Workers' Association (NFWA) from the ground up, one member at a time. By September 1962, they had 250 members and were ready to call their first convention in an abandoned theater in Fresno. It was a spirited meeting that set goals and planned actions for the betterment of the workers. Cesar always believed that talk is cheap and that only actions get results. He commonly urged his followers: "No philosophizing—do something about it."[21]

The Aztec eagle, which had been designed by Cesar's cousin Manuel, was unveiled at that first meeting. At first, there were some doubts about the symbol, but Cesar declared it to be a sign of hope. Manuel shouted, "When that damn eagle flies, the problems of the farm workers will be solved!" It was clear that La Causa now had a symbol.[22]

## The First Strikes

In 1965 the new farmworkers' association was still struggling to gain members and sustain its funds. It now had twelve hundred members, but only two hundred had paid the dues. Cesar did not think that they were yet ready for strikes, but there were pressures carrying them along into their first *huelga* (strike). In September of that year, the NFWA was asked to join Filipino workers against the grape growers in Delano, the very area where Cesar had set up headquarters. The farmworkers were asking a fifteen-cent-per-hour raise (up from $1.25) and a ten-cent-per-box-picked raise. Cesar was sympathetic to their modest requests but hesitant to enter a strike this early. But his style of leadership was to listen and let the people lead, so he called his members for a vote. A vote was taken and the cry of *"La Huelga"* went up throughout the hall. The fledgling association would now be a visible movement, openly picketing the wealthy growers.

The strike was a costly decision. The NFWA lost a $268,000 federal grant since it was illegal for farmworkers to strike. The local parish, Our Lady of Guadalupe, forbade the association to use its hall for meetings, and the growers attempted to break the strike by bringing in green-carders and illegal immigrants. Day after day the migrants would get up early and picket the miles of vineyards. Cesar believed that the picket line was the best school for organizers. He held that the line is where workers learn to make their commitment, and where they learn to gain their voice and speak out. Cesar could be poetic when speaking about picket lines: "Oh, the picket line is a beautiful thing, because it does something to a human being."[23] Cesar maintained that picketers were doing something for themselves and that this made them happy, while at the same time freeing them from self-pity. It also made them friendly and more open with their fellow strikers, as well as loyal to the cause. Strikers had taken their lives in their own hands, and they no longer needed to feel powerless or afraid.

## The First Violence

The striking farmworkers' association also got its first taste of violence from the growers. Ranch foremen marched around the perimeters of the vineyards, armed with shotguns and shooting at strike signs and car windows. While the police watched, the owners of the fields elbowed strikers, kicked them, stomped on their feet, spit on them, cursed them, brushed them dangerously with speeding trucks and sprayed them with chemicals. Cesar watched with indignation. He would shout out defiantly, "You people value your damn money more than you value human life!"[24]

The farmworker movement was no stranger to violence. Over the years many strikers had been hauled off to jail, beaten and even killed. One of the worst incidents was in 1933, when striking cotton-pickers were attacked by an armed posse—two strikers were killed and eight were wounded. Cesar felt the natural inclination to strike back, but he had quietly prepared his followers to avoid violence.

## The Nonviolent Response

Cesar was an ardent follower of Gandhi and wholeheartedly accepted his teachings on nonviolence. Cesar believed in the sanctity of human life and completely opposed the taking of life in any struggle, whether a labor movement or a war. He admitted that violence could get results, but believed that ultimately it fails because it does not earn respect for the one doing the violence. He deplored the Mexican tradition of "machismo," or manliness through violence, and declared that his union would not allow violence. He said, "*La Causa* must not risk a single life on either side, because it was a cause, not just a union, dealing with people not as green cards or social security numbers but as human beings, one by one."[25]

Cesar saw different dimensions to the violence inflicted on the farmworkers. There was the day-to-day violence that included beatings, threats, insults, attacks by dogs, people stripped, chained and taken to jail, as well as shootings and killings. But there was also the systemic violence that denied the personhood and human dignity of the workers: the horrible housing, lack of food and drink, poor healthcare, poverty, lack of sanitary facilities, exposure to pesticides, pathetic wages and denial of the right to organize, protest or bargain.

Chavez's nonviolent plan to overcome the opposition would have to be just as vigorously and systematically implemented as the plan of the growers. He knew that he would have to devise a plan of action around clear goals. Cesar was not a theoretician and maintained that "Non-violence by itself is impotent, but as a vehicle for action it is potent: it fails when it is not applied to concrete goals."[26] His use of nonviolence would be confrontational, aggressive and determined. As he put it: "We advocate militant nonviolence in our means of social revolution and to achieve justice for our people.... [W]e hate the agribusiness system that seeks to keep us enslaved, and we shall overcome and change it not by retaliation or bloodshed but by a determined nonviolent struggle carried on by those masses of farm workers who intend to be free and human."[27]

Cesar often told his followers that they were engaged in a struggle for freedom and dignity, but insisted that this must not be a violent struggle. He told them not to retaliate but to use love, compassion, creativity, tenacity, discipline and the legal system, as well as prayer and fasting.

For Cesar nonviolence was not passive, but thoroughly active. Neither was nonviolence to be equated with cowardice. Gandhi himself once said that he would rather be violent than be a coward. He had insisted that it requires courage to put your life on the line for a cause in the face of violence. Similarly, Cesar taught his followers that nonviolence takes guts and a strong character, whereas to be violent requires neither. Not only does nonviolence respect the lives of others, it also enables the persons practicing it to keep their own self-respect. Besides Gandhi, Cesar also turned to Jesus and to Saint Francis as his mentors and inspiration for nonviolence.

Cesar saw little value in simply talking about nonviolence. He stressed that nonviolence is something one *does* in the face of violence to bring about change. Violence was never to be the response to abuse. Cesar was adamant that violence only begets more violence, and that it even spreads among the perpetrators. He said, "When we become violent with others, then we will become violent among ourselves."[28] He would never allow his followers to return violence because he was certain that social justice could not be won by hurting others or by taking human lives.

Chavez had learned from the Civil Rights Movement that a nonviolent response to violence wins people over to your side. Consequently, every time there was violence against his people, Cesar would publicize it and the violence would be neutralized. He said, "By some strange chemistry, every time the opposition commits an unjust act against our hopes and aspirations, we get tenfold paid back in benefits."[29]

Cesar made sure that his people were well-prepared for the nonviolent approach. He knew that nonviolence requires rules, training, discipline; it must be creative and have strategy. Gandhi had described nonviolence as "moral jujitsu," always trying to keep the opponent off balance. Its first principle is non-cooperation with everything that humiliates the people in the movement.

According to Chavez, nonviolence is especially suited for the poor because it requires a lot of time and patience, both of which the poor often have in good supply. He also taught that nonviolence is more in the heart than in the brain. Love is its key ingredient, for love is stronger than hatred, which only saps one's energy and strength. While Cesar admitted that he had not yet learned to love the growers, he certainly did not hate them. He said with a devilish smile, "Of course, we can learn how to love the growers more easily after they sign contracts."[30]

## Use of Boycotts

When the strikes against the grape growers were weakened by the use of other workers, Cesar turned to boycotting grapes. His staff traveled across the country organizing the boycott, and longshoremen on both coasts gave their support, refusing to ship grapes out of the country. The boycott spread rapidly nationwide. It was a specific action that could be engaged in by large numbers of people, and it put tremendous pressure on the growers. Chavez put it this way:

> The whole essence of nonviolent action is getting a lot of people involved, vast numbers doing little things. It is difficult to get people involved in a picket line, because it takes their time. But anytime a person can be persuaded not to eat a grape—and we persuaded millions not to eat grapes—that's involvement, that's the most direct action, and it's set up in such a way that everybody can participate.[31]

## Gaining Power

Power was not a bad thing for Chavez unless it was misused. He came to realize that farmworkers had never been successful in their struggle because they had allowed themselves to become powerless. Cesar said, "I soon realized that you can't do anything by talking, that you can't do anything if you haven't got power."[32] Gradually, Cesar gained power by strikes, boycotts, marches, phone calls and press coverage. He also began to gain more support from Catholic bishops, from strong labor leaders like Walter Reuther and from powerful politicians like Senator Robert Kennedy. The struggle of the migrants even became linked to the black struggle for civil rights. At one point, Martin Luther King, Jr., wrote to Cesar: "The fight for equality must be fought on many fronts—in the urban slums, in the sweat shops of the factories and fields. Our separate struggles are really one—a struggle for freedom, for dignity, AND for humanity."[33]

## Marches

Cesar took another page out of Gandhi's book when he scheduled long, symbolic marches. In the spring of 1966, Cesar and a band of his followers began a march, or "pilgrimage," from Delano to Sacramento, a distance of over three hundred miles. The main purpose was to pressure the state to pass laws protecting farmworkers. But Cesar also saw this march to be an opportunity to train himself and his followers in endurance for the long struggle ahead. He wanted his movement to be both physically and spiritually fit, the marchers confident in what they were doing and united in their cause. He also wanted them to participate in Christian penance through the suffering and the pain of walking for nearly a month. This historic march would serve as a powerful weapon and organizing tool, and offer time for formation for all those who participated.

In many ways the march was a microcosm of the workers' struggle. There was the anticipation of achieving something, of getting started toward specific goals. There was progression step by step toward something ahead. A great sense of calm and peace came over the participants. There was also a strong sense of comradeship among the marchers, a feeling of personal sacrifice and the courage to face harassment from some of the drivers and townsfolk along the way. In addition, a feeling of solidarity developed with the poor folks they passed, who cheered them on and came out of their humble shacks to bring the marchers food and drink. There was the excitement of being joined by hundreds of others, including farmworkers from the fields along the way, as the ranks of marchers grew into the thousands.

For Cesar himself, the march was indeed a penitential ordeal from the start. He had for years suffered from back pain, and this was aggravated by the march. He had not adequately prepared for the march; he was tired, out of shape and wearing his worn-out street shoes. Soon he was miserable from back pain, a swollen ankle, blisters and a fever.

The first day the group marched twenty-one miles and was hosted by a woman who lived in a two-bedroom cabin—the only one around who would let its members use her lawn and cabin to rest for the night. Seeing Cesar's condition, the woman gave up her own bed to him so that he could rest. At 4:30 the next morning, the group was up and on the road again, and the walking deadened the pain in Cesar's ankle. His legs began to swell and the fever continued so that he had to ride partway in a station wagon. Eventually, someone gave him a cane which took the weight off his bad foot and enabled him to continue to the end of the march. As the march concluded, news came that one of the major growers had agreed to negotiate a contract—the first union contract in history for the farmworkers. When the marchers arrived at the capital, the governor was away, but they had made their point and were at a whole new level of spirit and sacrifice.

**Fasting**

Many in the movement were becoming impatient with Cesar's nonviolent approach. Strikes were often broken by green-carders and illegal immigrants. Boycotts were often thwarted when growers switched labels so buyers could not tell which products to boycott. Meanwhile, the owners hired roughnecks to intimidate the strikers, and police continued their use of harassment, shooting, intimidation and jailing. Some workers came to the conclusion that it was time for retaliation. It was suggested that a little violence—maybe some sabotage or terrorism—might bring the owners around.

Chavez decided to fast, a tradition with deep roots in his church. During his leadership, Chavez chose to fast a number of times: at times by way of protest, at other times as an act of sacrifice and penance. On certain occasions he saw these fasts as acts of love and prayer for his followers. This long fast would be specific in purpose—to stop the talk of violence among his followers. His fast would be an action of nonviolence, in part a warning to growers that he could not hold back his followers' inclination toward violence indefinitely, as well as a plea for nonviolence from his followers.

Once the word got out that Cesar was fasting, thousands of his followers came to office headquarters, now at Forty Acres, in order to be with him in spirit. Some of the visitors created art for the occasion; others brought religious pictures. A number fasted along with him, while others, both Protestant and Catholic, gathered around the altar with him for Mass. During that period Cesar took advantage of the time and read voraciously, especially the works of Gandhi and Thoreau.

After twenty-some days, Cesar's doctor warned him that continuing the fast could seriously harm his health and plans were made for him to stop. Senator Robert Kennedy attended the event and passed Cesar his first bread in twenty-five days. A Mass was celebrated and "*semita*," poor man's bread, was passed through the congregation. Chavez made a moving statement after Mass: "I am convinced that the truest act of courage, the strongest act of manliness, is to sacrifice ourselves for others in a totally nonviolent struggle for justice. To be a man is to suffer for others. God help us be men."[34]

The growers, of course, ridiculed Cesar's fasting as a publicity stunt or as a display of a holier-than-thou attitude. The growers also spread rumors that Cesar was cheating by having food sneaked to him. Cesar paid little attention to these criticisms, for he knew that most of his followers kept vigil during his fasts and thousands attended the daily liturgy. He knew that when the fast ended there was a closer unity and a deeper sense of commitment among the *Chavistas*.

### From Grapes to Lettuce

A banner year for the union came in 1970. The grape boycott was having its effect and bringing most of the grape growers to the table to sign contracts. The UFW now turned its attention to the vegetable and lettuce growers, and the growers turned to the Teamsters' Union for help. The growers knew that the Teamsters would push the NFWA out of the way, and then give the appearance of unionization when, in fact, they would do nothing for the workers. Cesar called for a nationwide boycott on lettuce, and when he refused to obey a court order to stop the boycott, he was arrested. As Cesar was led off, he shouted to his followers: "Boycott the hell out of them."[35]

## The Religious Dimension

Chavez's movement was deeply rooted in the Mexican Catholic tradition, so devotions and Hispanic spirituality played an important role in La Causa. As a boy, Cesar had sat at the feet of his grandmother, Mama Tella, to learn his catechism and his prayers. His mother, Juana, taught him many wise sayings about human dignity, justice and sacrifice, and always gave him a good example for sharing with the poor. She insisted that some of their food be shared with the needy, even when her own children complained that they were hungry themselves. His mother also urged Cesar to avoid violence, and she nurtured a faith in him that believed we must work and sacrifice to make things better.

Cesar was a devout Catholic. He attended Mass daily and spent an hour each day in prayer. He seems to have wanted himself and his people to live as the early Christians. He once observed, "Religion is a deep part of us.... We try to live as a community. We have a feeling for St. Paul and what he writes about the communities he struggled to build."[36] Cesar's love for his community was in a sense monastic and mystical. One of his followers once said, "He was entirely with the people, open to them, one with them, and at the same time that he makes them laugh, his gaze sees beyond them to something else."[37]

Cesar seemed to represent the ancient prophetic tradition that cried out against injustice and took action for human dignity. He wrote, "All my life, I have been driven by one dream, one goal, one vision: To overthrow a system that treats farm workers in that way, as if they are not important human beings."[38] He was deeply committed to the active faith of Jesus Christ. "I think Christ really taught us to go and do something. We can look at His sermons, and it's very plain what He wants us to do: clothe the naked, feed the hungry and give water to the thirsty. It's very simple stuff."[39]As with many other spiritual heroes, Jesus'

Beatitudes were at the heart of Cesar's vision.

In the marches, rallies and strikes, the banner of Our Lady of Guadalupe was carried proudly. This devotion is central to Mexican faith. The appearance of Mary to Juan Diego, a barefoot peasant who worked in the fields in the sixteenth century, symbolized for La Causa divine protection of the poor farmworkers in their struggle for justice. "*La Morenita,*" the dark-skinned mother, accompanied her children on their pilgrimage for human dignity, and her presence gave them hope and courage.

## The Church

Cesar's relationship with the Catholic church was often ambiguous. We have heard how, early on, Father Donald McDonnell befriended him as a young man living in Sal Si Puedes, and taught him much about the inequity in the economy and the social justice teachings of the church. Another Franciscan priest, Father Mark Day, worked closely with the farmworkers for many years. At the same time, in the early days of the union, Catholic clergy who did attempt to support the union were often forbidden by their bishops to support the farmworkers and their boycotts, and only a few priests and a number of sisters disobeyed and joined the movement.

Cesar also received support from many Protestant ministers, from prominent Jews and from many with no religious affiliation. Cesar was not hesitant to worship with other faith communities and learned a great deal about the power of singing and clapping from attending small Pentecostal services.

Following the Second Vatican Council, the California bishops began to support Chavez. By 1969, Cesar was prepared to appeal to the United States Catholic Conference for its support. Although the bishops were not yet ready to back the union's boycotts, they did agree to delegate a committee that could act as mediator in the negotiations. This brought Monsignor George Higgins, a veteran social action proponent, and Bishop Joseph Donnelly, a labor expert, into the picture. This was a strong boost for the union. Gradually, Catholics began to support the union's boycotts and, by 1974, Cesar was thrilled to be given a private audience with Pope Paul VI, who gave him a message of strong support.

## Political Support

The farmworkers were often on the outside, as far as many politicians were concerned. Richard Nixon, from the time he was a fledgling legislator and through his presidency, was hostile to the migrant workers. Governor Deukmejian of California and Ronald Reagan, both as governor of California and as president, opposed the union's struggle. At one point, Nixon and Reagan appeared for a photo opportunity eating grapes in defiance of the boycott. On the other hand, Governor Jerry Brown of California was most helpful in pushing through the state legislature laws in favor of the farmworkers. Senator Robert Kennedy was one of the most ardent supporters of the union until his assassination.

## Nonviolent Until the End

Cesar had to repeatedly reiterate to his followers his unflinching commitment to nonviolence. The violent provocations of the growers had pushed his movement to its limits. There were attempts to burn down the union office, and there were occasions when the office building was rammed by a truck and rocks were thrown through its windows. The union gas station had been bombed, putting many lives in danger. Cesar's house was barraged with crank calls and threats, and rocks and bottles were thrown through his windows.

Eventually, Cesar would allow guards to watch his office and home, but no one could be armed. He told them, "I've been getting threats on my life every day for the last six months, and I'm not armed, and I won't permit anybody with me to be armed."[40] Many threats were made on Cesar's life and there were several plots to assassinate him. As these were discovered, Cesar had to begin working out of a secret office and take greater care in his travels.

Violence against the Chavistas was a constant. In the fall of 1966 a grower's employee drove a truck into a picket line, seriously injuring one of the strikers. Had Cesar not intervened, the truck driver would probably have been beaten to death. The Teamsters' Union constantly competed with the National Farm Workers' Association and offered sweetheart contracts to the growers that did little for the workers. The Teamsters also regularly hired goons to intimidate Cesar's people. For instance, during the grape boycotts in 1973, truckloads of men attacked the strikers and beat them with sticks, pipes and chains, while a sheriff and his deputies looked on. On other occasions, thugs carried shotguns and shot out the windows of strikers' cars. In that same year thousands of strikers were arrested, while many others were beaten, maced and even killed by people hired by the growers.

The list of martyrs for La Causa grew longer as the years passed. There was Nan Freeman, a young college student who volunteered to picket the sugarcane growers in Florida in 1972; she was run down by a truck while she was on the picket line. There was Nagi Daifallah, a twenty-four-year-old Arab farmworker, who protested the unjust arrest of one of his picket captains and was chased and bludgeoned to death with a metal flashlight by a deputy in 1973. Juan de la Cruz was a Mexican who brought his family to work in the fields of California. While on a picket line in 1973 in the San Joaquin Valley, Juan was shot to death from a passing pickup truck. Rufino Contreras worked with his family for years as a lettuce cutter in the Imperial Valley. In 1979, he was striking in a lettuce field; as he walked toward some strikebreakers he was shot to death by employees of the grower, and fell face down in the very field he had worked for years.[41] And in 1983, Rene Lopez, the elected spokesperson for the dairy workers near Fresno, was shot in the face and killed during a strike. The bullet came from a car driven by a relative of the dairy owner.

Cesar spoke at the funerals of these martyrs, always praising them for their sacrifice, condemning the violence of the growers and urging his followers to remain nonviolent. He reminded his people that violence was born of frustration and impotence, while nonviolence required imagination and creativity. Cesar believed that with patience and faith in God, advocates of nonviolence could reach any goals. He said at Juan de la Cruz's funeral, "We are here because his spirit of service and sacrifice has touched and moved our lives. The force that is generated by that spirit of love is more powerful than any force on earth. It cannot be stopped."[42] Cesar himself is recognized as one of the martyrs of La Causa, because for many years he sacrificed himself in so many ways: strikes, boycotts, marches, fasts, confrontations with violent adversaries, lawsuits and interminable negotiations.

In his last years, Chavez focused on one of his constant battles with the growers for spraying pesticides on the crops—and even at times on the workers themselves—while they worked. He pointed out that incidents of cancer, skin disease and other ailments were much higher among the workers than on the rest of the population, and he traveled the country lobbying for a legislative solution.

Cesar died in his sleep in 1993, at the age of sixty-six. After his death, there was a special ceremony honoring him and the other martyrs for La Causa. Cesar's successor, Arturo Rodriquez, declared, "We remember! We honor the gifts of their lives by giving more of our own. We will continue to work together to build a farm-workers' union worthy of the sacrifice of their lives."[43] This is the way Cesar would have wanted it—not singled out or glorified, but honored among his own as one who led them in their struggle for freedom.

Cesar said that he worked for the day when children will learn early that being fully human means giving one's life for the liberation of those who suffer. In a prayer that he wrote for his farmworkers, Cesar said:

> Show me the suffering of the most miserable; I will know my people's plight.
>
> Free me to pray for others; for you are present in every person.

Help me take responsibility for my own life; that I can be free at last.[44]

## The UFW Today

The UFW is strong today and defends workers' rights against the agri-businesses notorious for undermining contracts, suppressing wages and failing to provide basic protections and benefits such as healthcare. The UFW also continues to protest the use of harmful chemicals sprayed on crops and applied to soil, which routinely poison agricultural workers as well as the food supply. More recently they have opposed "free trade" agreements by which small-farm owners are being pushed off their land. Such economic policies favor the single-crop interests of big corporations over the right of individual countries to have diversified crop production and to feed themselves. Once again the UFW is engaged in a struggle with grape growers, and has filed a sex-bias lawsuit against a dairy in Oregon. The work of Chavez continues, and the legacy he left behind lives on.

## CHAPTER THREE

## Harriet Tubman: Freedom for the Enslaved and Poor

It was the night of June 2, 1863, and the Union forces (which now included black soldiers) were planning a sneak attack on some of the richest plantations in Confederate South Carolina. A scouting group led by a small black woman had mapped out the area, located the Confederate mines on the Combahee River, giving three Union gun-boats access to the area, and had contacted a "fifth column" of slaves in the area prepared to assist in the liberation of the local slaves. Like clockwork, the boats slipped safely down the river, avoiding the mines, and the landing party disembarked and began to torch the wealthy slave-owners' estates and barns. The Confederate troops, caught by surprise, were unable to offer much resistance. Hundreds of slaves ran from their quarters, fighting off the whips and guns of their owners and approached the boats.

Since many of these slaves were just as suspicious of the northern-ers as they were of their masters, they had to be calmed and convinced that the gunboats were safe. The woman who had served as scout for the attack was asked to stand at the bow of one of the boats, sing Negro spirituals and encourage the slaves to run to the boats. The scout later commented, "Here you would see a woman with a pail on her head, rice smoking in it just as she had taken it from the fire, and a young one hanging on behind, one hand round her forehead to hold on, and the other digging into the rice pot, eating with all its might."[1] There were women with babies clinging to them, carrying squealing pigs and chickens, all wanting to be free. That night over 750 slaves were taken onto the gunboats and brought to freedom. The woman scout stood high on the bow of the boat that night, singing Negro spirituals to calm the fleeing slaves and encouraging them to get on the boats. This woman had long been in the business of rescuing slaves along the Underground Railroad. Her name was Harriet Tubman.

**Born Into Slavery**

Harriet was born Araminta ("Minty") Ross, the daughter of Harriet Green and Benjamin Ross, one of eleven children. She was born around 1822 (birth records of slaves were not kept since they were considered to be chattel). She was born around the same time and place as the famous ex-slave and dedicated abolitionist, Frederick Douglass.

Minty's grandmother had come on a slave ship from Africa, and the little girl had heard that she was an Ashanti from Ghana. Minty's African heritage brought her indomitable courage, a deep sense of community with her people and her family, and a passionate love for freedom.

The child was born into slavery on a plantation near Bucktown, close to Cambridge, Maryland. The Eastern shore of Maryland was good for growing grain and tobacco and logging timber for shipbuilding. The soil was fertile and abundant water flowed from the many marshes, creeks and rivers that flowed into the Chesapeake. The summers were scorching, and the population—planters, trappers, emancipated slaves and many still bonded in slavery—was hard-working.

**Slavery**

The first slaves in the United States were brought to the New World by the Spanish in 1526. Originally, slaves had been torn from family and culture in Africa by Muslim and Christian slave traders. Slaves were brought to the American colonies in 1619, some as indentured servants. By the middle of the eighteenth century, slaves in this country had lost their rights as human beings and could be bought and sold like property or farm animals.

Eventually, millions of human beings were brought here to work, many of them stacked together in the holds of squalid slave ships. Their marriages and parental rights were not recognized so that members of families could be sold off separately. They were also kept in a state of illiteracy so that they could not learn about the legal and social system binding them or forge the passes that they were required to carry in order to prevent escape. Many religious ministers taught them that they were created to be slaves and that to complain would be rebellion against the Creator. Any unauthorized movement, offense or mistake could be punished by a determined number of lashes. While it is true that not all masters were cruel, the fact remains that slaves had few rights and were subjected to whatever treatment they received. Many owners focused on getting the last bit of work from their slaves, and if they resisted or slacked off, punishment (even death) was often the result. Few owners were ever prosecuted for crimes against their slaves. "Lynch law" usually prevailed over court law.[2]

The idealized image of the house servant living harmoniously with the master's family applied to only a small percentage. Over 90 percent of slaves worked fifteen-hour days and were given little food and scant clothing. It is true that only a minority in the South actually owned slaves and many people there even opposed slavery. This was especially true of the many white small-farm owners who could not compete with the larger plantations whose many slaves worked for nothing. But those who did own slaves controlled the Southern economy and viewed their slaves as one of their most important investments.

By the time Minty was born, many slaves were needed from her people in Maryland as cheap labor in the deep South to harvest the enormous crops of "king cotton." In 1793 the cotton gin had been invented, and the spinning and weaving machines created the possibility of mass production for a world market. The entire American economy, including the northern banking, milling and shipping industry, now had a vested interest in slavery. Turning their backs on the Declaration of Independence and the Bill of Rights, both Congress and the Supreme Court supported slavery. Slavery has often been described as a "state of war," because only a fortress mentality that suppressed freedom of speech, assembly and the press as well as the guns of the big planters in the South could sustain a system so inhumane and irrational.

By 1808 the importing of slaves was forbidden, and even though the illegal smuggling of slaves continued, great pressure was now put on slaves' families in Maryland and Virginia to produce children, who could bring a great price "down the river" in the cotton fields of the deep South. Minty later recalled the horrible memory of seeing her two older sisters going off in a chain gang, wailing at being taken from their home and loved ones. She dearly loved her family, and lived in the fear that more of her brothers and sisters would be put in chain gangs and sold south. She would dedicate years of her life to rescue her family members from such a fate.

## Childhood

Minty was a very dark, wooly-haired child, small and frail and therefore considered to be worth little on the market. She later wrote that she really had no childhood: "I grew up like a neglected weed—ignorant of liberty, having no experience of it."[3]

At the tender age of six, Minty was hired out to a woman to clean and take care of a baby. Nearly a baby herself, Minty had to dust and sweep during the day, and sit on the floor all night keeping the baby quiet so that the master and his wife would not be disturbed. If she fell off to sleep and allowed the baby to cry or if she did her dusting poorly, she would be beaten with a whip. Little Araminta gradually got very homesick, lost weight, fell sick and had to be sent back to her mother—already deemed "worthless."

Minty's mother nursed her little girl back to health, praying at her side and telling her Bible stories. From the start, the little girl had a deep faith in God and became accustomed to praying "as a man talketh with his friend." She learned from her mother to bring her needs to God and to trust that things would be made right.[4]

After her recovery, Minty was hired out to a mistress who was so cruel that the little girl ran away and lived in a pigpen for five days, fighting the pigs for the scraps until she was found, brought back and whipped. As the girl grew older, she learned to wear a lot of thick clothes to protect herself from the blows of the whip. She eventually grew strong enough to resist the blows. On one occasion Minty stopped a master from punishing her by biting his knee!

Another master, a trapper, forced the young slave to wade into water up to her waist to check muskrat traps. One day, while she had measles, she was sent out to the swamp and got deathly ill. Again, her mother had to bring her home and nurse her back to health.

By age twelve it was decided that Araminta was hopeless as a domestic, and she was sent out as a field hand to dig, hoe and harvest. At one point, she was hired out to a man who worked her like a farm animal. She plowed, drove oxen and had to lift heavy barrels of flour and stack bails of hay. The outdoor work made the young girl extremely fit, and she actually surpassed most of the male slaves in physical strength.

**Youth**

When Minty was a young teenager, she was injured seriously while working as a field hand. One evening a young slave went into the village, the master followed him to punish him and Minty went along behind. The master asked her to tie him up for a whipping, but she refused. The slave bolted and she blocked the way of the master. He picked up a two pound weight and threw it at the slave. The heavy piece of metal fell short and hit Harriet in the head, breaking her skull and driving a piece of her shawl into her head. Minty lay at home for a long time in a stupor, and it took her months to recover. The aftermath left a large indentation in her forehead, and she suffered all her life from headaches, seizures and sudden sleeping spells. Such behavior led some to believe that Minty was slow-witted, while in actual fact, though uneducated, she was quite intelligent, resourceful and extremely strong-willed.

**Young Adulthood**

In her early twenties, Minty had good years working with her father, who was now freed, cutting and hauling lumber for John Stewart, a lumber business owner. Minty loved working outdoors, and the chopping and hauling of timber made her extraordinarily strong. By this time both she and her father were paid for their work, and young Minty began to put some money aside. While working the logging camps and the shipping wharfs, Harriet became part of a network among the black watermen who spoke of freedom and the dangers connected with trying to secure it. At camp meetings, market days and social gatherings she began to make contacts with people who would help her cause of freeing herself and her family later on.

In 1844 Araminta fell in love, married a free black man named John Tubman and took up residence on the plantation of her master, Anthony Thompson. It was then that she changed her first name to Harriet, possibly in honor of her mother. After trying for five years, the couple was not able to have children, which apparently put a strain on their marriage and drew pressure to Harriet's owner, who needed to "produce" more slaves.

In the winter of 1846, Harriet fell ill. She lay sick from Christmas to March, and eventually her master had people look at her to see if they wanted to buy her. As Harriet recovered from her long illness, she began to pray all the time. She said: "I was always talking with the Lord" as she washed, worked, sat quietly in the evening. She prayed, "O, dear Lord, change that man's heart…convert ole master." When Harriet heard that she was going to be sent to the deep South on a chain gang with her brothers, she prayed that her master would die. And he did! She felt pangs of guilt and says that she would have given anything to get him back. But he was gone, so she stopped praying for him.

The slaves with Harriet were now troubled. Now that their master was dead, what was going to become of them? Word came that they were going to be sold south, where slaves were treated even worse than in Maryland. Around that same time, Harriet says that she began to hear inner voices that called her to flee for her life. She began having dreams of horsemen coming to tear children from their mothers. She envisioned a boundary between the land of slavery and freedom, and dreamed of lovely white ladies on the other side waiting to welcome her and care for her. She saw herself and her people like the Israelites being called out of the slavery of Egypt, and began to feel a calling to carry out a special mission for the Lord.

When Harriet was in her mid-twenties, the word was whispered that she and her two brothers were going to be part of a chain gang and shipped south. The three agreed that it was time to run away. Since slaves were not allowed to congregate, Harriet had to find a way to say good-bye. She went from cabin to cabin singing in her low, husky voice. "I'll meet you in the morning, when you reach the promised land; on the other side of Jordan, for I'm bound for the promised land."

### The Escape

In the fall of 1849, the three headed out into the woods and swamps of the unknown, with no money and only the clothes on their backs. They knew full well that the bounty hunters and the bloodhounds would not be far behind, and that if they were captured they would be severely beaten and sold to the deep South to work in chain gangs. A notice was soon posted for the capture of the three slaves, and Harriet's description read as follows: "Minty, aged about 27 years, is of a chestnut color, fine looking and about 5 feet high. One hundred dollars reward will be given for each of the above named negroes…."[5]

Early into the escape, Harriet's brothers began to panic and decided to go back, leaving their young sister to fend for herself. Walking by night and following the North star and the moss on the north side of the trees, Harriet hid in holes and tree trunks by day. She later commented: "I had reasoned dis out in my mind; there was one of two things I had a *right* to, liberty, or death; if I could not have one, I would have de oder, for no man should take me alive; I should fight for my liberty as long as my strength lasted."[6]

Harriet's first stop was at the house of a woman she knew would help her. By the 1840s networks of houses had been set up in the area to help escaping slaves. This movement eventually came to be known as the Underground Railroad.

## The Underground Railroad

The Underground Railroad seems to have had its beginnings in the early 1800s, when those in sympathy with the slaves began to assist them to freedom. As time went on, many heroic people, both white and black, grew so bold as to risk going to prison, being beaten, being thrown out of their churches, and even losing their lives to rescue slaves. The leading religious group among them was the Quaker church.

The name "Underground Railroad" seems to have come from an event in Ohio, when slaves crossed the river and seemed to disappear out of sight by what seemed to be some mysterious passage underground. The name caught on, and a network of "stations" were set up throughout the country; "stationmasters" (hosts) and "conductors" (guides) were assigned, and precious "cargo" (fugitives) were encouraged to ride on the "liberty lines."[7]

The routes on the railroad varied. Some slaves from along the banks of the Mississippi would hide on shipboard, sail to the eastern part of Ohio and be within one hundred miles of the Great Lakes. From there they could be helped from station to station to Canada. There they often faced severe weather and harsh wilderness, but they were free. There were also routes through Illinois and Wisconsin to the Great

Lakes; routes up through Kentucky, across the Ohio River and from there to Cleveland or upstate New York to the Great Lakes. There were sea routes up the east coast to Boston and then up through Maine to Canada. For Harriet, the route was usually from southern Maryland, through Wilmington, Delaware, to Philadelphia and from there to upstate New York to the Niagara River and across the great gorge at Niagara Falls into the area around the city of St. Catherines, Canada.

Of course, all this activity was against the law, for in 1793 Congress passed the first Fugitive Slave Act, which placed heavy fines and even prison time on those assisting runaway slaves. In 1850 another law would be passed that required that captured fugitives be returned to their masters. The "slavocracy" at this time controlled the presidency, the Congress and the Supreme Court.

## Harriet's Trip

At her first stop, Harriet was given a "pass," a piece of paper with names on it, which would identify her as "cargo" and be recognized at the next stop. At the next house she was told to pose as a servant until transportation by wagon could be provided to the next stop. Moving by wagon and on foot from one station to the other under the cover of darkness, she made her way north, always on the lookout for slave-catchers out of Dover and Smyrna, Delaware. These men lived off the high rewards offered for the capture and return of slaves. Runaways who were captured and returned were often branded or maimed so that they could not escape again. Often they were put in chain gangs and shipped to the harshest areas in the South.

## Fear of Rebellion

By the time Harriet fled, there was much anger, fear and hatred in the air on the part of slaveowners. Conspiracies and rebellions had made them well aware that slaves could be dangerous. Rebellions were not new. As early as the seventeenth century, there had been uprisings in Massachusetts, Virginia and New York. During a rebellion in New York

City in 1712 black and Native American slaves killed nine whites and wounded seven more. In 1739 a large uprising occurred near Charleston, South Carolina, where about one hundred slaves destroyed plantations and killed some whites. In the late eighteenth century there had been many violent struggles for freedom by the shipboard slaves as well as those in New Jersey, South Carolina and Florida. Though the slaves were from Africa, they now breathed the air of a country that, at least in theory, was dedicated to freedom and liberty. They wanted their portion of this!

At the beginning of the nineteenth century, a blacksmith named Gabriel, along with many others, hid hundreds of pikes, bayonets and knives and planned an attack on Richmond, Virginia. They were betrayed by one of their own and were executed. In 1822, a free black, Denmark Vesey, who worked as a carpenter in Charleston, South Carolina, was accused and convicted, along with many of his followers, of organizing a violent insurrection.

The uprising that put the most panic into the hearts of slaveowners was that of Nat Turner in Virginia in 1831. Turner and his followers killed his master and then went from house to house hacking slaveholding families to death. They killed more than sixty white people before they were stopped by state and federal troops. Sixteen conspirators were hanged, and Turner, who stayed on the loose for several weeks, was also executed. Terror set in throughout the South, legislatures met to strengthen the Slave Codes, and many who were merely suspected of rising up were lynched.[8] While Nat Turner was portrayed as a savage by Southern whites, he became a hero and martyr for many slaves.

### Crossing the Line to Freedom

It probably took Harriet several weeks of dangerous travel over eighty miles of rivers, swamps and woods to reach Wilmington, Delaware, a main station on the "railroad," where the bridge crossing into the city served as the line to cross to freedom. There the leader was a Quaker named Thomas Garrett. Garrett ran a blacksmith shop, hardware store and cobbler shop. He, along with other locals, offered help to the fugitives, providing them with lodging, food and clothing, and often with a brand new pair of shoes from Garrett's shop. Slaveholders threatened to shoot Garrett on sight, and on one occasion he was beaten up and thrown off a train trying to help a black woman. In 1848 Garrett was tried for aiding slaves and fined five thousand dollars. He lost his business, his property and all his possessions. But Garrett refused to give up his work with fugitives, and defiantly told the judge who asked him if he had learned his lesson: "Friend, if thee should see a fugitive slave in want of help to-day, thee will please send him to me!"[9] Even after his conviction and being stripped of all his holdings, Garrett defiantly continued his rescue efforts, and by the time of the Civil War helped bring over twenty-five hundred slaves to safety.

### Pennsylvania

From Wilmington, Harriet crossed into Pennsylvania and was now about thirty more miles from her destination, Philadelphia, which for a time provided haven for runaways. As she crossed the line from slavery to freedom, there were no ladies in white dresses to welcome her with outstretched arms. She says that her liberation was bittersweet, because she was alone and without her loved ones, yet she was a free woman and would never call a person "master" again. She says that as she entered the "heaven" of freedom, she felt that she was reborn. She recalls, "I looked at my hands...to see if I was de same person now I was free. Dere was such a glory ober eberything, de sun came like gold trou de trees and ober de fields, and I felt like I was in heaven."[10]

Harriet couldn't seem to enjoy this freedom on her own because she was so closely bonded with her family and all her relatives and wanted them close to her. She knew that she would have to go back for her blood relatives, friends and some others who wanted their freedom. She later noted, "There was no one to welcome me in the land of freedom. I was a stranger in a strange land; and my home, after all was down in Maryland; because my father, my mother, my brothers, and sisters and friends were there. But I was free, and they should be free."[11] This point of view was at the very core of Harriet's determination to keep returning to her homeland and making so many attempts to rescue her family members and neighbors.

## Life in Philadelphia

Philadelphia was a culture shock for a young woman who had just a few weeks before been a slave on a plantation. It was a bustling urban area with nearly twenty thousand blacks—about 10 percent of the city's population. The same year that Harriet fled, over two hundred slaves had also come there seeking freedom. Here she could just fade into the crowds and move about freely among black vendors, sailors, churchfolk and a growing black middle class. The city had hosted the first black national convention in 1831, and was one of the centers of the abolitionist movement. Blacks had their own organizations, schools and businesses.

Harriet could now freely walk in the public parks and go to lectures and cultural events. She could attend her own church and attend discussions on black rights and freedom. The life of freedom opened up a whole new world for the young woman, and she soon secured a job as a domestic and began saving her money. She became friends with William Stills, the son of a fugitive slave who for many years interviewed and recorded the stories of incoming fugitives.

There were still many problems and dangers for Harriet in Philadelphia. There were slavecatchers, those who would kidnap fugitive slaves and return them to the South for auction. There was a strong racial prejudice on the part of many whites, especially the new immigrants who competed for jobs against the former slaves and who felt that blacks drove down the wage scale. Blacks were often blamed for high crime rates and urban disturbances. Many blacks lived in poor neighborhoods, and often found it difficult to find work in white industry. White gangs roamed the streets at times, looking for trouble with blacks. There were race riots and violent attacks on the abolitionists.[12]

Just a year after Harriet arrived in Philadelphia, the Fugitive Slave Act was passed, which allowed federal officials to capture fugitives and send them back to the South. Fees were provided as an incentive to capture fugitives and Harriet knew that she would no longer be safe in Philadelphia. Many fugitives began to migrate to Canada, where they would be safe from being apprehended. Those who remained often purchased firearms and were prepared to defend themselves.

It was in Philadelphia that Harriet began to be politicized and started to attend meetings on abolition and women's rights. She began to network with other black women who were dedicated to fundraising, demonstrations and community programs to benefit blacks, whether freed or enslaved.

## The Abolitionists

Harriet soon became part of the abolitionist movement and joined the protests against the Fugitive Slave Act. The abolitionist movement was led by people like the fiery, eagle-eyed William Lloyd Garrison in Boston and the eloquent former slave Frederick Douglass in Rochester. Both black and white abolitionists thwarted the recapturing of slaves, at times with armed resistance.

The abolitionist movement goes back to the founding of this country. Deep in the conscience of the United States there was always a feeling that slavery was wrong. Abigail Adams wrote to her husband, John, that slaves had as much right to freedom as they did. Thomas Jefferson, a slaveholder himself, drafted a denunciation of slavery into the Declaration of Independence, but the founding fathers did not allow it to be included. Still, the publication of such a declaration on freedom moved many slaveowners to free their slaves. Slaves were enlisted into the Continental army with the promise of emancipation, and many slaves went over to the British who promised complete emancipation. A good number of slaves fled to Canada, rightly believing that after the Revolution many would be re-enslaved.

Slavery first began to collapse in the North. In 1787 Congress had banned slavery in the Northwest Territory (a region comprising the present states of Ohio, Indiana, Illinois, Michigan, Wisconsin and the eastern part of Minnesota). By 1804 the other Northern states were beginning to end slavery in their territories. The long winters when the slaves had to be supported, as well as industrialization, rendered slavery no longer attractive. By 1807 the slave trade was made illegal in the United States, and though many continued to smuggle slaves illegally, slavery was gradually abolished in the North. In 1827 it was abolished in the state of New York.

Preachers among the Baptists, Methodists and especially among the Quakers gave sermons against slavery and acted as circuit riders, denouncing slavery and telling the slaves that freedom was a goal of Christianity. Later, the strong movement of evangelical revivalism in the North in the mid-nineteenth century also promoted the abolition of slavery.

In 1852, Harriet Beecher Stowe, the daughter of a Connecticut clergyman, published *Uncle Tom's Cabin,* which exposed the horrors of slavery to the general public. The book quickly became a best-seller and deeply affected antislavery feelings in the North, while it drew outrage from the South. Many believe that this book was an important factor leading to the outbreak of the Civil War.

Although the North was moving toward the abolition of slavery, many there still retained a strong racism, which maintained that blacks were biologically inferior to whites and were intellectually and morally incapable of self-government. This moved both states and the federal government to pass legislation that limited the rights of free blacks.

William Lloyd Garrison had a long history with the abolitionists. As a young man, he began to speak out strongly about how ashamed he was of his country, which proclaimed liberty and equality and at the same time supported the barbarity of slavery. Initially imprisoned for a short time for denouncing the slave ships in Baltimore, he returned there and rented a room where he set up a printing press and, in 1831, published his first issue of his abolitionist newspaper, *The Liberator*. In this issue he declared: "I will be as harsh as truth and as uncompromising as justice.... I am in earnest—I will not equivocate. I will not excuse, I will not retreat a single inch—and I WILL BE HEARD!"[13]

For the next thirty years, Garrison never let up in his fight against slavery. He started a small group that called themselves the National Anti-Slavery Society, which helped blacks find jobs, pressed for the admission of blacks into public schools and investigated cases in which slaves were kidnapped and scheduled to be returned to slavery. The society also advocated for legal intermarriage, distributed free groceries to poor blacks and raised money to educate black youths in the trades.

As this society began to spread, it was the target of verbal and physical abuse, terror and shunning at churches and schools. The abolitionists had to endure threats, rotten eggs and brickbats. Garrison and his followers were hated by many in the North and South, often even by those who opposed slavery but feared that its abolition would rip the country apart and destroy the economy of both North and South. Harriet fearlessly threw in her lot with the abolitionists.

### The Abductor

As we have seen, though Harriet enjoyed her new freedom, she was lonely, homesick and deeply desired to share her freedom, precarious as it was, with her loved ones. She became determined to return and bring her family out of slavery. Harriet began to study the workings of the Underground Railroad, learned the names of the dedicated conductors, became familiar with the vast network of trails stretching from the South to Canada, New England, Florida and Mexico. She would assume the dangerous and unusual role of being a female "abductor," that is, one who would go south and actually seek out fugitives.

Harriet's first mission was a very personal one, the rescue of her favorite niece, Kizzy and Kizzy's two children, who were about to be sold into the deep South. Harriet arranged to meet them in Baltimore where they were carried by boat by Kizzy's husband from the eastern shore of Maryland. Then Harriet provided secret transportation, probably by wagon, to Pennsylvania and freedom. Harriet had made her start in freeing as many of her people as she could.

Her next expedition was into an area north of her old plantation, where one of her brothers had been hired out. She arrived secretly one night, scooped up her brother and two coworkers and led them through the swamps to Wilmington and then on to freedom in Philadelphia.

Her third trip was to be the most risky: to go right into the lion's den, the very plantation where she used to be enslaved and bring out her beloved husband, John. Harriet saved up her money for the trip, bought her husband a new suit, and longed to be united with her beloved, whom she had not seen for two years. Fully aware that she was risking apprehension and severe punishment, Harriet made her way during a number of nights over the difficult eighty miles and hid in the town of Cambridge, near the plantation where her husband worked. How she longed to see him, embrace him and spend the rest of her life with him in freedom.

Harriet furtively sent word to her husband that she was ready to lead him to the North where they could once again have a life together. The answer that came back shocked Harriet and broke her heart. John had a new wife, and neither wanted to leave with Harriet or even to see her! Harriet was grief-stricken and angry and at first wanted to storm into his cabin and give her husband trouble. But she decided that would be of little value and eventually said that she would simply drop him out of her heart. She later said that "if he could do without her, she could do without him."[14] Harriet decided to get on with her life and dedicate herself to freeing other members of her family. By this time Harriet says that she was convinced that she had a unique call from God to free others.

On her next trip, Harriet brought out eleven of her family members, and to be sure of their safety took them across New York and into

Canada at Niagara Falls. It is possible that on the way her group was sheltered by Frederick Douglass, at his "station" in Rochester. She began to return south a number of other times, and became known along the "railroad" as "Moses." She carried forged passes, pictures of comrades, which had to be recognized by the conductors before she trusted them, and always her trusty pistol. Often she would pose as a feeble woman and even ride the trains south for her expeditions. When she was ready for a rescue, she would hide in the woods, give the signal by singing a spiritual, and then gather her flock on a Saturday night. Sunday was an off day and it would take Monday before the owners got their game together to search. By then, Harriet's latest group of slaves was long gone.

Harriet was a master of disguise. At one time she would be a fine lady in a silk dress, traveling south on a train. Often, though young and strong, she would be a bent-over old woman. On one occasion she went right by one of her former owners, chasing her chickens like a crazy old woman. At times she would dress like a sturdy young man. No one guessed that under these disguises was one of the most clever and enterprising conductors of the Underground Railroad.

During the summers, Harriet would often work at vacation resorts in Cape May, New Jersey, cooking, cleaning and saving her money for the next rescue mission. Then she would sneak back south and suddenly show up at one of the cabins. A frightened group of her relatives as well as some other slaves who were willing to risk all for freedom would go running off with her through the thick woods at night. Often there were treacherous swamps and rivers to cross and, since many of the slaves could not swim, they were terrified. Harriet would have to go in the rivers first to make sure that the water was not over their heads. In the raw, cold weather, this was very difficult and often gave Harriet severe colds. There were constant dangers of being discovered, so the groups had to move in silence. The cry of a baby could alert the bounty hunters, so Harriet and others would carry the babies in baskets, and drug them with paregoric so they wouldn't cry.

## Go Free or Die

At times, a "passenger" would drop to the ground exhausted and afraid, wanting to give up and go back. Harriet knew that such a person would be forced to reveal the names and places where help was given, and the routes of escape. That would spell the end for the Underground Railroad! On these occasions, she would simply reach into her dress, take out her gun and say something like: "We got to go free or die." That surely motivated the passenger to continue. Harriet proudly maintained that she never lost a "passenger" on any of her rescue missions.

The travelers were passed along the "railroad" by dedicated "conductors" both black and white. Traveling by carts with false bottoms, by boats and on foot, they were fed, clothed and cared for along the way. One station was the home of Sam Green, a free black in Maryland, who was a good family man and a preacher. He was later arrested and sent to the state prison for ten years. The charges? Having a copy of *Uncle Tom's Cabin* in his possession.

Over the years she returned about a dozen times to Southern Maryland to bring to freedom more members of her family and some others (perhaps sixty to seventy in all).[15] Her example also inspired many other slaves from her area to escape, and she was able to instruct many of them on how to gain their freedom through the Underground Railroad. We will never really have an accurate account of all these amazing adventures because it was all done clandestinely and records were not kept. But we do know that "Moses" became a well-known symbol among those who wanted to see the slaves freed. She was known and admired by such leaders as William Seward, William Lloyd Garrison, Thomas Garrett, Frederick Douglass, John Brown and Sojourner Truth. Garrett stood in amazement of her and once commented that she seemed "to have a special angel to guard her on her journey of mercy…and confidence that God will preserve her from harm in all her perilous journeys."[16]

## Mysterious Powers

Many felt there was something mystical about Harriet. She had strong intuitive powers, with a sixth sense for danger or an ambush, and often seemed to have a mysterious way of discerning and "envisioning" the way through the forests to safe houses. Governor William Seward said: "I have known Harriet long, and a nobler, higher spirit, or a truer, seldom dwells in human form."[17] Harriet knew the natural signs for travel (moss, the direction of a stream and the stars), but she also believed that she followed the unseen presence of God along her way.[18] She was a believer in omens and dreams and warnings, and these often helped her escape close calls and find her way through the woods to the next station. She was never afraid because she never went anywhere unless the Lord sent her. She seemed to have a "guide" within her that helped her find her way, get out of tough situations and be able to find money, food and clothes just as they ran out. She knew that she could survive even the harshest winter weather because "I jest asked Jesus to take keer of me."[19]

## Close Calls

Along the way there were many occasions when Harriet came close to being caught. On one such occasion the group had reached a "station." "Who are you?" someone asked, and she gave the customary rap—no answer. Then they were told that the former owner was asked to leave for helping negroes. Harriet knew that the person would reveal them, so she took her group to a little island in a swamp, waited in the tall grass and prayed. After dusk a man came by the swamp and whispered that his horse and wagon were waiting for them. They were saved and made it to the next stop!

Another time Harriet and her group heard their pursuers hot on their trail. They were exhausted, out of food and terrified. Harriet hid each one in the woods and then went off to scout for a "safe station" that she knew of. The group waited, frightened and trembling, scarcely breathing so they would not be discovered. It seemed like an endless time that she was away, and then suddenly out of the darkness they heard her voice softly singing: "Oh, go down, Moses, way down into Egypt land, tell old Pharaoh, let my people go." The coast was clear. Harriet had brought food and led her passengers on to the next safe stop.

### The Rescue of Her Brothers

In the early 1850s Harriet began to plan to rescue three of her brothers, Ben, Robert and Henry, from slavery. They had made several attempts to escape themselves, but each time had failed. After hearing that they were to be sold south at Christmas, Harriet decided that it was now or never to plan a rescue. She started by sending a coded letter, telling her brothers to be "always watching unto prayer, and when the good old ship of Zion comes along, to be ready to step on board."[20]

Just before Christmas, Harriet made her way to the eastern shore and arrived on Christmas Eve, an opportune time to escape, for then the masters eased up on their slaves. Harriet left word to meet her brothers, along with Jane, Ben's fiancée, whom they dressed up like a man, to meet at her father's cabin. Harriet did not know that Robert's wife was expecting a baby very soon. The birth delayed him, but nonetheless he was able to tear himself from wife and family and join Harriet and the others at the plantation where her parents lived. At the homestead, Harriet was able to contact her father, and there was a brief reunion when Ben brought them some food. All that time the father kept himself blindfolded, so that when asked he could say that he didn't see his sons or anyone else leave. They couldn't make contact with their mother because she was so excitable that she would make a fuss and raise suspicions. But they looked through the window of the cabin and saw their mother "by the fire with a pipe in her mouth, her head on her hand, rocking back and forth as she did when she was in great trouble, and wondering what new evil had come to her children."[21] They watched with their eyes streaming and then they sadly crept into the night. Their father accompanied them a few miles, still blindfolded, and then stopped, let them go and returned home alone. When they reached Philadelphia, William Still recorded that Harriet now had nine in her group. He took down all their names and made plans to secure passage to New Jersey, across to New York and into Canada.

Arriving in Canada, the group joined other escaped slaves and had to endure the difficult winters, often experiencing cold and hunger. They were able to obtain some work, chopping trees for lumber. Harriet kept house for her family and other poor of the area. She worked hard for her people and often went out begging for food and clothing for them. In the spring Harriet would return to the States, where she would work in hotels or cook for families before returning to Maryland to gather up more slaves.

### Saving Her Parents

In 1857, Harriet decided to take on an extraordinary mission: She would once again risk being apprehended by her now well-alerted and furious master and rescue her aged parents, Ben and Rit. Technically, her parents were not slaves. Her father had been emancipated by his master's legal will and had purchased the freedom of his wife. But the old couple still lived in slave quarters on a plantation and had been separated from their children and grandchildren, who had either been sold south or had escaped with the help of Harriet. The urgency of their rescue arose when Ben was threatened to be tried for sheltering some runaway slaves in his cabin and for working with the Underground Railroad. It was time for Harriet to make her move.

Harriet stealthily traveled south to the eastern shore of Maryland. Harriet arrived at her parents' place and prepared for the escape, knowing full well that the couple, now in their seventies, were too old for the usual routine of traveling on foot by night and hiding by day. Harriet was able to secure an old horse and hitch it to a makeshift cart in which she hid her parents. Traveling by night, she was able to cover the eighty miles to Wilmington, Delaware, where Garrett gave the old couple the money they needed to take the train to Canada. There they had a wonderful reunion with their children, grandchildren, great-grandchildren and cousins. Harriet thoroughly enjoyed reunion celebrations with all the joyous hugs and kisses, and she was always deeply satisfied to see all her risks and efforts reunite her family. But Harriet did not stay around long; she soon returned to Maryland, hoping to lead more of her family and others to freedom.

### Securing House in Auburn

In 1858 Senator William Seward, an admirer of Harriet's work on the Underground Railroad, offered to sell her a house in Auburn, in upstate New York, which she could use to house her family and other needy ex-slaves. Seward later served as secretary of state for Lincoln, and was stabbed as part of the assassination plot that ended Lincoln's life so tragically. Seward was fiercely antislavery and had himself harbored runaway slaves on his own property. Harriet was attracted to Seward's reasonable and flexible terms for the house, and she accepted his offer. She was eager to relocate her family to the United States, in part because the winters in Canada were so harsh. Southern slaves were not prepared for such frigid weather, and inadequate clothing, shelter and food brought on much suffering and illness.

The routes to southern Maryland were now closed to Harriet. The many escapes of slaves from southern Maryland had caused such an uproar there by owners, that Harriet was prevented from returning for more rescues. In addition, Harriet wanted to get more strongly involved in the abolitionist movement in her own country.

### Harper's Ferry, 1859

Harriet met John Brown in 1858 and at the time he told her of his plot to begin a violent rebellion against slavery. Brown had always been strongly opposed to slavery, and he trained his large family to oppose hypocritical Christians who went to church and at the same time enslaved their brothers and sisters. His opposition intensified over the years, and he was further inflamed at the death of a newspaper editor, who was murdered by a mob in Illinois for his antislavery views. After that Brown said he would "consecrate my life to the destruction of slavery."[22] He moved from state to state, hatching plots to get slaves to rebel. In 1856 he directed the executions of a number of men who were proslavery. After that he was determined to give his own life, if necessary, to destroy slavery.

Brown had not been well-received by mainstream abolitionists like William Lloyd Garrison and Frederick Douglass. They and many other abolitionists opposed his violent ways and thought that his plans to lead an army into the South to fight slavery were ill-conceived and extreme. But Harriet strongly supported Brown, thrilled to see a white man take up the cause of the slaves. Brown in turn deeply respected Harriet and was encouraged by her support. Brown had high hopes that Harriet would participate in the uprising, calling her "General Tubman, the best officer he had ever seen who could command an army." Harriet began a lecture tour to raise funds for Brown's cause and apparently had hoped to join in his plots to free slaves. Meanwhile, Brown went on some trial forays, rescuing slaves and killing their owners. In August of 1859, Brown moved to Harper's Ferry, Virginia, with several of his sons and commenced plans to invade the federal arsenal there in order to obtain the weapons needed for his war against slavery. But by this time Brown's "army" consisted of no more than several dozen men, and his money was running out. After delaying the attack on the arsenal until October, Brown finally made his move. Harriet was at that time unaware of the change in plans and had also fallen ill from her old head injury. The raid was poorly planned and Brown's hopes of slaves rising up with him were thwarted by lack of advanced planning. John Brown knew little of military tactics and was soon trapped in the arsenal. After two days of battling, Brown tried to negotiate for hostages, but his hold-out was stormed by federal troops led by Robert E. Lee, and Brown was led off to jail, broken and bleeding. Most of his men, including two of his own sons, were killed in the battle. Brown was tried for treason and hanged.

It would seem that John Brown was more effective against slavery in death than he was in life. News of his raid held the headlines nationwide, and his hanging turned him into a martyr who sacrificed himself to stop slavery. His composure during the trial, the many moving letters he wrote while awaiting his execution, and the dignity with which he held himself at the gallows made him into a hero. Before he died he wrote: "It is a great comfort to feel assured that I am permitted to die for a cause...."[23]

Harriet was deeply moved by Brown's sacrifice. Indeed, she greatly admired his courage and said that she saw the power of God acting in him. She saw the whole affair as a turning point for her in that she sensed that her days on the Underground Railroad were winding down and that she was being called into a great and violent conflict that seemed to lie ahead. She had seen many slaves gaining their freedom, but now she prophetically sensed that the time was drawing near for all of her people to be free from slavery.

She began to show a great deal of enthusiasm for emancipation. At times she would walk along singing and shouting that her people were going to be free. One morning, years before the Emancipation Proclamation was issued by Lincoln, Harriet had a dream while staying with a minister that her people were free. She came down to breakfast shouting, "my people are free, my people are free!" The minister tried to quiet her down and said that they would never see that in their lifetime. But Harriet insisted that freedom was coming to her people very soon. And come it did, but not before this nation's costliest war was waged.

### The Rescue of Charles Nolle

In 1860 Harriet was on her way from her home in Auburn to speak at an abolitionist meeting in Boston. By now Harriet was a popular speaker on the circuit and the stories of her rescues were well-known. When she stopped on the way at Troy, New York, she was confronted with a dramatic scene. A runaway slave, Charles Nolle, had been captured by a Virginian slavecatcher and was being held in a federal courtroom, pending his being shipped back south. A large crowd of antislavery protesters had gathered around the building and the police were nervously guarding Nolle. Harriet immediately sprang into action. She disguised herself as an elderly woman and slowly worked her way through the crowd, wending her way up the stairs into the courtroom. Once she was next to the guards, she knocked them down, grabbed Nolle and dragged him downstairs. Harriet took many blows from police clubs, but she was able to hand Nolle over to some abolitionists, who put him on a boat to cross the Hudson River.

On the other side of the river, the police once again took Nolle into custody and kept him in a judge's office. Harriet and a group of men broke the door down, and in a hail of bullets, which felled some of her companions, she and some other black women stepped over the bodies, and grabbed Nolle. Harriet threw him over her shoulder like a sack of meal, and with bullets whistling by her, got him onto a waiting wagon that brought him to safety.[24]

**A Pivotal Election**

In 1860 the abolitionists were heartened when the Republicans began to support Seward, a staunch opponent of slavery, for president. The party eventually decided that Seward was too radical and would narrow the focus of the election to slavery. There were many other issues: tariffs, homestead lands to be distributed, and railroads, so the Republicans turned to a safer candidate, a politician from Illinois who had gained notoriety debating Stephen Douglas in a Senate race. He had been born in the South, was self-educated and was opposed to slavery but cautious about how to deal with it, at times favoring recolonization or government payments to those who would lose slaves should the law on slavery be repealed. His name was Abraham Lincoln.

Lincoln's name did not appear on southern ballots, and when he was elected president the southern states saw his election as a victory for the abolitionists. The South began to arm, train volunteer forces and make plans for secession. Trade ceased between North and South, and the banks tottered when the South refused to pay millions in debt. Even though Lincoln was still ambiguous about what to do about slavery, many slaves began to believe that freedom would come from "Massa Linkum."[25]

Harriet at first didn't warm up to Lincoln. She felt that his main objective in going to war was to preserve the Union, and that he was too cautious about the abolition of slavery. She believed that the North would be wasting its young men's lives if the slaves weren't emancipated. She said: "God won't let Mister Lincoln beat the South till he does the right thing."[26] She used the analogy of a snake. If the snake bites and the doctor keeps fixing the wound and the snake keeps biting, the solution is to kill the snake. She believed that Lincoln should kill the snake!

Later, even after Lincoln wrote his Emancipation Proclamation, Harriet objected to the way black soldiers fighting for the Union were given lower pay, had to buy their own uniforms, and were segregated when they were wounded and even when they were buried. But eventually, Harriet grew to admire Lincoln for his courage and sound judgment.

**The Civil War**
When the federal post at Fort Sumter was captured by South Carolina troops in 1861, the gauntlet was thrown down and both North and South began mobilizing for war. Both the North and the South had misjudged each other. Many in the North did not think the South was serious about succession, and many in the South did not think that the "immigrants" of the North would be willing to fight to preserve the Union. Now, Fort Sumter was a clear symbol that both sides were prepared to fight each other. There was a lot of flag-waving and recruiting and parading on both sides, but no one realized what an apocalyptic destruction was ahead.

All the advantages seemed to favor the North. The twenty-two states that would remain in the Union (three more would come in before 1865) had a combined population of twenty-two million. But the eleven states that made up the Confederacy had a population of nine million, which included almost four million black slaves. The North was far superior in its industrial capability; its railroads and its navy could control the rivers and ports. But this was all counterbalanced by the fact that the South had to defend its position, while the North had to invade the South, defeat its forces and destroy its government. The North underestimated the determination of Southerners to fight for their land and their way of life.

Many on both sides thought the war would be short, and at first the federal militia was called up for just ninety days' duty. Such optimism was dismissed after the First Battle of Bull Run in Virginia, where the Union forces were soundly defeated by the Confederates and had to withdraw to Washington in a state of panic. It was now clear to many that the Confederate army was going to be a formidable foe, and that the war might go on for years with heavy casualties on both sides.

### Harriet's War Duty

One of the early victories for the Union was the capture of the Confederate forts on the South Carolina coast. In November 1861, the Union sent seventeen wooden cruisers into Port Royal Sound and pounded the shore batteries so effectively that after several hours the defenders evacuated the forts. Supply ships and twelve thousand men landed with little opposition and took possession of the forts. Thus, early in the war, the Union established a key base of operations along the southern coast.

As the Union army battled into the South from these forts, thousands of slaves came over to them wanting to be free. They were poor, sick, half-dressed people who were running from their masters. A common problem was that the slaves often did not know whether they could trust the Yankees. In May of 1862 Harriet was called from her home in Auburn, New York, where she cared for her parents, her relatives and other poor blacks. She was asked to work with these fugitive slaves, or "contrabands," because it was believed that she would be able to gain their trust. Harriet arrived on the South Carolina seacoast in sweltering weather and began her work with the masses of slaves who were swarming into Port Royal, Ladies Island and Hilton Head. Despite strong opposition in the South and in Congress, the fugitives grew in number until hundreds of thousands of men, women and children flooded into the Union camps.

Harriet at first experienced a culture shock because these ex-slaves seemed to be quite primitive and spoke in dialects that she could not understand. Harriet got down to work acting as a nurse among the contrabands, fighting malaria, typhoid, yellow fever and cholera among the slaves and soldiers as well. The skill with herbs and roots that she had learned from her parents came in handy, and her healing powers soon became legendary. Harriet was able to gain the confidence of the slaves with whom she worked by her cheery words, her songs and sacred hymns. With her own funds she built a laundry so that the ex-slaves could have clean clothes, and she provided protection for the young women who were vulnerable to the lusts of the soldiers in the camps. Harriet was also able to obtain valuable information from the former slaves about the southern armies that was useful to her officers.

By this time Harriet had a reputation because of her work on the Underground Railroad. It is said that many of the officers and soldiers recognized that the famous "Moses" was among them, and they tipped their hats when they met her.

**Emancipation**

Lincoln had been gradually moving toward the abolition of slavery, and in September 1862 he published his Emancipation Proclamation. It said that as of January 1, 1863, "all persons held as slaves within any State…the people whereof shall then be in rebellion…shall be thenceforward and forever free." The abolitionists saw this as half a loaf since it was more of an unenforceable moral statement which allowed the slave states three months to make their move, and was silent about a million slaves in the border states. But when January 1 arrived, the

Emancipation Proclamation took effect, and abolitionists and slaves alike held great celebrations. The slaves were free! Now northern soldiers who were perhaps reluctant to fight for the Union now had a more concrete cause—the defeat of the slavocracy.

A military draft was now put in place, and even though for a time blacks and abolitionists rioted against it in New York City, major victories over the South calmed the atmosphere and gave purpose to the northern cause. Blacks were now incorporated into the armed forces and thousands more slaves packed up and headed for freedom in the Union camps.

### Working as a Nurse

Harriet was called upon to work as a hospital nurse with the wounded soldiers. Her familiarity with the herbs and roots of the area enabled her to concoct healing potions and salves at a time when few medicines were available. Early reports tell how Harriet was able to nurse many soldiers suffering in the hospitals from malignant diseases back to health.[27] Rising early each morning, she would attend to the wounds of the soldiers until late at night. Even though many of the soldiers had dysentery, smallpox and other contagious diseases, Harriet jumped right in to help, never worrying about her own health. "The good Lord will take care of me," she would say. Then at the end of a long day with her patients, the indefatigable Harriet would go home to her little cabin, bake pies and make gingerbread and root beer to sell to support herself.

### Working as a Spy and Scout

Harriet also worked as a spy, sneaking through enemy lines, with shots flying by her and surrounded by carnage. Her job was to find out the position and strength of the enemy troops and bring this information back to the Union army. Her knowledge of the woods and survival techniques enabled her to carry out such dangerous missions and also enabled her to lead Union forces through the thickly wooded areas and dangerous swamps.

One of Harriet's most challenging missions occurred in June 1863, when she was asked to accompany a river expedition up the Combahee River. The incident was described at the opening of this chapter. Harriet said that she would always remember a comment made by one old slave that night: "I'd been yere seventy-three years, workin' for my master widout even a dime of wages. I'd worked rain-wet sun-dry. I'd worked wid my mouf full of dust, but could not stop to get a drink of water. I'd been whipped, an' starved, an' I was always prayin', 'Oh! Lord, come an' delibber us!...' Oh! Praise de Lord!...an' now he's come an' we's all free."[28]

Harriet would continue her work as a scout for over three years. In the fall of 1863 she took a leave to see her family back in Auburn, New York. After visiting her family, she moved on to see her kin in Canada and then went on to Boston to raise money for herself and her family. Money was constantly a problem for Harriet. She had received some small sums for working as a scout in the war, but was never paid for her work as a nurse.

After her leave, it appears that Harriet went to Florida to continue her care for the troops. She got another furlough in June of 1864 during which she visited with family and reconnected with abolitionist friends in New York City and Boston. Then, on her way back to South Carolina, she stopped to talk to the troops outside of Philadelphia. The newspapers recorded her rousing speech and pointed out that she was now well-known among the military there as a "great Underground Railroad woman" and patriot. Just before going to South Carolina, she was persuaded by some nurses to help them with sick and wounded black soldiers in Hampton, Virginia. While she was there, the South surrendered and the war ended. Harriet's next mission would be to help her family and friends recover from the hard times of this devastating war.

The war had lasted for four long years, and hundreds of battles were fought in dozens of states, with men standing in fields, hacking and shooting each other to death in what turned out to be a national bloodbath. At places like Shiloh, Tennessee, 25,000 perished in one day;

at Antietam, Maryland: 23,000; Fredericksburg, Maryland: 18,000; Chancellorsville, Virginia: 24,000; Gettysburg, Pennsylvania: 50,000; Atlanta: 12,500; Wilderness, Virginia: 27,000; and at the Peninsular Campaign in Virginia: 36,000. In the end over 600,000 Americans died of wounds or disease, more than the total casualties from all the wars this country has ever fought.

The war brought the South to its knees, causing a great loss of life and property and bringing wide-scale economic destruction. The Confederate states lost two-thirds of their wealth during the war. The loss of slave property through emancipation accounted for much of this, but the economic infrastructure in the South was also severely damaged in other ways. Railroads and industries were leveled, and nearly half of all farm machinery and livestock was destroyed.

For many in the North, it was time for celebration. The Union had prevailed, four million slaves had been freed, and the Underground Railroad was officially closed forever. But then the dark news came— the president had been assassinated. Abraham Lincoln, who had bravely led his nation through this horrible war and who had ended slavery here forever, had been killed by an assassin.

After the war, in December 1865, the Thirteenth Amendment banning slavery was passed. Blacks were given citizenship and the right to vote, and the long, chaotic and often violent road toward Reconstruction began. The South fought back with Black Codes that severely restricted blacks, and bands of white-robed klansmen roamed the South, attacking Union supporters and blacks.

The slaves now moved to the arena of the white working man, which many came to see as a new form of slavery. The economic power of the slave master now passed to the stockholders and the captains of industry in the North.

### Harriet Goes Home

On the way back home from the war, Harriet soon discovered that ending slavery had not ended discrimination. She had taken a train from

Philadelphia to New York, using her half-fare military pass. When the conductor came around, he didn't believe that a "nigger" could have such a pass and told her to go to the smoking car. When Harriet refused, the conductor tried to physically remove her from her seat but couldn't deal with her strength. He called several other officials to help him, and they were able to drag her and throw her into the smoking car. Harriet suffered injuries to her arms, shoulders and ribs. So much for welcoming home a war hero!

Harriet returned home to Auburn penniless and applied for a pension for her military service. Her application read:

> My claim against the U.S. is for three years services as nurse and cook in hospitals, and as commander of several men (eight or nine) as scouts during the late war of the Rebellion under directions and orders of Edwin M. Stanton Secretary of War, and of several Generals.
>
> I claim for my services above named the sum of Eighteen hundred dollars. The annexed copies have recently been read over to me and are true to the best of my knowledge information and belief.

The document bears Harriet's X and someone wrote in "Harriet Davis, late Harriet Tubman."[29] Harriet's request was turned down for lack of adequate proof of her service to the government.

Harriet soon found the conditions to be overcrowded in her home in Auburn. Besides her relatives, there were always blacks coming back from Canada, returning veterans, boarders or people just passing through. Her parents were now dependent upon her, and often turned their scoldings and complaints on her. That winter they were short of food and had to burn the fences for firewood. Harriet was unable to earn any money to help because of the injuries she suffered on the train. She had to go into town and get the food she needed on credit. Fortunately, she was able to receive donations from some of the abolitionists she had worked with. Meanwhile, Harriet continued her struggle to receive back pay for her services during the war effort. Her appeals were all turned down, even though she secured high recommendations from the Union officers.

In good weather Harriet organized events to raise money to support the education and advancement of the many slaves now freed in the South. She also channeled donations into projects for needy people in her town—orphans, disabled veterans, widows and the homeless. One citizen of Auburn wrote: "All these years her doors have been open to the needy…. The aged, the babe deserted, the demented, the epileptic, the blind, the paralyzed, the consumptive all have found shelter and welcome."[30] To help her, the neighbors often left bags of food and clothing on her porch.

### Her Biography

In the spring of 1868, Sarah Bradford, a writer of short stories and novels who lived near Auburn, offered to help Harriet's cause by publishing a book about her life. Bradford did extensive interviews with Harriet and also contacted people who knew her for testimonials. The final text, which was written in haste because Bradford was leaving for Europe, contains many romanticized exaggerations as well as some white bias from the author. Still, it is a charming and useful text, and Bradford generously turned over all the profits to Harriet, enabling her to pay off some of her debts. The text raised Harriet's life and work to mythic level, and in time she emerged as "New Moses," "the Black Joan of Arc" for school children. It would be only in recent times that the "real" Harriet Tubman could be recovered by scholars and historians.

### A Home for Needy Blacks

Harriet did not wait long before she began to dream of her next project—a home for needy black people. In 1864 she drew up plans for a kind of freedom plantation on a piece of land that adjoined her own property. She was able to persuade her pastor to help her with the down payment. She struggled to run the place for poor people for the next thirty years. She extended hospitality to numerous people and always enjoyed visits from notables like Sojourner Truth and Booker T. Washington.

## Marrying Again

In 1869 Harriet fell in love again, this time with Nelson Davis, a veteran and one of her boarders, who was more than twenty years younger. Her first husband, John Tubman, had recently been gunned down in Maryland, and Harriet apparently felt that she was now free to marry again. The couple was married in the local Presbyterian church in the presence of many family members, friends and dignitaries in Auburn. This family togetherness had been her dream during all the years of rescuing her family from slavery. Together the couple opened a brickmaking operation behind the house that Harriet now owned outright. Both of them worked in the brickyard and on their farm. Nelson suffered from tuberculosis and was frequently ill, so Harriet had to often fill in for him and also took up domestic work for some of the wealthier families in Auburn. By this time, many of Harriet's family and friends had moved to residences of their own in Auburn.

Though Harriet was now happily married, there would be setbacks. In 1872 her longtime protector William Seward died and was buried in Auburn. The newspaper pointed out the poignant gesture when she put a wreath of field flowers on his grave. In 1873 she was beaten by a pair of con men and cheated out of two thousand dollars. In 1874 a bill made it to Congress pointing out the great service she had given to the government as nurse, scout and spy and seeking just compensation. The bill passed the House, but was rejected by the Senate. In 1888, after nineteen years of marriage, her husband Nelson died. The following year, her brother John Henry Stewart passed away.

## On the Circuit

During the postwar years Harriet was popular on the lecture circuit and often gave her support to suffragettes. Her down-home style and the fascinating stories of her adventures on the Underground Railroad and in the war riveted her audiences. In 1896 she spoke at the founding meeting of the National Association of Colored Women. In 1907 the New England Women's Suffrage Association honored Tubman in Boston, and in 1904 she was introduced by Susan B. Anthony as a "living legend" to the New York State Women's Suffrage association. It was on this occasion that Harriet said, "I was conductor of the Underground Railroad for eight years, and I can say what most conductors can't say— I never ran my train off the track and I never lost a passenger."[31]

The fees for talks on the circuit helped Harriet's financial situation. Things improved even more when the government decided to give a modest payment to the widows of war veterans. Her ill husband, Nelson, qualified as a veteran, but Harriet had to produce a great deal of paperwork proving his identity, his military record and their marriage. In 1892 she was granted the grand total of eight dollars per month. In addition, her persistent appeals to the Congress were finally heard, and it was decided that in view of her wartime services she would be allotted a total pension of twenty dollars per month.

**Her Last Years**

In 1903 Harriet turned the home for the aged and its property over to her church, with the agreement that it would be maintained as a home for "aged and indigent colored people."[32] When she was eighty-five she was able to attend a gala anniversary celebration for the Harriet Tubman Home, which was now thriving. As she circulated among the crowd, she noted that it was one of the happiest moments of her life. "Moses" was still leading her people out of poverty and oppression. In 1904 another such home was established in Boston and named after Tubman.

Harriet began to slow down in 1911, when she was hospitalized for a lengthy period. Early in 1913 she became severely ill and knew that she would soon die. News of her condition was noted in the *New York Times* and *New York Tribune* and tributes were paid to her work rescuing slaves and serving during the war. Harriet died on the evening of March 10, 1913—the same year Rosa Parks was born. Harriet passed on surrounded by her family and friends. The local paper reported that she whispered to those around her the same message while many of her loved ones were in slavery: "I go to prepare a place for you."[33] Her good friend and protector William Seward has given us what might have been the epitaph for this great woman: "The cause of freedom owes her much; the country owes her much."[34]

C  H  A  P  T  E  R      F  O  U  R

## *Thea Bowman: Freedom From Prejudice*

All the bishops of the United States had gathered in South Orange, New Jersey, and were in for an unprecedented experience: They were about to be "lectured" by a black nun! There she sat in front of them, dressed in brightly colored African fabrics, her hair gone from chemotherapy treatments, and her huge dark eyes searing into their souls. Suddenly Sister Thea sang out in her magnificent voice: "Sometimes I feel like a motherless child / A long way from home." Then she called for their attention: "Can you hear me, church?" She reminded the bishops that as a black person she had been told that the church was her home, and now she asked them to help her get home.

The nun then gave the bishops a history lesson about her people, going back to the great nations of Africa, and the cultural treasures they brought with them as they were chained and shipped over to America as slaves. She reminded the bishops how black folks helped build this nation and gave their lives for it in war. Then she shouted: "You know what I am talking about, church? I mean, are you walking with me church?" The "old lady" had some words to say to her bishops, and she wanted to make sure they were "lis't'n up!"

She reminded the bishops how her people have suffered from prejudice, even within the church, and she called them to give black

Catholics their due recognition in the church. She asked that the bishops educate blacks, consult them and call forth their unique gifts. She said, "Today we're called to walk together in a new way toward that land of promise and to celebrate who we are and whose we are."[1] Then she did an amazing thing: She told the bishops: "You all get up!" She asked them to get close, cross their arms, hold hands and sing with her, "We Shall Overcome." Awkward and even a bit giddy at first, the bishops soon got into it and sang their hearts out, some with tears in their eyes. The woman who had touched the bishops' hearts was Sister Thea Bowman. In many ways, this was the climax of her life's work, to stand up for the dignity of her people and to free the church and society from prejudice. The very next year Thea died from cancer at the age of fifty-three.

**The Early Years**

Thea was born in 1937 in Yazoo City, Mississippi. This was the Deep South, the land of the great river, bayous and magnolia trees made famous in the novels of William Faulkner. It is an area where segregation was strictly enforced, a place where horrible racial violence and lynchings had taken place. Just north of Yazoo City is the small town of Money, where in 1955 Emmett Till, a fourteen-year-old Chicago youth was shot and savagely beaten to death for whistling at a female store clerk. Just south is Jackson, where Medgar Evers, a leading civil rights leader, was murdered in his own driveway in 1963. To the east is the town of Philadelphia, where three young civil rights workers were brutally beaten and shot to death by the Ku Klux Klan (KKK) in 1964. From Thea's teenage years on, Mississippi burned with racial hatred and violence.

Baptized as Bertha, the Bowmans' only child later changed her name to Thea, after her father, Theon Bowman. Thea's father was a doctor who gave up a promising career in New York to serve black people in Mississippi, where most white physicians would not do so. Theon had to get up at dawn to serve his patients before they started work, and he cared for them after working hours far into the night. Dr. Bowman didn't receive much for his services and was often paid in vegetables, a piece of beef or car repairs.

Thea's mother was Mary Esther, a generous and loving teacher by trade, who carefully looked after the future of her only child. Thea says that her mother was "sweet and cultured," and wanted her daughter to be the same, but instead had to settle for a "little rowdy" for a child. Mary Esther taught her daughter to never return insult for insult or hate for hate, and to respect and pray for those who abused her, realizing that they needed help. She would say, "You know they crucified my Lord and he never said a mumbling word."[2]

### Old Folks' Child

Both parents taught Thea to be proud that she was black and to value her culture. She learned that her grandfather had actually been a slave, and she always considered herself to be "an old folks' child." Her parents were older, and their friends were grandparents and great-grandparents who taught her the music, songs, faith and stories of survival in difficult times. They taught her about the trials of slavery and segregation, and how to stand up against prejudice with courage and dignity. She says that though most of her people were poor, she "knew people who live rich lives and continued to inspire me."[3] One such woman was "Mother Ricker," who would feed twenty to thirty children at her house, and have rousing sessions singing the many great songs from their culture. Thea remembers wonderful gatherings in her own home, when thrilling stories of the past were told and the folks joined in laughter and in the singing of the old songs.

The old folks taught Thea about the days of slavery, when their people were brought from Africa in the holds of ships, stacked next to each other amidst stench and filth. They described how slaves worked from dawn to dusk in the scorching heat; how children were torn from their mothers' arms by slave traders; they recounted how young girls were molested; they described the blood around the whipping post; and they told of the hounds trained to hunt them down and tear their flesh. They had been taught that God created them to humbly serve their masters. Thea learned about how slaves were freed, only to be forced into the bonds of segregation just a few years later, where they were set apart in schools, churches, restaurants, hotels, buses, restrooms, even hospitals. In Mississippi, the lands given to blacks were often marshy areas filled with mosquitoes, frogs and land crabs.

The old folks taught Thea to "pass on" the wisdom of her African heritage, where community was so valued. They encouraged her to recognize her gifts and to be responsible to her community. Thea says that the old folks used to say: " 'Each one teach one.' If you know how to cook, you teach somebody; if you know how to raise a child, you teach somebody; if you know how to get a job, you teach somebody.... To be responsible is to know your best and to give your best. Don't ask for money in exchange for your gifts. You help me and I help you."[4]

**Moved to a Catholic School**

After five years in the poor and understaffed segregated school, Thea could still neither read nor write, so her mother made a decision that would change the direction of her daughter's life. She sent her to a Catholic school, which was not an easy decision. The Catholic Franciscan sisters had come to town recently, and many of the townsfolk thought they worshiped statues and spoke in foreign tongues (Latin). The nuns had constructed army barracks, where all children were welcome. In spite of the prejudice against Catholics in the town, the generous and loving service the sisters offered began to win over many of the people.

Thea was enrolled in the school and immediately began to make real progress in her studies. The sisters borrowed desks and books and taught the children the same lessons that their elders had passed along: to use their gifts to teach others. Thea was weak in math and got help; she was strong in reading and helped those who were not. The sisters also worked with their students' parents, teaching them how to help themselves and showing them how to raise funds to educate their children. Thea found a home in the school and liked to hang out with the sisters every moment she could. She says that she was inspired by them—not by their doctrine, of which she knew little, or by their rituals, but by the example of their love and service. Though most of the children were black and not Catholic, the sisters were totally dedicated to them as children and as learners.

**Conversion and Vocation**

Within a few years, Thea decided to become a Catholic. She was baptized at age ten and confirmed a year later. She had experienced Catholics as people who loved others and who reached out to the poor, the hungry and needy children. She later wrote, "I was drawn to examine and accept the Catholic faith because of the day-to-day witness of Catholic Christians who first loved me, then shared with me their story, their values, their beliefs; who first loved me, then invited me to share with them in community, prayer and mission."[5] At fifteen, Thea announced that she wanted to join the Franciscan sisters, and she left her beloved home and community to become the only black member of a convent in La Crosse, Wisconsin.

The convent in Wisconsin was a culture shock for Thea. At home she said she had seen "more poverty, filth, disease, and suffering than many people see in a lifetime."[6] She had witnessed the deep racial prejudice and violence of the South. The other sisters had led rather sheltered lives and had no experience with blacks. The sisters carried their own biases, and Thea had to endure their comments about "nigger toes" and "nigger heaven," as well as their patronizing remarks that they liked her—even though she was black. She learned that there was a deep prejudice against her race among many Catholics, and that the community would prefer that she act like a nice Midwestern white girl. She found the motherhouse to be "cold and white," and she missed the liveliness, energy, song and down-home lifestyle of her people back in Mississippi. But Thea felt called to be a sister, and she was willing to go along and put up with whatever she had to in order to become the best sister she could be. She adjusted, made good friends and moved toward her goal.

When she was eighteen, Thea developed tuberculosis and was sent to a sanatorium. While recovering there for a year, she took a course in writing and produced a revealing essay called "Away f'om Home." Written in southern black dialect, it tells how she longed for her parents and relatives back home and how difficult the winters were without green grass and flowers. She writes,

> [W]hen meal time comes, it really sets my mouth a waterin' fo' that there chicken Southern fried, an' for some hominy grits or some o' them fluffy, nice, high hoe-cakes like ole Mama cooks.... Then there's the nights; I lies abed an' dreams that I'as stranded in the sno', and I can heah the old folks callin'.... I ain't complainin', but you all can see that this yere ain't at all like home. Nossuh! I ain't complainin', but this yere ain't like home a'tall.[7]

Once Thea had recovered, she started her studies at Viterbo College in La Crosse, Wisconsin. There she blossomed as a student and joined with many teachers who shared her love for learning. She writes, "I was an English major with a minor in drama and I was just having fun. I loved literature and I met teachers who were able to help me open up the books, teachers who realized that I had some gift. That was something that had never occurred to me: to realize that I could do things like think, read, write."[8] At the same time, Thea still experienced a deep loneliness, for she had little opportunity to be in touch with her past, her family or the contributions of her own people.

**Thea the Teacher**
After college Thea was assigned to be a teacher. As was typical of the times, she was put into all kinds of teaching situations—at both primary and secondary schools—where she had to sink or swim. Fortunately, Thea was a natural teacher and was much loved by her stu-

dents. In teaching, she used the wisdom she had learned from the old folks and the Franciscan sisters who taught her. First, she went against the educational system she had seen so often where some children are taught that they are superior, while others are told that they are inferior. Thea taught all her children, "You're somebody special because you are God's child."[9] Secondly, she taught each student to discover his or her gift. Thea had a knack of sizing people up quickly. Her students have commented that she seemed to be able to look right down into their souls, see what they were capable of, and then push them to do it. She also had the talent of asking just the right question to spark a lively discussion. "We are all folks together," she would say, and then launch into a song. She saw learning as a community effort and asked all her students to participate in teaching each other. "Each one teach one" became her motto.

Thea loved to teach Shakespeare, and his plays gave her an opportunity to be the minstrel and troubadour she was born to be. She and her students went to any place where the plays were put on, and then would come back to sing the songs and dramatize the scenes themselves.

But teaching wasn't always comfortable for Thea. She had much difficulty teaching high-school biology because it was not her field, and she didn't think the students studied enough. Thea could just not understand how students wouldn't put forth good effort the way she had always done, and she would come home from class discouraged.

Thea's next assignment was exciting for her. She was sent to teach in a Catholic high school in Canton, Mississippi, where she could be once again with her parents and friends, once again back home in the South. This brought Thea back to her roots, but at the same time she found teaching high school students to be very demanding.

### The Catholic University of America

The Franciscan superiors decided that Thea would perform better at the college level, and they sent her to The Catholic University of America in Washington, D.C., in 1968 to gain her doctorate in English.

This was heady stuff for a sister from Mississippi, who had been a schoolteacher for ten years. Now she would be part of a city and university where she would encounter much more diversity and be challenged by graduate studies.

The late 1960s were turbulent times in the United States and especially in the nation's capital. Martin Luther King, Jr., was assassinated the year Thea came to Washington. She would remain an admirer of King's and would later reflect on those days in Washington: "We are here to celebrate a dream—a dream of freedom…. A dream that men and women and children can find life and liberty and happiness and wholeness. Men, women, children, black, red, white, brown, yellow and all the colors and hues between—have lived, have died to make that dream a reality."[10] The Civil Rights Movement was in full force, with marches in Birmingham and D.C. in 1963, civil rights legislation in 1964, the march on Selma in 1965, and the Poor People's March in D.C. in 1968. Thea also witnessed many demonstrations against the Vietnam War during those years.

In the late 1960s, the Vatican II explosion hit the church, and Thea got caught up in the enthusiasm of church renewal. The idea of the church as "people" was just what she had experienced growing up, and she knew well what it was to "celebrate" liturgy in a community of closely bonded folk. She cheered the notion of going "back to the roots," the promotion of religious freedom, and the church being actively involved with the world's issues of poverty, prejudice, injustice and violence. She had been brought up on ecumenism and she had learned from her early school days with the sisters that love had to be the center of catechesis.

### Going Back to Her Roots

It was during this period at The Catholic University that some other significant changes took place within this young nun. Meeting fellow black students there, Thea got back in touch with values she had learned from the old folks in Mississippi, who sang about their woes and their joys, who supported each other in community, and who talked with God throughout the day. As she would say later, she discovered more intensely than ever that: "I like being black. I like being myself and I thank God for making my black self."[11]

At the same time, Thea found that at the university, where many religious orders gathered for study, racism existed within higher education and even the best of Catholicism. And she observed how educational institutions like The Catholic University of America seemed to be often dedicated to a "melting pot" or "common destiny" approach, where racial and ethnic minorities are expected to give up their identities and blend into the dominant white culture. She discovered that the university taught "white" history and "white" literature and even "white" Catholicism. She continued to observe that there was little place for black culture in Catholicism itself. She didn't see the achievements or gifts of her culture being recognized, and at the same time she observed that negative stereotypes were still perpetuated.

Thea often told people that they could not expect her to melt into and fit into other cultures. She treasured her own roots and was not about to give them up. But her minority position often gave Thea the impression of being shy, intense and even reclusive. She often put herself down with comments like "my big ol' head" as she worked to flatten her hair. And she found herself often reminding her fellow students that "Black folk won't bite."[12]

Two things helped Thea during her time at The Catholic University. First, she met many outstanding black religious and priests at the university who valued black culture and religious celebrations. She realized that she was not alone in her love for the energy, compassion and strong bonds in the black community. She was not alone in her love for the "ol' time religion," with its rich songs, dances and rituals.

The second saving feature was the opportunity to study the oral literary traditions while working on English literature. In her studies she came to realize that the oral tradition in literature was still alive and developing among many black people. Thea steeped herself in the study of literature and linguistics, always with an eye on how all this related to the oral tradition and songs of her people. At one point she wrote a paper on the oral literary tradition. She taught the first black studies course ever offered at The Catholic University. At one point, she even presented and "sang" a paper on the Negro spiritual at Howard University. After that, Thea began to be in demand on the college circuit, singing the spirituals of her people, while still dressed in the modified habit of her order.

Her mission in life was beginning to take shape: the promotion of racial understanding and freeing people from prejudice. As Thea puts it:

My favorite approach toward promoting racial understanding is to bring people into situations where they can share their treasures. I mean treasures such as art, food, prayers, history and traditions. I think as people share those treasures we get to know one another. Then we reach a point where we can talk about our concerns and issues and needs. As I grow to understand your needs and you grow to understand mine, we can see our common needs and begin to work together.[13]

Thea finished her Ph.D. in English in 1972, spent the summer traveling in Europe and studying at Oxford, and then began her teaching at Viterbo College (now University) in La Crosse, Wisconsin.

### Viterbo College

Thea taught English at Viterbo for six years and was now at her peak in teaching and in sharing her songs and culture. She found herself sometimes going against the current. She says,

I was surprised to find that so many of the students I met as freshmen were spending most of their time trying to figure out what somebody else wanted them to think and what somebody else wanted them to say. I tried to show them that surviving college was simple: one of my primary objectives was that I should have a good time, that my students should have a good time and enjoy what we're doing. That got me into trouble sometimes....[14]

Naturally, Thea dedicated herself to teaching her students how to think for themselves.

Thea liked the close family atmosphere of Viterbo and saw herself as a Franciscan troubadour teaching the good news with joy and singing. She said: "Somebody like me, a teacher of English language and literature, was made to be a minstrel and troubadour."[15] For her, there had to be serious work, but always time for laughter, fun and play. Humor was part of her life, and she liked to make fun of herself. When someone said more Theas were needed, she replied: "One's enough, you ask my friends. They'll tell you that's plenty."[16]

## Reaching Out to a Larger World

At this time, Thea began an effort that would remain central to her mission: to help students to know and be proud of their culture and races. She wanted her students to step out of their cultural "bubbles," learn to appreciate other cultures and races and become free of their prejudices. Thea studied Native American cultures and others, and she began to do intercultural workshops for elementary school children in La Crosse and surrounding areas. This was all new and challenging for that part of the Midwest!

In 1978 Thea's parents' health had grown to be such a concern that she returned to their tiny clapboard house in Canton to take care of them. At the same time she assumed a post in the Office of Intercultural Awareness for the Diocese of Jackson. This job enabled Thea to continue her mission to free people from cultural and racial prejudice.

## Blackness as a Gift

Thea knew from her personal experience that many people—including people of her own race—were taught that black people were inferior. Therefore she was determined to use her talents and energy to bring to light that blackness was a gift to be proud of and to be admired. She studied the history of her people and pointed to the great cultures of Egypt and Africa with their contributions in art, mathematics, architecture, religion and crafted articles in textiles and gold. Thea liked to point to blacks in the New Testament—Simon of Cyrene, who helped Jesus carry his cross, and the Ethiopian eunuch who came to believe in Jesus after being instructed by the apostle Philip. She would point out that her people didn't come to the New World on the Mayflower, but on slave ships in chains. Subjected to horrendous suffering, they came as "Proud, strong men and women, artists, teachers, healers, warriors and dream makers, inventors and builders...." They brought with them the treasured spiritual and cultural gifts of Africa, and clung to their African ways of thinking, celebrating, singing and being together in laughter and tears.[17] They came to North America, the Caribbean, Central and Latin America, where they mingled their blood with Europeans, Hispanics, Native Americans and Asians.

Thea was proud of her people and recognized the place of honor they should have in this country. She would proclaim: "[W]e are here in this land, and this is our land."[18] She would point out how her people helped build this nation, picked its crops, constructed its buildings, taught and raised its children and defended this country in all the wars, starting with the American Revolution.

Several trips to Africa deepened Thea's understanding of her roots. She was moved when she was accepted as belonging to Africa and delighted to be mistaken for an African. She loved the scenic beauty, the art, music, dance, drama and prayer of the African people, and felt that they ministered to her with shared stories, laughter and tears. Each time, Thea returned home more determined to share the beauty, wholeness and spirituality of the African people with Americans of all colors.[19]

Thea became completely dedicated to her mission to help her people be proud of their race and to free them from low self-esteem and feelings of inferiority. In the schools Thea taught the children to be proud of their black skin, of their culture and music. During a *60 Minutes* interview, she told Mike Wallace: "When I work with my kids, I say, 'black is beautiful,' and I make them say to themselves, 'I am beautiful.' Until they have found the beauty in themselves, they cannot appreciate the beauty in others."[20]

Thea taught her people their forgotten history. It was the story of a people who had a tremendous capacity for work, yet had to watch others benefit from their slave labors. They were a people who had enormous capability to maintain their dignity amidst slavery, where they experienced degradation, humiliation and severe punishments. They were a people who had developed enormous potential for dealing with hardships. They knew how to heal and forgive: "Our history has given us black men and black women who could tend to the wounds inflicted by evil. They could mend a broken heart; they could hang on to a battered woman; they could overcome rejection; they could look beyond prejudice; they could find new strength in the face of adversity."[21]

Thea called her people to an inner freedom of the heart: She said, "The worst slavery is not the slavery that comes from outside, that comes from the whips or from the dogs, or from the forced labor. The worst slavery is the slavery in your own hearts and slavery in your own homes. Harriet Tubman said she was free from the time she was six years old because she was free in her heart."[22]

### The Struggle of Her People

Thea was saddened by the plight of her people. In spite of the Civil Rights Movement, African Americans were still disproportionately poor, lacking in employment, education, healthcare and housing. She was saddened by the high incidence of violence, suicide, addictions and imprisonment among black males. She pointed out that her people were "still trying to find home in the homeland...still struggling to gain access to equal opportunity."[23]

This would be her mission: to alert others of their calling to break down barriers. As she once said in an address celebrating the life of Martin Luther King, Jr.:

We are all called to free ourselves and to free one another.... Some of us walk around, and we think we're free. Some people think, well, I have a good job and my children are in school and the Klan is not at my door. Folks are not insulting me on a regular basis. But there's poverty, there's still ignorance, there's still aggression. It's not over....[24]

In an impassioned speech, she urged the people of Milwaukee "to work together, all of us, work together for freedom for all of us, for all God's children...to be about peace, to be about justice, to be about freedom, and to be about unity."[25]

**Black Spirituality**

Thea especially appreciated the uniqueness of black spirituality. She saw this spirituality as one that actively testified to the glory of God and the compassion of Jesus. It was spirituality that was dedicated to affirming God's children. Unlike much of Western spirituality, black spirituality was holistic, in that it was not afraid to express emotions and was comfortable with the movements of the body. She believed that there are uniquely African ways of embodying and celebrating the work in song and dance. Thea once pointed out that she tried to help people sing and praise God with their bodies. She felt that clergy had no training in "body work," and so she attempted to teach techniques of relaxation, rhythm and communication that come from the black community. She knew that deep in her culture there were African feelings of oneness with nature, of sorrow from being enslaved, of yearning for freedom. These deep emotions were openly expressed in their celebrations and were partly the way the people could survive their desolate conditions. And many were able to survive indescribable miseries because of their deep faith in themselves, their own wisdom and power, and in their God.

Another unique aspect of traditional black faith is that it is not rooted only in the individual as it is so often in the West. Black faith is a participatory faith, springing from Africa's high regard for family and community. Thea encouraged blacks to journey together in faith, holding on to one another, supporting and loving one another. She called them to march together toward home, where they will feel they belong and be loved as they are.

Thea honored the prayer tradition of her people, which tries to go to God with deep feelings and passions. She said that her people wanted to have the same feelings as Jesus as he hung on the cross, his anguish and abandonment, the love and compassion that motivated Jesus to give life and salvation to the world.[26]

## The Black Family

Thea was seriously concerned about black families. She knew how the family structure of her people had been torn apart by slavery, which did not recognize slave marriages, which condoned sexual demands upon slave women by their owners, and which routinely destroyed families by selling off slave children to the highest bidder. Thea was concerned about so many single mothers and grandmothers raising children in fatherless homes. She decried the high incidence of crime, addiction and imprisonment among black men.

While working for the diocese of Jackson, Mississippi, Thea edited a book that promoted healthy black family life. Here she encouraged black families to strengthen their racial roots and to celebrate their wonderful traditions in their homes. She demonstrated that black families have had to endure slavery and segregation and yet have been able to survive with many of their cultural treasures. She encouraged blacks to continue their struggle for liberation from both external domination and internal contradictions. Thea wanted the book to demonstrate that in spite of the problems in black families, the black family is alive and well and still has much strength and beauty, and is able to foster deep faith and strong family bonds.[27]

Thea constantly referred to the wisdom of the elders, from whom she had learned the stories of how patience and forgiveness can overcome hatred and bigotry, how endurance and compassion can survive the most horrible oppression and cruelty. She often spoke of the "moans" whereby her people expressed their strength and courage to survive the painful journey. From the old folks she learned how to walk with her head high and "lean on the everlasting arms" of the Lord.[28] They had taught Thea to sink her roots deep into the black experience of God and to spread the love she found there to people of all cultures, classes and religions. One of her fellow black sisters describes this mission as follows:

> Thea's interaction with the many and varied cultures sensitized and refined her own intensity for outreach and further expanded the boundaries of her heart so that all persons had a feeling of self-worth as they experienced the warmth of her magnetic love. Yes, Thea learned the lessons of her elders well. Her message was always "We are all God's children and there is room for all of us."[29]

## Mission to Black Catholics

Thea felt a special calling to help black Catholics realize the unique gifts they brought to the church and to help the church openly receive and appreciate these treasures. She called for recognition of black Catholics within the church, for positions of leadership. Thea knew full well that the "invisibility" of black Catholics in the American church was due to the legacy of racism. She agreed with the black Catholic bishops of the United States when they wrote: "Blacks and other minorities still remain absent from aspects of Catholic life and are only meagerly represented on the decision-making level…. This racism, at once subtle and masked, still festers within our Church as within our society."[30] Thea recognized that unless the Catholic church responded, many of the gifts of the black community would be lost to the church.

As we saw earlier, toward the end of her life Thea had a rare opportunity to address the American bishops. Now one of the "old folks" herself, Thea gave them an earful. She first posed a question: "What does it mean to be black and Catholic?" and then with her magnificent voice

burst out with the answer: "Sometimes I feel like a motherless child...."
She told them how proud she was of the few black bishops among
them. "[T]hese bishops are our own.... [W]e raised them.... [I]n a
unique way, they can speak to us and for us.... [Y]'all talk about what
you have to do if you want to be a multi-cultural church: Sometimes I
do things your way; sometimes you do things mine...."[31] She called for
more black priests and bishops, because "The leaders are supposed to
look like their folks, ain't that what the church says?"[32]

There she sat, weary from advancing cancer, yet vibrant with those
flashing dark eyes and her colorful African robes. She was there to tell
them what it meant for her to be black and Catholic. She told them: "It
means that I come to my church fully functioning. That doesn't frighten
you, does it? I bring my self, my black self. I bring my whole history, my
traditions, my experience, my culture. I bring my African-American
song and dance and gesture and movement and preaching and teaching
and healing and responsibility...."[33] She instructed the bishops on black
spirituality, which is contemplative, biblical, holistic. It is an embodied
faith that values the entire person; a communal faith that wants to be
together, even with the bishops. Thea leaned forward, looked these
ecclesiastics in the eye and said: "You know, when our bishop is around,
we want him to be where we can find him, where we can reach out and
touch him, where we can talk to him. Don't be too busy, you-all."[34] She
encouraged the bishops to be one with their people and candidly
addressed the high walls of separation that exist in the church. She said:
"That's one thing black folk can teach you. Don't let folk divide you or
put the lay folk over here and the clergy over here, put the bishops in
one room and clergy in the other room, put the women over here and
the men over here."[35] She reminded the bishops that blacks see themselves as "Spirit-filled" and like to shout out and express their feelings.
No "feeble service" for her people! If the church is calling for participa-
tion in liturgy as well as in ministry, it has to be open to the diversity
and richness that blacks have to contribute in both of these areas.

She reminded the bishops that they have to stop looking at blacks as a minority, because there are more black Catholics in Africa than there are in the United States. Moreover, the church in Africa is growing much faster and has many more people choosing to serve as priests and religious than the American church. She wanted the bishops to realize that the Roman Catholic church is a world church, which includes people of all colors. People should be able to bring their culture with them to the liturgy, teaching and service of the church.

Thea reminded the bishops in this country that "To be black and Catholic still, though, often feels like being a second- or third-class citizen of the holy city."[36] There are black laity, priests and bishops, she said, but they are invisible in that they are not consulted when decisions are made. Black Catholics are patronized and treated with the old "mission" mentality. Thea asked them to drop their prejudices about blacks and accept their unique religious ways of expressing themselves. She complains: "When we attempt to bring our black gifts to the church, people who do not know us say we're being non-Catholic or separatists or just plain uncouth."[37]

Thea urged the bishops to help blacks get education, which she believed was the way out of poverty. She had known the poor educational opportunities in a segregated public school and her life had been changed radically by the Catholic education she had received from the Franciscan sisters. There she met a diversity of faiths and met sisters and priests who truly loved all the students. Years later she attended a reunion with her classmates, and they all agreed that the Catholic school was a graced experience for them.

Thea stressed that Catholic schools can offer a unique opportunity not only for black children but for children of all different faiths and races. If the diversity she experienced is maintained, these schools can prepare young people for the pluralistic world in which they live. She believed that such diversity can witness to a central Christian teaching that we be loving and open to all persons. Catholic schools can also teach students of different faiths a rich mutuality of exchange of religious beliefs, which can help all the students clarify their own personal beliefs. Such schools can also develop attitudes and skills so necessary for ecumenical and interfaith dialogue and cooperation.[38]

Thea sees diversity as an integral part of Catholic education because there is so much to learn from other traditions. Native Americans can teach us a love of nature; Asian religions can show us the value of meditation and prayer; Buddhists can show the value of involving the young in ministry; and Muslims can teach us how to connect faith with social and political issues.[39]

She firmly held to the conviction that much is lost if Catholic schools remain as ghettos closed to the diversity of religions and races. The schools must move beyond the European cultures and the middle class and reach out to other cultures wherein the poor and disadvantaged so sorely need education. They must be committed to learning from the rich cultures of these "outsiders" and dedicated to empowering all students. As we saw earlier, Thea closed by inviting the bishops to join her in the black religious experience. They had encountered a black woman who seemed sure of herself as priest and prophet, and they had been preached to by an elder of the black community.

**Black Songs of Faith**

Thea believed that black spirituality was best articulated through song. Slaves brought their spiritual chants from Africa and were encouraged by their masters to sing as they worked as a way of keeping track of them (keeping them within earshot). At first they sang songs from Africa, but gradually developed their own songs and expressed all their moods and feelings in hymns, chants, moans and psalms. There were songs to express their weariness at work, their longing for freedom, their grief over separation from their children and loved ones. There were happy and excited songs as they marched through the woods to the great house on allowance day; plaintive melodies for camp meetings and revivals; and consoling chants when someone had died or been sold off. Many became expert musicians and composers, and after emancipation some went on tour to give concerts. In the twentieth century, gospel music came into its own and singers like Mahalia Jackson and Edwin Hawkings became well-known. With the Catholic liturgical renewal of the 1960s, Father Clarence Rivers brought black liturgical music into the Catholic community in the United States.[40]

From her childhood, Thea was taught to sing songs of faith about Bible stories. She heard these songs sung by her Mama as she went off to sleep, heard them sung by her neighbors as they tended their gardens, and joined in with others in home gatherings. These songs bonded them in church, provided their religious education and were the instruments of their prayer.

Once Thea was a teacher, she would gather black children and teach them the songs of their culture. In her hometown she organized a fifty-voice choir and made an album. On it one can hear Thea proudly speaking for the children:

> Though our forefathers bent to bear the heat of the sun, the strike of the lash, the chain of slavery, we are free. No man can enslave us. We are too strong, too unafraid. America needs our strength, our voices to drown out her sorrows, the clatter of war…. Listen! Hear us! We are the voice of Negro America.[41]

At The Catholic University of America she pursued her study of black music and when she returned to Viterbo College to teach, she organized another chorus that toured the Midwest singing black sacred music. And, of course, as Thea toured the country as a Franciscan troubadour, she offered countless people "the Thea experience," moving them with her powerful songs and drawing them to join into the black experience.

### Thea and Vatican II

When Thea was twenty-eight, the Second Vatican Council closed and published documents that would cause a sea change in the Catholic church. She embraced the progressive ideas of reform, especially when she saw that they confirmed many things she had already learned from her community. She had always seen the church as people, as community, as disciples of the Lord. Now she began to address her audiences as "church." She had learned from the old folks in her community that the church has to be concerned about the modern world and, in particular, about freeing the oppressed and poor from injustice. She grew up respecting other faiths and appreciating dialogue and cooperation with those who believed differently than she. She also had learned from her elders the value of religious freedom and evils of persecution. She had come to see herself as a preacher, even though she had no access to church pulpits, and she knew that she, as well as all Christians, had a call to holiness and to service in the church. Her particular mission would be to help free her church from racial prejudice and open it to the treasures of black spirituality.

**The Thea Experience**
Once Thea's talents in singing and speaking were discovered, she became popular on the religious circuit. Many have described her appearances as "the Thea experience." Listening to recordings or watching videos of her reveal how she would light up an auditorium and work hard to loosen up the whites in attendance. It wasn't always easy getting ordinary Catholics into the black experience!

Cardinal Josef Suenens of Belgium once characterized Catholics as "God's frozen people." The typical Western Catholic doesn't talk in church, rarely shows emotions in a religious service and often sings faintly. Silent, stoical and solemn would be the words to best describe many Catholics in church. When Thea started her speaking tours in the 1970s, this is the kind of attitude she was often facing.

Thea would arrive bundled up and often looking like a bag lady, with those large dark eyes shining out from under her bonnet. People reacted to her in different ways. Someone said you either loved her for her frankness and vivacious spirit, or loathed her, because she could come on strong about her tradition and shake people up about their prejudices. Thea could be blunt. Once she overheard someone at the break say, "I've heard her before." She acknowledged the remark to the audience and then told them that her message, because of its importance, could indeed bear repeating.

Thea offered her audiences a new experience of religion. Typical was her appearance before a Louisiana conference of religious educators in 1987.[42] On stage, the mere sight of her—dressed in colorful African prints with a marvelous head-wrap—was enchanting. She would begin with a song, filling the room with her spirit-filled voice: "Give me that old time religion." She'd chide the audience for sitting like they sit in church, and she would encourage them to "lighten up," to *be* church, and to *do* the Word. She was bringing the gospel to them, and that was supposed to be "good news." It was supposed to make them happy! "Tell your faces that," she would kid her audience.

It was her experience that love was what communicated the Word most effectively. She always said that the love of the sisters for her as a child turned her to Catholicism long before she had any knowledge of doctrine. She would tell them that the gospel is good news if it feeds the hungry, gets jobs for the unemployed, and gives self-respect to the outcast. The gospel has to be lived, she would shout out. Parishes can't be places closed off from the world. They have to be centers where people live the faith and are actively engaged in the real problems around them. She told a group of religious educators that many of them lived in white parishes surrounded by blacks who are unemployed and illiterate, with high rates of teenage pregnancies and death. Catholics have to be concerned about the real world and "take care of business."

The audience would often resist Thea's challenge, but she would stay after them. Like a good teacher, she would gently remind them: "Some of you aren't listening to me. I can see it in your eyes. I see you squirming, rattling papers, and talking." Once she regained their attention, she would persist and tell them that people come to them because the church was promising something—loving care. In the early church people were attracted to the movement because it offered love and care. Thea reminded them that they are the church, they are the community of believers called to reach out in love. "We must celebrate who we are and whose we are." Thea reminded her listeners that they must not only tell the gospel stories, they must live them. They need to know their people personally and be involved in their lives. They need to be *doing* the Word with loving actions of service. She told them that she hears so many people complaining that the people in ministry don't seem to have time to listen. She encourages them to listen carefully to the children, the teens, the poor, the elderly. Their message should not be, "I don't have time," but, "God is here for you."

Part of the Thea experience was to teach her audiences how to be "fully functioning" in singing. She would tease them about their first meager efforts. She'd say something like: "Most of you sound like somebody's got you around the neck!" Some of you might be thinking: 'I prefer something more intellectual.' Well, we are going to try to put our hearts and bodies into this song." Slowly and surely she would get the audience swaying, raising their hands and singing spirituals with real feeling.

Thea would urge members of her audience to get to know people of other colors, other religions, other ethnic backgrounds. She would remind them that as Christians they belong to a two-thousand-year-old religion that embraces all colors and nations. They are the church, and are for all nations! She would urge them to be free of prejudice, free from all the barriers that cut them off from the children of God, to spread the Good News of God's love to addicts, the mentally challenged, the abandoned. "Are you with me, church?" she would shout. By then most were indeed with her, inspired by her message. There would be more songs and then a final urging to let the spirit take over in their lives and go forth to bring the good news. Another group had been touched by the Thea experience!

## The Power of Liturgy

Thea was always deeply interested in liturgy, especially in its potential power to bond diverse people and move them to work for a more just world. She observed that Catholic liturgies are often tired, ineffective, even boring. She believed that Catholics forget that liturgy is about bonding. So often Catholics come into silent churches, where no one looks at them, acknowledges their presence, smiles or hugs them. She points out the irony in that it is possible to come to church and have no human contact whatsoever.

Having grown up in a very different culture, this shocked Thea. She said that her people come to church to have a good time. "Now that means if you are in sorrow, you will find comfort and consolation. If you are in grief, you will find someone to share your burden. If you are tired, you will find rest. If you are burdened, you will find relaxation and relief. If you've got a tear, you'll find joy."[43] The church community should be offering love, support and care for all those who enter.

Thea says Catholics need to begin with "gathering," the first act of liturgy. The liturgy should start with "the bonding of minds and hearts and goals and purposes and faith and love and joy, the leaning on the promise that where two or three are gathered in Jesus' name, he's going to be with us, the celebration of our realization that we are brothers and sisters gathered in Jesus' name, the joy of reaching out to touch somebody."[44]

Thea thought that liturgy should mean the coming together and uniting of all kinds of people, rich and poor, young and old, outcasts and accepted, people of all colors. For her, the table of the Lord is the place where people can be freed of their prejudices. It is the place where we can "touch one another across the customary barriers and boundaries, across race, and sex and class, elitism, defeatism, holier-than-thouism."[45]

Thea believed that liturgy was also about bonding with the larger church, and coming to awareness that the majority of people in the world church are of color and poor. Liturgy is about conversion on our part to be in union with all of these brothers and sisters and dedicated to seeking justice for them. By justice, she meant "everyday justice," which includes reaching out to the pain of others, visiting the sick and lonely, withholding judgment of addicts, the homeless and prisoners, refusing to participate in violence, and speaking out against discrimination and oppression. For her, liturgy is all about commitment to do something each day for justice. In our pulpits, Thea believed that there must be concern about real issues, real problems, and that we should be challenged to make a difference. She says, "Preach justice and teach justice every Sunday. And get rid of the tired, poor, theoretical, worn-out homilies."[46] For Thea, liturgy should be a profound communal experience where those gathering are shown that they aren't alone in their efforts. The work for justice is through the power of Jesus, who works through the community, the church.

Thea believed that we talk too much about liturgy and don't do enough celebrating. By real liturgy, Thea meant "some real stomp-down celebration that leaves you spent and tired because you have given every ounce of energy from your whole being, because you have shared so much of faith, hope, love, and joy." She was convinced that liturgy should make us say before going to bed each night: "What have I done this day to make my world more just?"[47]

### Her Final Years

The year 1984 was a difficult one for Thea. Both her parents died and she was diagnosed with breast cancer, which eventually spread to her bones. Thea decided that she "would live until I died," and for the following years maintained an arduous schedule of speaking engagements. In the last few years she had to use a wheelchair and lost all her hair from chemotherapy, but that did not stop her.

### Cosmic Spirituality

In her final years, Thea expanded her spirituality and began to speak about "cosmic spirituality," by which she meant spirituality that is prepared to serve a multicultural church and world. It is a spirituality that is willing to learn new languages, new customs, new ways of glorifying the Lord. It means being serious about welcoming and taking people from different cultures into our communities. To extend such a welcome, people have to value their history, their experience, their art, music, songs and ways of prayer. "Cosmic spirituality means we come together, bringing our gifts, bringing our histories, bringing our experience, all that we have, all that we hold."[48]

Thea wanted people of all kinds to share prayer, share styles, ways of life. She urged her listeners to not write anyone off "because they don't read right, they don't write right, they drink too much, they smoke the wrong thing, they don't walk right, they don't talk right, their sexual preferences are not in agreement with ones you claim."[49] She was convinced that people of diversity have to hear each other's stories and sing each other's songs. She believed that the church needed to reach out to everyone needing love, security and nurturance. Thea spoke especially for the outcasts, the alienated, the hurting. "All my life my mama told me to stand up straight, hold up my head, and speak out."[50]

**Almost Home**

In her last months of life, Thea allowed people to come into the tiny home where she was raised and where she wanted to die. Her journey was almost over now and she wanted to share her gifts for the final time and show people how to deal with suffering and death. Thea knew that her mission had its limits: "Maybe I'm not making big changes in the world, but if I have somehow helped or encouraged somebody along the journey then I've done what I'm called to do."[51] She pointed out that in her difficulties she still drew strength from the wisdom she gained in the black community that raised her. She was still in a listening posture, listening to God, to nature, to her own heart and to other people. She now listened to the earth and had come to realize how we must sustain the earth as our home. Love for her was still what binds us together, overcomes our fears and moves us to share with others.

Thea came to realize that her days were few: "What can I do with the time that's left me to help somebody? Sometimes it's just a song, just a tear, just listening with an attentive ear, to help somebody, to teach somebody, to reach somebody, to share laughter, life, love, joy, to leave the world a better place than I happened to find it."[52]

In her last days she wanted to help people face death. She shared how she was trying to face death and deal with the fears that continually crept up on her—fears of pain, fears of helplessness. She commented on how difficult prayer had become and how difficult it had been for her to accept her death. She told how cancer had shifted her priorities, taught her what really is important, and helped her to be more patient and tolerant of things that before had been bothersome. Facing death had made her relationships, especially her relationship with God, of the utmost importance.

Thea insisted on speaking about death and helped others deal with this difficult topic. She spoke to children and helped them talk with their dying parents and bring them the comfort they needed. She showed people how the dying need companions to be there with them as a caring and loving presence. Like Saint Francis, the founder of her order, she wanted to continue to be an instrument of peace and serve God until her last breath. She refused to choose death, but instead chose to live for others and for herself. She continued her songs in a faint voice, and more than ever appreciated how the old folks gained comfort by "moaning." From her bed, her head now wrapped just above those still shining dark eyes, Thea asked her friends to sit with her, pray with her and count their blessings with her. When asked how she wanted to be remembered, she said: "I want people to remember that I tried to love the Lord and them, and how that computes is immaterial." Her last moving words on a video she made were said with tears running down her cheeks: "Keep on keeping on!"[53]

Thea died on March 30, 1990. Just before she passed on she was asked by a priest-friend what he was to say at her funeral. She told him,

"Tell them what Sojourner Truth said: 'I'm not going to die. I'm going home like a shooting star.'"[54]

Joseph Brown, s.j., a friend and fellow professor with Thea at Xavier University, has said, "Like the prophets of Israel, she used her life, her thought and her activities as a medium and the message. In this regard she was authentically black.... She took on, became possessed by, the voice of the beloved community, called the 'old folks,' the 'elders,' the 'ancestors' in the African-American theological tradition."[55]

## Nelson Mandela: Freedom for His People

It was a clear, sunny February day in Cape Town at the end of the African summer in 1990. The prisoner awoke at 4:30, did his usual exercises, ate breakfast and telephoned some friends. He was given a brief physical checkup, and then stood among some crates of papers and books as he waited to be released after twenty-seven years of confinement. The inmate embraced the officials of the prison, thanked them and proceeded to the gate. Much to his surprise, he was greeted by a huge crowd of people who were cheering and yelling, as well as hundreds of reporters and television cameras. Stunned by all the chaos, the man recoiled when a furry object was thrust toward him, thinking the object was a weapon. He was told that it was just a modern microphone.

The prisoner was Nelson Mandela, and he was experiencing freedom at the age of seventy-one, after ten thousand days in prison. He raised his clenched right fist in the power salute and a roar went up from the crowd. He was taken to city hall in Cape Town and spoke before a sea of celebrating people. He proclaimed:

> Friends, comrades, and fellow South Africans. I greet you all in the name of peace, democracy and freedom for all! I stand here before you not as a prophet but as a humble servant of you, the people. Your tireless and heroic sacrifices have made it possible for

me to be here today. I therefore place the remaining years of my
life in your hands.[1]

Mandela had entered prison as a vigorous young man, and now was
coming out an old man, although still fit and healthy. For his struggle
to free his people from oppression, he had spent one-third of his life in
prison. Now, he would begin the final stage of his efforts to lead his people to freedom.

## Tribal Background

Nelson Mandela was born on July 18, 1918, in a small village that was
part of the Transkei area, located in southeastern South Africa. This
beautiful area of green rolling hills and rivers was the home of the
Thembu people, part of the Xhosa nation into which Rolihlahla
(Nelson's tribal name) was born. Nelson's more common name was
"Buti." His father, Hendry, was a tribal chief, who acted as a counselor
to several tribal kings. He was known for his stubbornness and rebelliousness, characteristics that Nelson believed were passed on to him.
His mother, Nosekeni, was one of the chief's four wives and was known
for her loyalty and quiet wisdom, also aspects of Nelson's character.

When Nelson was still a baby, his father was deprived of his position and lost his income, land and cattle. All this was a punishment for
refusing to recognize a white magistrate's authority over him. Nelson
had learned an early lesson about opposing white domination. He and
his mother were forced to move from their comfortable thatched hut
and well-stocked homestead to another village, where they had to live
in a mud hut with a cow-dung floor. Their diet now also would be sim-
pler—usually corn, beans and pumpkins. Village life was difficult. The
men were generally away working in remote farms or in the goldmines.
The women carried water, did the farmwork, cooked, and looked after
the babies and children.

Nelson remembers his childhood days in the village as happy ones.
At five he became a herd-boy, tending the sheep and cattle in the fields.

He discovered the mystical attachment that his people had to their cattle, seeing them as a blessing from God, and he also acquired a love of nature and open spaces. In his free time he played with his friends, learned stick-fighting, and swam and fished in the cold streams. In the evenings, his mother would fascinate Nelson with the tribal legends and fables, and if his father was visiting he would hear heroic stories of Xhosa warriors. He learned to cherish a strong sense of community with the people of his village, the importance of custom and tradition, and the value of honoring one's ancestors.

Often around the night fires, the elders would tell Nelson stories of the good old days before the arrival of the white man. Those were the days when his people lived peacefully under the democratic rule of their kings and could freely move throughout the country and enjoy the forests, the rivers and the mountains. The land, the main means of production, was owned by the whole tribe and not by individuals. There was no such thing as a rich class or a poor class, for all were equal and this was the foundation of their governmental system. All participated in "council" discussions and decisions, whether they be chief, subject, warrior or medicine man. Hearing of these so-called "primitive" days, where there was freedom from servitude and poverty, would be always remembered by Nelson in his later struggles for political freedom.[2]

### The Mission Mentality

In those days conversion to Christianity was synonymous with being civilized. Nelson's father did not buy into this and remained faithful to his native religion, acting as a priest in the traditional rituals, such as harvest, weddings, funerals. This religion celebrated a cosmic wholeness and did not see the distinction between the secular and the sacred. Nelson's mother, however, was attracted to Christianity, converted and had her son baptized into the Methodist church. When he was seven, Nelson was enrolled in the mission school to receive a British education. To attend school the boy had to exchange his native blanket for his father's pants, cut off at the knee, and when he showed up the first day he was given the name he would carry for life: Nelson.

## A Turning Point

When Nelson was nine, his father died suddenly of an apparent lung disease. Soon after, the regent of the Thembu people offered to become Nelson's guardian. It was an offer Nelson's mother could not turn down, so she took her boy by the hand, trekked for a whole day to the regent's royal residence, and handed her son over to his new home. Though Nelson and his mother were very close, the boy quickly got into his new world as a member of the royal family. He received new clothes, attended a good school in a crude building, dutifully performed his chores as a plowboy and shepherd and was excited about going to dances.

At this point, Christianity began to become more a part of Nelson's life. The church provided education and a future for this life as well as security in the next. Nelson recalls the minister's booming fire-and-brimstone sermons and women kneeling and begging for salvation. In the world of the regent, religion was an integral part of life, and Nelson was expected to attend services with the family every Sunday. Although Nelson would hold a respect for the church, he usually kept his distance from organized religion.

## Learning to Be a Leader

Nelson learned a great deal about leadership during his years with the regent. He was able to attend the tribal meetings and noticed that the regent would gather with the elders and anyone else who wished to attend. During the meetings anyone who wished to speak was given a chance. Conversations were candid, and even the regent himself was not above criticism. Only when all had had their say would the regent say his piece and work toward some kind of unanimity. If that could not be achieved, the meeting would be continued or another meeting would be held until there was a consensus. Nelson would later sum up how his own leadership would be affected by all this: "I always remember the regent's axiom: a leader, he said, is like a shepherd. He stays behind the flock, letting the most nimble go out ahead, whereupon the others follow, not realizing that all along they are being directed from behind."[3]

Nelson always valued his close relationship with his household and clan. From prison he once reflected how wonderful it had been to be accepted as a beloved household member "where you can call at any time, completely relaxed, sleep at ease and freely take part in the discussion of all problems...."[4]

At these meetings Nelson had more opportunities to hear about African history. He listened to the stories of how the white man shattered the fellowship among the tribes, divided them against each other and took their land from them. He heard stories of how the brave African patriots fought and died in wars against Western domination. He learned that he was part of a conquered people who were slaves in their own country and lacked any power or control of their own futures. Nelson later pointed out how these indictments against the white man angered him and made him feel cheated of his birthright.

## Leaving Home for School

At sixteen Nelson left home for secondary school at Clarksbury with a pound note in his pocket and brand-new boots on his feet. In his first Western school with degreed teachers, he began to see his abilities measured against those of others. He also became close for the first time to white people—Reverend Harris, the head of the school, and his wife. Still a country boy, a Thembu through and through, Nelson began to broaden his horizons slightly.

At nineteen Nelson moved to Methodist College at Healdtown, where he joined over a thousand students, both male and female, in order to receive an English-Christian liberal arts education. It was a rigorous institution, where Nelson was able to meet students from all over the continent, and he began to sense his identity as an African. It was here that he met Oliver Tambo, who would be his close comrade for the rest of his life. In college, Nelson began to take up the sports of long-distance running and boxing. On Sundays he taught Bible classes in the surrounding villages.

During this time a Xhosa poet came to the college and made
Nelson deeply proud of his tribal heritage, as well as stirring him with
the possibility of standing against the white man. The poet said: "We
cannot allow these foreigners who do not care for our culture to take
over our nation. I predict that one day, the forces of African society will
achieve a momentous victory over the interloper. For too long, we have
succumbed to the false gods of the white man. But we will emerge and
cast off these foreign notions."[5]

## On to University

From Healdtown, Nelson moved on to the elite University College of
Fort Hare, home of some of the greatest African scholars. Here he continued his studies and did further research on how the British had suppressed the African tribes, tricking them out of their land with fake documents and false promises, tearing down their houses and killing those
who resisted.[6] Nelson also continued his interest in athletics, got
involved in acting, and became an enthusiastic ballroom dancer. On
one occasion he sneaked out of the dorms to go fox-trotting, spied a
lovely young woman and began dancing with her, only to learn that she
was the wife of one of his professors. Nelson quickly apologized, conducted her back to her husband and made a hasty retreat.

Early on at the university, Nelson began to get into conflicts with
the authorities over student rights. He was elected a student leader, and
soon found himself involved in a controversy with the principal. He
returned home for the summer with the understanding that he change
his view or be expelled.

Over the summer Nelson's benefactor informed him that he had
arranged marriages for both Nelson and one of the regent's sons.
Neither of the boys found the decision acceptable, and they decided to
run away from home together. They ended up in the huge and bustling
city of Johannesburg, where Nelson's life was about to be dramatically
changed forever.

**Life in the Big City**

When Nelson came to Johannesburg in 1941, it was a sprawling metropolis with much industry, particularly gold mining. Hundreds of thousands of Africans, unable to sustain themselves in the barren reserves, had migrated to the city for work. While there were jobs, there was little housing for blacks and most had to stay in crowded barracks in the "non-European" township. The "lucky" ones were crammed into fenced-in compounds of municipal housing.

For a time the young men were able to fake their way into jobs at a gold mine, but eventually the regent tracked them down and they were forced to leave the mine. A cousin took in Nelson and introduced him to a prominent businessman and black leader, Walter Sisulu, who would be a close associate for the rest of Nelson's life. Sisulu secured a job for Nelson in a large Jewish law firm. There he met many bright and well-formed people and enjoyed the vibrant social life of the city. His living conditions, however, were substandard, for he could only afford a room in a boarding house with a dirt floor and no electricity, running water or heat. His income was so low that he often had to walk the six miles back and forth to work, study to finish his degree by candlelight, and wear a tattered, patched suit to work. The room was located in a township that was a noted slum with a high crime rate. Eventually, he was able to move in with a family of his tribe, and things improved.

Nelson enjoyed the urban life, with its vibrant politics and its exciting African subculture, fueled by local writers and musicians along with American movies and jazz. Nelson met many Africans who held professional careers, as well as doctors, lawyers and educators. They were determined to see the promises of Western culture to be realized on their continent. A new spirit of African nationalism and freedom was in the air!

**Entering Into Politics**

It was during these early years in Johannesburg that Nelson was first introduced to the African National Congress in 1944, and then had his first taste of taking part in a protest and boycott against the raising of bus fares. He began to change his goals from preparing for a successful career and a comfortable salary back in Transkei to "see that my duty was to my people as a whole."[7] His interests now shifted to racial oppression, the few opportunities for his people, and the laws that subjugated them. To follow this mission, Nelson enrolled in the University of Witwatersrand. There he experienced deep prejudice, and although he did not do well in his studies, Nelson met several key white people who would play roles in his future: Joe Slove, an ardent communist, and Bram Fischer, a brilliant lawyer and freedom advocate. This period opened his mind to a whole new world of ideas and political positions. He also encountered many who were dedicated to the freedom of the Africans. He was moving from his African exclusivist views and coming to see that if his country was to be liberated, all of its citizens would have to have an international mentality.

**A Freedom Fighter**

Nelson had been discriminated against and oppressed all his life, and gradually he came to the point of having enough. His anger and rebelliousness deepened, and he began to be resolved to stand up and fight the system that held his people in captivity. He began to realize that his black skin could be seen as beautiful, and that his people had every right to enjoy the beauty and resources of their own country. Nelson became ardently committed to the cause of African nationalism.

Along with Sisulu, Oliver Tambo and others, Nelson helped form the Youth League, designed to moving the "slumbering" African National Congress (ANC) into action. Nelson at this time was a tall, handsome athletic lawyer, but still felt insecure, politically backward and lacking in confidence as a speaker. The league's goals were to create a nation out of the many tribes, rid their people of their sense of inferiority and overthrow white supremacy. With youthful enthusiasm, they vowed to bring more intelligence and power to the movement for African nationalism, and to use direct actions as a means of protest.[8]

The ANC Youth League Manifesto, which Nelson played a central role in drafting, gives a snapshot of the situation in South Africa in 1944. It points out that two million whites with superior military strength had decided that they had a "race destiny" to rule eight million Africans. The whites had thus claimed ownership of 87 percent of the land and in order to consolidate their position had segregated the Africans in state, church, industry and commerce. This situation was designed to ensure that the Africans would never have any power to resist "white domination."[9]

The Manifesto goes on to reject the white domination and insists that Africans determine their own future by their own efforts. The Youth League openly rejected foreign leadership in Africa, believed that all Africans must speak against domination in one voice, vowed to oppose discriminatory laws and promised to struggle for full citizenship for the Africans in a democratic society. It set up policy for land redistribution, mass education, the elimination of all color bars in trades and professions, and the establishment of labor unions. The league extended its services to the national liberation movement and expressed its conviction that the cause of Africa "must and will triumph."[10]

At the same time that Nelson was beginning to get involved with the Youth League, he met Evelyn Mase, a student nurse. The two fell in love and were married in Johannesburg. A year later, they had their first child, a son, whom they named Thembi. Nelson's political involvement, however, left him little time with his family. His little boy once asked, "Where does Daddy live?"[11]

Nelson continued to watch the oppression in his country. In 1948 the Afrikaner Nationalist government came to power and put in its program of apartheid, designed to separate and dominate the black population. The Afrikaners took away colored representation in parliament, made it illegal for whites and nonwhites to have sexual relations, and segregated each racial group into separate areas.

In retaliation, the ANC called for strikes, boycotts, demonstrations and other mass nonviolent actions of civil disobedience, a model developed by Mohandas Gandhi in earlier decades. Coal miners attempted to strike, and the government brutally stopped their march, killing two miners. On May Day 1950, eighteen protesters were killed, and the ANC called for a national work stoppage. Nelson and the Youth League moved for a more revolutionary leadership in the ANC. Nelson led the Defiance Campaign, in which trained groups went through "European Only" entrances to railway stations and post offices, broke curfews and broke other apartheid laws. Indians were told where they could reside, were restricted in owning property, and their leaders were jailed—a harbinger of things to come for blacks.

By 1952 Nelson had become a major leader in the ANC and was extremely busy traveling throughout the country, firming up branches of the organization, getting new recruits and raising money. In that same year, Nelson was arrested, charged with opposing the government and scheduled for trial. He and twenty-one others were convicted and given a sentence of nine months in prison, which was suspended for two years. Nelson remarks how proud he was to have been a part of this campaign of defiance, saying: "I had come of age as a freedom fighter."[12]

Nelson was soon chosen one of the presidents of the ANC, but the government made a serious effort to stop him by banning him from attending any meetings. Since he was banned, Nelson had to have his presidential address read on this behalf. In this speech he reviewed how for the last fifty years the African people have raised their voices against white domination, only to see the repression increase and their sacrifices made to seem futile. But now, the young Mandela saw that there was a new spirit and many fresh ideas gripping the people. He says, "Today the people speak the language of action: there is a mighty awakening among the men and women of our country and the year 1952 stands out as the year of this upsurge in national consciousness."[13] He proudly points to the Campaign for the Defiance of the

Unjust Laws, which joined Africans as comrades-in-arms and put extreme pressure on the government. Now Africans suffered from government reaction with arrests, fines, bannings for leaders and gatherings. The government provides for and protects the Europeans, but the African's situation continued to worsen and many lacked food, clothing, housing and medical care. Many farmers still lived and worked in slave conditions and were subjected to flogging and torture. He sums up the attitude of the government to have been: "Let's beat them down with guns and batons and trample them under our feet. We must be ready to drown the whole country in blood if only there is the slightest chance of preserving white supremacy."[14] Nelson points out that the foundations of colonialism are being shaken all over the world and that "[t]he day of reckoning between the forces of freedom and those of reaction is not very far off."[15]

Nelson viewed nonviolence not as a principle but as one tactic among others to be used when appropriate. As the oppressive relocations widened and more people were seriously hurt or even killed by the police, Nelson began to believe that "violence was the only weapon that would destroy apartheid."[16] As he became more outspoken in this way, the leadership of the ANC became nervous and reprimanded him. Later, when Nelson looked back, he reflected: "[T]hey were the actions of a hotheaded revolutionary who had not thought things through and who acted without discipline."[17]

Nelson recognized that the organization itself would soon be banned, so he devised a plan whereby the members would be part of small cells that would report to the central leaders without the necessity of meetings. The plan had only modest success.

### A Law Career

Nelson gave up his studies at the university and decided to become an attorney by taking the qualifying exam. Once he passed the exam, he teamed up with his friend Oliver Tambo and opened a law office that could serve the huge numbers of blacks who found themselves charged with breaking many of the apartheid laws. Needless to say, they were swamped with cases and had to steel themselves for the contempt they often met in the courtrooms.

Nelson became a "man-about-town," wearing fine suits and driving a splendid car. To keep in shape, he worked out regularly at a local gym and became quite an accomplished boxer. But the authorities quickly moved to neutralize him by banning him further and requiring his resignation from the ANC. He was now thirty-five years old and his activities for the struggle for freedom would have to be secret and illegal. Meanwhile, the ANC continued its fight for freedom and sponsored a strong Freedom Charter, which laid out all the demands of the African people for equal rights and opportunity, the right to vote and govern and share in the country's wealth and land. Nelson was sent on a factfinding mission to the area where he grew up and to other areas. After several months of having his bans expire, he was again banned, this time for five years.

**Arrested for Treason**

In 1956 Nelson was arrested along with most of the ANC leadership, charged with high treason, then released on bail. When Nelson returned home, he found that his wife, Evelyn, had taken the children and moved out. The marriage, which had been shaky for several years due to his obsession with work in law and politics, her rigid commitment to the Jehovah Witness religion, and rumors of Nelson's infidelity now collapsed. Nelson stated that he no longer loved Evelyn and requested a divorce.

During the months of the preparatory period, the evidence for treason among ANC leaders proved to be muddled and the witnesses confused. Nevertheless, after thirteen months, the magistrate said that there was sufficient reason to put most of the defendants on trial. It was during this period that Nelson met Winifred ("Winnie") Madikizela. The two fell deeply in love, were married in 1958, and began what would turn out to be a long and difficult marriage.

The repression continued. In a general election in 1958, three million whites participated, while thirteen million Africans were forbidden to vote. The people of color (70 percent of the population) were permitted to live on 13 percent of the land, and nonwhites were barred from the universities.

Mandela continued to write articles against the repression. He openly condemned colonialism and imperialism and how these forces exploited the mineral and agricultural resources of Africa and Asia. Nelson warned of the dangers of the new American imperialism, which comes from a country that emerged from the two world wars as the richest and most powerful country in the West, in a position to dominate through investments and trade monopolies. He was severely critical of his government for pretended secure seaports, communications systems and power plants for the Africans, when in fact these facilities were designed to exploit the native people and export their wealth to Europe.[18] He denounced his government for situations where his people were deported, separated from their children, wounded and deprived of medical care, flogged and murdered by European farmers for disrespect, beaten up and thrown in jail by police for protesting. He attacked the government for dividing his people into hostile tribes and then instigating violence among the tribes. African youth with intelligence and education were persecuted for not wanting to be slaves in the mines or the farms. The government was deliberately designing separate and inferior education (Bantu Education) on all levels to prevent young Africans from getting ahead.

Nelson spoke up at a conference: "You must defend the right of African parents to decide the kind of education that shall be given to their children. Teach the children that Africans are not one iota inferior to Europeans. Establish your own community schools where the right kind of education will be given to our children."[19]

He openly denounced his government as fascist and warned his people that the official policies for ruling over Africans were similar to those designed by the Nazis. He warned that the specters of the Nazi concentration camps loomed ahead if his people did not actively resist. Meanwhile, he was banned from attending conferences and had to watch from afar in various disguises.

In 1959 the treason trial finally began and the state began to build its case against the leaders of the ANC. Suddenly, the trial was interrupted by an event that would change the history of South Africa: the massacre at Sharpsville. It started with a protest against the infamous passes needed by Africans to travel or work. The response to the call for protest was sporadic, but in one small township, Sharpsville, thousands of demonstrators showed up and surrounded the police station. They were a controlled and armed crowd. Without warning, the police opened fire on the crowd, causing them to run in panic. In the end, sixty-nine Africans were killed and four hundred were wounded, including many women and children. Most of them had been shot in the back. The slaughter provoked a strong reaction throughout the country, as well as around the world.

As the trial proceeded, Nelson used it as an opportunity to press the government with the ANC demands for voting rights and representation in the parliament. Ultimately, the government was not able to prove its charge that the ANC was a communist organization bent on overthrowing the state by violence. All the accused were declared not guilty and discharged.

### A Move Toward Violence

Nelson saw the government gathering enormous forces and watched the nonviolent demonstrations crushed. He began to be convinced that only some sort of violence would be the answer. He wrote: "[I]t was precisely because the soil of South Africa is already drenched with the blood of innocent Africans that we felt it our duty to make preparations as a long term to use force in order to defend ourselves against force."[20] The ANC was committed to nonviolence but did permit Nelson to form a military organization independent of the ANC, called

Umkhonto (spear of the nation). Amid thunderous applause at his last conference of the ANC, Nelson made it clear that Africans now had only two choices: "to accept discrimination and humiliation or stand firm for their rights."[21]

## Going Underground

Nelson then decided to disappear underground and began to see himself as a soldier, a revolutionary dedicated to "make government impossible."[22] He would have to leave his wife and children and his law practice and live as an outlaw in his own land, continuously hunted by the police. Nicknamed, "The Black Pimpernel," Nelson thrilled his followers by changing lodging nearly every night, hiding by day, traveling by night and showing up in many different places in various disguises. He would now lead a sabotage movement that would perform acts designed to destabilize the government. The attacks were aimed at military installations, power plants and telephone lines. Strict instructions were given that the rebels not be armed and that there be no loss of life. Nelson wrote a letter to the South African newspapers, which declared his destiny: "For my own part, I have made my choice. I will not leave South Africa, nor will I surrender. Only through hardship, sacrifice and militant action can freedom be won. The struggle is my life. I will continue fighting for freedom until the end of my days."[23]

The ANC decided that it needed help from other African countries involved in revolution. They sent Nelson to speak at a conference in Ethiopia in 1962. In his address to the conference, he thanked the independent African states that had helped the Africans in South Africa by boycotts, sanctions and offering asylum to refugees and freedom fighters. He pointed out that his was a country "torn from top to bottom by fierce racial strife and conflict and where the blood of African patriots frequently flows."[24] He reviewed the many massacres, the persecution of leaders, the banning of organizations and the unjust trials and executions. He denounced the rule by the gun of the government and said that his people were slowly turning from peace and nonviolence to other methods. He told them about the sabotage and that the government was striking back viciously. He promised the conference: "I should assure you that the African people of South Africa, notwithstanding fierce persecution and untold suffering, in their ever-increasing courage will not for one single moment be diverted from the historic mission of liberating their country and winning freedom, lasting peace, and happiness."[25]

Nelson then began to make contacts for help with money and military training. He was well received as he traveled around Africa, and said that, "For the first time in my life, I was a free man."[26] He was awed at the vastness of the continent and the variation of lifestyles. He was inspired by the strength of tribal traditions and at the same time depressed by the extreme poverty. Africa was recovering from colonialism and rediscovering its own history and personality. Freedom was in the air! Besides Ethiopia, where Nelson met the famed Haille Selassie, he visited many countries, such as Egypt, Nigeria, Ghana, Tunisia, Morocco, Algeria, Sierra Leone and Tanganyika, where he was deeply impressed by the leadership of Julius Nyerere. Nelson even took a brief tour of London. Then he began a six-month military training program in Ethiopia, which was cut to two months because he was called home by the ANC.

He returned to South Africa, and though warned that the police knew of his return, he carelessly attended a party, and then drove into Durban in a new car, armed with a pistol. He was quickly flagged down, arrested and charged with incitement to strike and leaving the country without a passport.

### Another Trial

When the time came for the trial, Nelson entered the courtroom wearing a leopard skin to symbolize the culture of his people, and he defiantly conducted his own defense. He pointed out that it was impossible for him to gain a fair trial in a system totally controlled by whites and where the Africans have no representation. He declared: "The white man makes all the laws, he drags us before his courts and accuses us, and he sits in judgement over us."[27] He defiantly protested: "I hate race discrimination most intensely and in all its manifestations. I have fought it all during my life; I fight it now, and will do so until the end of my days."[28] He insisted that the highest human aspiration is the struggle against color discrimination and the pursuit of freedom. The whole time, Mandela put the Afrikaner government on trial and denounced the injustice and invalidity of its authority and laws. He recalled how in the days before the white man came he lived in peace with democratic rule and moved freely and confidently up and down the country, enjoying the forests, the rivers, and the mineral wealth of their beautiful country. The Africans had lived in freedom and equality and there was no exploitation. He closed his arguments with a stirring speech pointing out that the past peaceful and democratic tribal way of life contained the seeds of revolution against the slavery and exploitation of his people. He ended his speech defiantly with the words: "Posterity will pronounce that I was innocent and that the criminals that should have been brought before this court are the members of the government."[29] Nelson was convicted and sentenced to five years in prison.

### His Final Trial

In 1963, after Nelson had been in prison for one year, the government invaded ANC headquarters and discovered many incriminating documents about plans for revolutionary movements and acts of sabotage. Nelson and most of the ANC leadership were brought to trial on charges of sabotage and conspiracy. The penalty could be death.

In his testimony Nelson eloquently spoke of his desire for nonracial democracy for his country. He did not deny the acts of sabotage and the military preparation of his people to defend themselves in the event of civil war. He said that he had planned sabotage but insisted, "I did not plan it in a spirit of recklessness nor because I have any love of violence. I planned it as a result of a calm and sober assessment of the political situation that had arisen after years of tyranny, exploitation and oppression of my people by whites."[30] Nelson spoke at length about the oppression of his people and the policy of white supremacy and made demands for equal political rights for his people. He closed his remarks steadily, though facing a possible death sentence:

> During my lifetime I have dedicated myself to this struggle of the African people. I have fought against white domination, and I have fought against black domination. I have cherished the ideal of a democratic and free society in which all persons live together in harmony and with equal opportunities. It is an ideal which I hope to live for and to achieve. But if needs be, it is an ideal for which I am prepared to die.[31]

In the end, the leaders of the ANC were convicted and sentenced to life in prison. The group was sent to the infamous Robben Island, where Nelson would spend the next eighteen years of his life. Young Mandela's career as a guerrilla leader had been short, and he was now about to spend nearly three decades of his life incarcerated. As he was led off to prison, on the world scene, the United Nations was voting to impose sanctions on South Africa, and the United States and Russia were squaring off in the Cuban Missile Crisis.

**Imprisoned**

The conditions in the Pretoria prison where Nelson was first sent were grim: no books, few visitors, a garb of short pants to humiliate the prisoner and solitary confinement if one complained. Their work was sewing vermin-infested mailbags. After six months, Nelson was transferred to Robben Island, a remote area offshore, which from time to time had been used to punish rebels. At first, the prisoners were bullied, shoved about and threatened with blows. Nelson would have none of it and challenged his jailers with: "If you so much as lay a hand on me, I will take you to the highest court in the land. And when I finish with you, you will be as poor as a church mouse."[32] The officers began to shake and quietly withdrew from the cell area.

Robben Island is the Alcatraz of South Africa. It is surrounded by cold, rough waters that prevent escape. At this time Robben Island had been designed to be an inhuman and brutal place where white guards were trained to inflict harsh punishment on these new political prisoners. Nelson and six others arrived there and settled in for a long ordeal.

Nelson was combative from the outset, protesting the short pants. (It took him three years before he could gain long trousers for himself and his men.) The cells were small, about eight feet by seven feet, and were equipped with only a straw mat and several threadbare blankets. Life would be harsh, with no radio or newspapers and only one letter to and from the immediate family and one visitor every six months. Yet, from the outset, Nelson and the others were resolved to remain hopeful and confident, knowing that the ideas they stood for would never die and that ultimately their cause would prevail, whether they themselves survived or not. At one point, Mandela prophetically wrote: "In my lifetime I shall step out into the sunshine, walk with firm feet."[33]

The daily routine was extremely difficult and designed to be punitive. Up at 5:30, the prisoners had to clean their cells and wash and shave from a bucket of cold water. Breakfast was taken in the open courtyard and consisted of almost inedible porridge, along with a drink of boiled corn in water. After a brief inspection, the men worked until noon, sitting in the sun in rows and hammering rocks into gravel in silence. At noon, there was a lunch of boiled corn, and then more rock-breaking until four o'clock. At four they could wash in cold seawater, speak briefly to each other and then have a supper of soggy vegetables or gristle in their cells. In the evenings, they were left to their solitary thoughts while guards patrolled.

Early in 1965 the thirty political prisoners, who were kept separate from the others, were assigned to harder work in a lime quarry. They worked in the quarry for thirteen years, in the winter cold and the summer sun, hacking into the rocks to get at the layers of lime, and then digging the lime out and hauling it away. The glare on the white rocks did permanent damage to their eyes. Nelson would later explain how he survived: "[T]he human body has an enormous capacity for adjusting to trying circumstances. I have found that one can bear the unbearable if one can keep one's spirits strong even when one's body is being tested. Strong convictions are the secret to surviving deprivation; your spirit can be full even when your stomach is empty."[34]

Occasionally, a writer or reporter would visit the island, and the prisoners would be issued jerseys to sew instead of their usual work on the rocks. Nelson would use these occasions to blast the conditions in the prison and give bad publicity to the government. He was able to influence visitors from the Red Cross, Parliament and the British government and was able to gain improvements in the prison.

It was obvious to these visitors that Nelson had risen to a strong position of leadership in the prison. Helen Suzman, a progressive member of Parliament, visited him many times and reported that: "He had a commanding presence over both prisoners and warders."[35]

After three years or so, conditions began to improve in the prison. The atmosphere became more humane and civil.

Nevertheless, Nelson continued with his complaints and wrote strong letters of protest to the officials. At one point he wrote a letter to the Minister of Justice, pointing out that political prisoners are often released early and asking the same for his group. Mandela was always quite outspoken about the injustices of his government and had to be regularly reminded that he was a prisoner!

In 1970 the government had had enough and unleashed a reign of terror on the prisoners. A brutal commander was installed, and the prisoners were subjected to persecution and severe punishments for offenses. At one point, they were forced to stand naked in the cold while their cells were inspected. Some of the prisoners were beaten bloody when they returned to their cells.

Throughout this nightmare, Nelson remained calm and stood strong. He led a delegation to face down the commander and sent out letters exposing the abuse. When some judges were sent to the island, Nelson accused the commander face-to-face before the judges and ultimately had the commander transferred. At the same time, he was able to win over the commander who departed on friendly terms. Nelson had come to see the prison as a microcosm of the ANC's struggle for freedom—a place where he could learn of the good and bad sides of the Afrikaners, gain knowledge about how to win them over, and be able to be reconciled in the long run. These would be valuable lessons for his life of leadership after prison.

At the end of 1971, matters began to improve on the island. A new officer was installed who maintained a professional relationship with the prisoners. The Red Cross began to play a stronger role in the improvements, and gradually it seemed as though the prisoners were running the prison. The prisoners could work at their own pace at the quarry and often did not work at all. Often they were allowed to go to the beaches to collect seaweed. There they could enjoy the sea breezes, watch the wild birds and even have fish fries with the warders. They were given more clothes, warm water for showers, a better diet, and they were even allowed to build a tennis court in the yard where they once broke rocks. They were also permitted to play rugby, cricket and board games; a cinema was set up where they could watch movies. Nelson and his mates were also allowed to have a small garden, where they grew fresh vegetables and melons. They established a "university" atmosphere, where the prisoners could teach courses and work for higher degrees through correspondence courses. Often intense academic and political discussions went on among both the prisoners and the warders. Later on, the prisoners were even allowed to put on plays and learn to play musical instruments. Religious services were regularly held for the different denominations, and Nelson, though a Methodist, attended them all.

## Personal Trials

While in prison, Nelson underwent many personal trials. He dearly missed his wife, Winnie, and the rare times she could come for visits were brief and heavily watched. Winnie became deeply involved in political activity. As a result, she was often arrested, interrogated, assaulted by the police, banned, imprisoned and even put in solitary. A gunman was once found prowling in her yard, two men attempted to strangle her in her sleep, and her home was attacked, the windows smashed, and the Mandela house was eventually burned down. Winnie became more and more strident, out of control and given to violence. At the same time, she remained an important source of information for Nelson and served as a strong spokesperson for him and the ANC. Many believe that, without Winnie, Nelson's name would have become forgotten while he was in prison.

Nelson also grieved the loss of his mother in 1968 and then his son Thembi was killed in a car crash in 1969. For Nelson, one of the most severe punishments of prison was the feeling that his children were becoming strangers and that he was losing his beloved family.

## The Prison as Laboratory

Nelson continued to use the prison as a laboratory in which to learn how to deal with the Afrikaners in the future. When the young warders arrived, the political prisoners would speak with them in the Afrikaner language (Afrikaans), attempt to get acquainted with them, learn their mindset and attempt to reeducate them. The prisoners learned African history, literature, and, most importantly for the future, how to negotiate with them. Mandela was the leader in all this and persuaded his fellow prisoners to be calm and to laugh at the brutalities they had to endure. Mandela remained always optimistic and never gave into depression. He said: "...I know that my cause will triumph."[36] Ironically, it was in prison where Nelson achieved true liberation. He lost all fear of his oppressors, and though filled with anger, gained complete control of self. He achieved a coolness and gentleness, under which lay a steeled and hardened person. Self-disciplined, he intently avoided getting shaken at any time, believing that persons who get rattled can make serious mistakes.

## Writing an Autobiography

Now that the prison atmosphere provided time for reflection, Nelson was persuaded to write his autobiography. Writing through the nights, Nelson turned out ten pages per day and finished the book in four months. Each day, he would pass the finished pages to an inmate who was soon to be released. The inmate would copy the material in tiny script and put the pages in his own books, which were eventually smuggled out. The document was given to the ANC leaders in exile, but remained unpublished for twenty years. It ultimately became the basis for Mandela's autobiography, published in 1994. The original manuscript was buried in plastic containers in the courtyard. The authorities at one point discovered this cache, and Nelson and several others were deprived of study rights for several years.

## The Struggle Wanes

By the early 1970s things looked bleak for the freedom movement. The ANC was nearly dead, with all of its leaders long gone to prison or into exile. The whites were enjoying a booming economy and were able to squelch any resistance from blacks. Some hope came to the ANC when it was learned that Angola and Mozambique had been liberated. This raised the possibilities for more military training and for guerrilla warfare in South Africa. In addition, the black trade unions were gaining strength and there was growing resistance to apartheid from white liberals, students and church leaders like Archbishop Desmond Tutu and Archbishop Denis Hurley.

Sanctions from other nations were also putting pressure on the Afrikaner government. The Black Consciousness Movement, founded by Steve Biko, a young intellectual who was killed by the government, was still working underground. Militants were also encouraged by the Black Power Movement and the Civil Rights Movement in the United States.

In 1976 another event brought South Africa closer to the brink. In Soweto ten thousand young blacks marched against the school system that was forcing the teaching of African language. Soldiers fired on the marchers, and Soweto became a bloody battlefield with 618 blacks killed. The slaughter was reported around the world, and the ANC was encouraged to see that the young were eager for freedom. Mandela wrote a letter smuggled out from prison, encouraging his people to unite in their resistance to apartheid: "Even as we bow at their graves we remember this: the dead live as martyrs in our hearts and minds, a reproach to our disunity and the host of shortcomings that accompany divisions among the oppressed, a spur to our efforts to close ranks, a reminder that the freedom of our people is yet to be won."[37]

As the young freedom fighters were sent to Robben Island, Nelson and the others were challenged to win them over. Many of them saw these older men as out of touch and had even heard that Mandela had sold out. He patiently listened to them, and gradually won their loyalty and friendship. He turned many of them away from their hatred toward whites and helped them envision a nonracial South Africa. Intense debates took place about different forms of government, the merits of Communism, and the use of violence. Throughout it all, Nelson kept a cool restraint and balance, and was always open to the views of others. With regard to dealing with apartheid, Nelson always stood for a position of reconciliation and forgiveness, but only after uncompromising confrontation and sacrifice. Once again, he was rehearsing for his later role as leader of his country.

In 1980 Nelson was once again allowed to resume his studies for his law degree. He and the other political prisonerss were also permitted to listen to the radio and read newspapers. Some of the news was good. There was a petition in Johannesburg to "Free Mandela," and the students at the University of London nominated him for chancellor of the university. (He received 7,199 votes but lost to Princess Anne!) More often the news was bad. Margaret Thatcher, the Prime Minister of Britain, as well as President Ronald Reagan of the United States, opposed the ANC and sided with the whites in South Africa. Most of the African nations that had gained freedom were now experiencing dictators and corrupt governments, and were locked in coups and wars. The Western world did not want to invest in Africa, except for South Africa, a fact that gave this country more leverage against its black population. Nelson and his men saw the United States engaged in a new kind of imperialism. Not finding military support from the West, the ANC had turned to the East and Marxism for assistance.

**Leaving the Island**

In March of 1982 the commander of the prison came to Nelson's cell and shocked him by telling him to pack up his things and get ready to be transferred. He and three others were whisked off without a chance to even say good-bye to their mates and sent to Poolsmoor Prison in Pretoria. The prisoners were given the entire top floor of the prison and now had spacious rooms and beds in place of the mats on a stone floor that they had known for so long. While all this was an improvement, the leaders realized that they were being deliberately cut off from the strong influence they had on Robben Island, a place that had become mythical in its symbolism to the black struggle. Nelson was now given many privileges and allowed "contact visits" with his family.

Outside the prison the armed struggle was escalating. The government made an offer it had made before, that it would free him if he would reject violence as a political instrument and return to the tribal place of his origins. Once again, Nelson refused because he did not want to be marginalized and did not believe that nonviolent actions could be effective against a military that crushed such actions with brutal force. He says: "I told them that I was a Christian and had always been a Christian. Even Christ, I said, when he was left with no alternative, used force to expel the moneylenders from the temple."[38] Nelson turned down his own freedom, and in his speech that was read by his daughter, Zindzi, at a rally in Soweto, he declared: "Only free men can negotiate. Prisoners cannot enter into contracts.... I cannot and will not give any undertaking at a time when I and you, the people, are not free. Your freedom and mine cannot be separated. I will return."[39]

Even though Nelson would not accept his freedom by rejecting violence, he was convinced that now was the time for negotiations lest there be a bloodbath. Since he had recently been given a cell three floors away for his comrades, he would now have the opportunity to make secret plans for "talks about talks."

**Negotiations Begin**

The first opportunity for negotiation came when the representatives from the British Commonwealth of Nations came to South Africa on a fact-finding mission to determine whether or not they would enforce sanctions on the government for supporting apartheid. Nelson was given all new clothes, including a pin-striped suit and looked like a "prime minister...not a prisoner."[40] In the ensuing talks, Nelson made it clear to the group that he was only speaking for himself and that he was committed to a nonracial nation where both blacks and whites would be secure. He suggested that the government needed to withdraw the military and police from the townships and suspend armed struggles so that talks could begin. The answer came swiftly when President Botha ordered air raids and attacks on ANC bases. The "talks" ended abruptly and the Commonwealth visitors left the country.

Violence escalated and the ANC ordered their people to render South Africa "ungovernable." Nelson next asked to see the Commissioner of Prisons and the Minister of Justice. Surprisingly, Nelson was taken to the minister's residence for an extensive conversation. Nelson gained the impression that the government wanted to talk, so he asked if he could speak with the president and the foreign minister. Months passed. Meanwhile, Nelson was taken on a number of pleasant excursions around the city, perhaps, he thought, to get him in a compromising mood. Then, in 1987, a committee of senior officials was appointed to conduct private conversations with Nelson.

Mandela knew it was time to consult with his colleagues in prison and with Oliver Tambo in exile. On hearing about his talks, they were all worried that Nelson was being used. He assured them that his only goal was to arrange official meetings between the ANC and the South African government and that he was only acting as a go-between. His colleagues decided to go along, but with apprehension and reluctance.

Nelson continued his talks with the government committee for months, explaining to them the real goals of the ANC and discussing its alliance with the Communist party, its commitment to majority rule and racial reconciliation and its attitude toward the use of violence. With regard to the latter, Nelson insisted that the ANC's use of violence was done in self-defense and would stop once the violent oppression of his people ceased.

As the talks proceeded in 1988, the country was in chaos. International sanctions increased and many companies left South Africa. President Botha was prepared to talk with Mandela. Nelson suddenly came down with tuberculosis and was sent for six weeks of treatment at a luxurious clinic, where he could continue his talks with the secret committee. In early December of 1988, he was sent to Victor Verster Prison, where he was given a house on the grounds with a private cook and a swimming pool. Here he could host his ANC visitors and continue with high-level talks. He wrote letters to President Botha with his proposals for majority rule and internal peace.

In July of 1989, Mandela was taken to see Botha for a "courtesy call." At the president's office, Botha, known as the "Great Crocodile," was quite courteous and friendly. After a breezy exchange, Nelson asked that all political prisoners be released. After a tense moment, Botha said he could not do that. They shook hands and Nelson left. He felt that there had been no breakthrough, but that Botha had crossed the Rubicon, and now "there was no turning back."[41]

## The De Klerk Era

Soon after Mandela's meeting with Botha, the latter resigned and was replaced by F.W. de Klerk. Nelson viewed de Klerk as a party man and had little respect for him, and was thus surprised when de Klerk eased up on restrictions on demonstrations, seemed open to negotiations and began dismantling apartheid. Nelson consulted his colleagues and began to prepare for a meeting with de Klerk. At the outset, Nelson pointed out that the first steps toward peace would be the rejection of apartheid, the release of all political prisoners, the removal of bans and troops from the townships and a mutual cease-fire. Nelson made it clear that if he were to be released, he would continue in the struggle for freedom. Nelson saw that de Klerk listened carefully and seemed open to his proposals. Soon after de Klerk brought Nelson's proposals before Parliament, Nelson was told that he was about to be free. But even in the release, Nelson remained resolute and was clear that he would go when it was timely for him and would go where he wished, not where he was told to go.

## Free After Twenty-Seven Years

As described earlier, Nelson was released in February 1990 and was put up at the residence of Archbishop Desmond Tutu in Cape Town. Nelson immediately held news conferences and called meetings with his associates. Nelson realized that he would not truly be a free man until his people were freed, and there was much work still to be done. He was flown to a stadium in Soweto, the key city in black urban South Africa, where he gave an impassioned speech before a throng of 120,000 people. He proclaimed his joy on returning but also revealed his sadness at the poor housing, schools and few job opportunities, and he decried the high black-against-black crime rate. He made it clear that he harbored no hatred of the whites but abhorred their system of repression. He made it quite clear that his plan was one of inclusion: "No man or woman who has abandoned apartheid will be excluded from our movement toward a nonracial, united and democratic South Africa based on one-person one-vote...."[42]

The next order of business for Nelson was to meet with his associates and assure them that he had not been co-opted by the government and would still work closely with the ANC. He then began a six-month tour of Africa, during which he was hailed as a hero. While traveling, Nelson was able to discover the many changes that had come about since his imprisonment. He ended the trip with a meeting in Stockholm, Sweden, with Oliver Tambo, who encouraged him to now lead the ANC. Then he attended a concert held in his honor by many international artists in London.

Once at home, Nelson had to face the horrors of tribal violence. The negotiations with the government were stalled by incidents in which the military fired on black demonstrators with live ammunition. De Klerk was now being revealed as a "gradualist," a political pragmatist who, in fact, opposed majority rule.

In May the talks began and "[h]istoric enemies who had been fighting each other for three centuries met and shook hands."[43] Black and white leaders met as equals at the table. The three-day meeting ended with some significant agreements and the commitment to continue negotiations.

**An International Tour**

Nelson decided to begin an international tour to urge countries to continue their support with sanctions. He was feted in France, Switzerland, Italy and the Netherlands. He next moved on to the United States, where he was given a one-million-person ticker-tape parade in New York City, visited Harlem, spoke before a packed Yankee Stadium, addressed a joint session of Congress and met with the president. He then visited Canada, where he closely related to the Inuits at the Arctic Circle. Then he visited Ireland and went on to have a cordial meeting with Margaret Thatcher in London.

When Nelson returned home, he found that the violence had increased and that the death toll in 1990 was fifteen hundred. Nelson learned that the government was using a "Third Force" of renegade security men to manipulate violence between the ANC and the opposing Inkatha tribes.

The ANC finally agreed to suspend armed action to speed along the negotiations, but violence continued to escalate and negotiations were suspended in July 1991. Some criticized Nelson for being out of touch and for engaging in personal negotiations, but he was nonetheless elected president without opposition by the first ANC conference held inside South Africa in thirty years. The ANC now had to move from being an outlawed liberation movement to becoming a central political party.

**Formal Negotiations**
Formal negotiations began in December 1991 at the Convention for a Democratic South Africa. The government spoke of power-sharing and even offered apologies for apartheid. Mandela boldly stressed that government derives its legitimacy and authority from the consent of the governed and that this is now the time to put together such authority with a free election and a new constitution.

Most at the convention agreed on an intent to create a democracy with multiple parties based on universal adult voting. It was agreed that de Klerk have the last words, and though he initially was positive, he suddenly turned on the ANC and denounced them as dishonorable. Mandela would not stand for that and took the mike to have his own final words, angrily rejecting de Klerk's betrayal and abuse of authority in the interest of making political gains. Mandela ended on a more positive note; the next day he and de Klerk were able to shake hands, but the negotiations were now quite shaky. Eventually, de Klerk decided to put the decision to negotiate up to a national vote. The results turned out in favor of the negotiations, but this gave de Klerk and his people a stronger bargaining edge over the ANC.

In between negotiations, Nelson announced his separation from his wife, Winnie. He praised her for her constant support, but noted that their long separation and the differences they had on issues and approaches to the freedom movement called for a separation.

Negotiations resumed but were stalled by charges of corruption in the government, continued violence against the ANC and de Klerk's resistance to majority rule. Black-against-black violence continued, thought to be manipulated and "allowed" by the government. Many ANC supporters wanted to turn to violent revolution, but Mandela insisted that negotiation was the way to freedom and called for strikes and marches against the government.

At one march, the people were fired on; twenty-nine were killed, and over two hundred wounded. The bloodshed, while tragic, opened the way for new negotiations and an ultimate agreement to have free elections for a government of national unity with a multiparty cabinet. The historic election was set for April 27, 1994, and plans were made for a parliamentary form of government. In 1993 Mandela and de Klerk were awarded the Nobel Peace Prize for their efforts toward national unity. In his speech Nelson said that he stood with all those who suffered and died for freedom in his country and with all those throughout the world who struggle against tyranny and injustice.

Nelson now became an extremely effective campaigner, holding town meetings throughout the country, promoting the ANC's vision for South Africa and declaring the group's intentions of creating jobs, distributing land more fairly and providing good housing, healthcare and education for the people. He called for patience, since it would take time to eliminate a system that had been unjust for hundreds of years. He urged all the people to put the past behind them and contribute to the building of the future.

### A Free Election

Blacks had to be taught how to vote since they had never done so before. Nelson's advice was: "On election day, look down your ballot and when you see the face of a young and handsome man, mark an X."[44] On election day, undeterred by violence, bombs and other efforts to sabotage the election, the people lined up for as many as five hours to cast their first votes ever. One person remarked: "After nearly 350 years, 350 minutes is nothing."

## A New President

Nelson and the ANC carried 62.6 percent of the vote; he was now president of his country. He wryly commented that the very generals and police chiefs who were now saluting him would just a few years before have arrested him! At the victory celebration, jet fighters that had been purchased to defend the country against black insurgents now flew overhead in tribute to the new black president. Nelson congratulated de Klerk for his strong showing and, accompanied by Coretta King, used the words of her husband in his acceptance speech,

> This is one of the most important moments in the life of our country. I stand here before you filled with deep pride and joy— pride in the ordinary, humble people of this country. You have shown such a calm, patient determination to reclaim your country as your own, and now the joy that we can loudly proclaim from the rooftops—Free at last! Free at last![45]

## President Mandela

President Mandela at his inauguration celebrated the freedom and political emancipation of his people and pledged to dedicate himself to the liberty of all the people of South Africa. He began his term by encouraging reconciliation and trust and by immediately forming a new democratic and nonracial government.

In the first few months Nelson enjoyed a political honeymoon and presided efficiently over his new cabinet, with ANC members intently working with their ex-enemies. He seemed to often use the old tribal chief approach of listening to all sides and then coming to a decision. He never trusted de Klerk, and when he made it clear that he was the president, de Klerk soon became alienated. In spite of the conflicts, a new constitution was gradually formulated.

The economy became a major concern early on. International aid was not forthcoming, and investors were still avoiding South Africa. Political corruption and bribery were rampant. The housing problem proved difficult to solve, and illegal immigration from impoverished neighboring countries was putting more pressure on housing and jobs. Nelson later remarked: "It was more difficult to defend the freedom we have won…than struggling or fighting to gain it."[46] Nelson faced all of this in his usual disciplined and steely fashion, determined to fulfill his destiny of creating a new and free nation.

### Reconciliation

One of Nelson's priorities was reconciliation among the ex-enemies. He was sensitive to the racial and tribal differences and intent that the minorities, especially the Afrikaners, be protected and properly participate. He visited Botha, many of his former judges and prosecutors, past black and white leaders and their widows and wives, and even appointed some of his former enemies to posts in the government. He said: "Courageous people do not fear forgiving, for the sake of peace."[47] In February 1996 Nelson initiated the Truth and Reconciliation Commission, led by Archbishop Tutu. The purpose of the commission was not so much forgiveness of all the atrocities, but to discover the truth so as to grant amnesty. The goal was understanding rather than vengeance, reparation rather than retaliation.

### Mandela Steps Down

In 1996, Nelson was seventy-eight years old and saw that it was time to begin withdrawing from power in favor of younger leaders. He announced the end of his leadership of the ANC at the end of 1997 and then left government after finishing his five-year term in 1999. Meanwhile, he continued his efforts at diplomacy at home and abroad. His was on a mission to promote peace, tolerance and the recognition of human rights throughout his country, the whole of Africa and the world. To do this, Nelson traveled a great deal with his new wife, Graca, and spent less and less time in his homeland.

Mandela gave his last speech as president to parliament in February 1999. Much had been achieved: equality, the right to vote in free elections and freedom of speech; much more remained to be accomplished. There were still deep divisions and even hatred between blacks and whites; many whites had lost privileges and were now citizens of a developing country with an impoverished population moving into the cities; there was a growing black middle class that had achieved wealth and left the black poor to sink into unemployment and poverty. The economy was struggling, and corruption was widespread in business and government. Violent crime was rampant, hundreds of white farmers had been murdered, and there were still dangerous factions among the military. Many whites, especially from the professional class, were leaving the country. Mandela ended his final speech with the words: "The long walk continues."[48]

### The Mandela Myth

Nelson Mandela is now wrapped in multilayered mythology. He has been a freedom fighter, an exiled yet surviving prisoner, a tribal leader, president, international statesman, political showman, elder grandfather. Some say he lacked the ruthlessness to achieve his goals, while others say that his power to forgive prevented a bloodbath in his country and brought the nation to where it is today. Some say he was naïve, while others say that his simplicity and steely commitment to negotiation brought the best out of even his enemies. Nelson admits, "I'm no angel," but indeed he seems to have been the man that South Africa needed at a crucial time in its history.

### The Present State of Affairs

Today South Africa is a country of forty-four million people, an area rich with natural resources including gold, diamonds, copper, coal and iron ore, a wide variety of livestock and agricultural products and a strong industrial base. It is a young country, with the median age in the mid-twenties, but the life expectancy is only forty-four years, due in part to the fact that a significant percentage of the population is suffering from HIV/AIDS. The economy is growing, but there is a high unemployment rate—27 percent and over half of the population lives below the poverty line.

Nelson Mandela, now nearing ninety, lives quietly in the place of his birth, Quni in Transkei. He is actively engaged in the fight against AIDS, and in 2005 lost his eldest son, Makgatho, to the disease. While many women and men sacrificed and even gave their lives for the cause, Mandela stands as "the single most vital symbol not only of liberation from the tyranny of apartheid, but of a new way of life in South Africa."[49]

# C H A P T E R    S I X

## *Jean Vanier: Freedom for Those With Special Needs*

It was a glorious Easter morning. Thousands of suffering people from all over the world had gathered at Lourdes. They had come great distances to this Marian shrine with its baths of healing waters in southern France to pray together. Many came in wheelchairs, some walked with great difficulty, and others were severely disfigured. All wore ponchos of different colors and style, and as the celebration began everyone broke out in an explosion of joy. Standing in the midst of these broken pilgrims was a tall man with an angular jaw and gray hair, dressed in simple clothing. This man, standing straight and shepherd-like among his flock, was Jean Vanier, the founder of L'Arche, a worldwide movement to provide homes and care for those with special needs.

### Early Life

Jean Vanier is a French-Canadian but was born in Geneva, Switzerland, in 1928. He was one of five children of his father Georges, a decorated World War I hero (he had lost a leg) who later served as the governor general of Canada. Jean's mother was Pauline Vanier, a woman who was heroic in her efforts to care for refugees during World War II and dedicated to humanitarian causes. The Vaniers spent most of the 1930s in London, where Georges worked with the Canadian High Commission. Jean ("Jock") went to a prep school in England and then, during the war, joined his father in France and studied there. In 1940 the family had to leave France due to the war, and after a time in England returned to Canada. At thirteen, Jean asked to join the war effort and his father's permission meant a great deal to him. He writes: "[I]f a much loved and respected father will trust you to do something apparently so foolhardy, then you can trust yourself."[1] With a confidence and determination that would characterize him for the rest of his life, young Jean set off on a troop ship for Liverpool amidst the dangers of torpedoes in the Atlantic and German bombers headed for England flying overhead. Upon arrival, Jean entered the Royal Naval College in England, and after graduation spent several years in the Navy, preparing for warfare. By the time he was ready to be commissioned, the war was coming to an end, so Jean saw no action. He was assigned as an officer on an aircraft carrier in the Royal Canadian Navy.

Life in the Navy had trained Jean's body, showed him how to live simply and use his energies in constructive ways, but it was not the life for him. He believed that he was hearing a calling to give his life to God. His brother's entrance into the Trappists, a friendship with a Carmelite nun and reading Thomas Merton's *Seven Storey Mountain* had all influenced him in this decision. He says that he soon became more interested in praying in the evenings than attending the night watch, and he began to pedal his bike to Mass each morning.

**Pursuing a Calling**

In 1950, Jean resigned his commission in the Navy in order "to know God better" and to find his place in life.[2] He wrote letters of inquiry to the Jesuits and to his mother's spiritual director, Père Thomas Philippe. The Jesuits didn't answer, but Père Thomas wrote him a warm and enthusiastic letter. After trying the simplicity of several Christian communities, Jean joined Père Thomas's community, Eau Vive, a widely diverse lay community in a poor area near Paris. The prayer and dialogue shared among the Catholics, Orthodox, Protestants and Muslims were once admired by a visitor named Angelo Roncalli, who would

become Pope John XXIII. Jean was profoundly influenced by the philosophy and spirituality of Père Thomas and by the ecumenism and
openness of his community.

Père Thomas fell ill and asked Jean to take his place. The parent
Dominican community did not like the idea of a layperson being in
charge, even though he was now studying for the priesthood. The
Dominicans asked Vanier to leave, so he withdrew from the community
and quit his studies at Institut Catholique, now filled with uncertainty
and without his mentor Père Thomas.

Jean decided to stop preparing for the priesthood and lived on his
own for several years, spending some time at a Cistercian abbey, then a
small farm, and then in a cottage in Fatima, Portugal. Eventually he
decided to return to Paris, where he finished his doctorate and then
began teaching philosophy at St. Michael's College in Toronto.

At one point Jean decided to pay a visit to his old mentor, Père
Thomas in France, where the priest was now chaplain in a home for
men with special needs in Trosly-Breuil. Jean was impressed with the
studies of the disabled being conducted there, especially with the finding that when those with special needs were crowded together, they
became withdrawn. On the other hand, research showed that when they
were given their own space, they were usually much more outgoing.
Even more importantly, it was discovered that once the disabled were
approached with love, they responded with extraordinary warmth and
generosity. When Jean experienced this sense of community with those
with special needs, he began to see where his calling was taking him.

Jean returned to his teaching, where he packed the halls with his
lectures on love, friendship and sexuality. During break he returned
again to France and Père Thomas, and he began to visit the asylums,
where families were frequently encouraged to turn over mentally disabled children. At that time, there were few schools or workshops for
the mentally disabled. In these institutions patients were packed into
dorms smelling of urine and disinfectant, and lived amidst chaos and

violence. Inmates went about aimlessly in miserable conditions, some crying out for love, others hitting their heads on the floor. Vanier could see that their greatest pain was from rejection. They felt ugly, dirty, of no value and unwanted.[3]

But Vanier also observed that changes were in the air. Parent associations were urging better conditions for their disabled children, and governments were beginning to move to finance projects for their care. He sensed a strong movement to treat the disabled with care and dignity and thought that he might be part of that movement to free them from inhumane and prison-like conditions.

Jean continued to visit the institutions, and would often just sit and watch the men walking in circles with nothing to do. Strangely, he began to experience the presence of God in the midst of all this anguish. He decided to resign his professorship in Toronto and, on Père Thomas's advice, he bought a little house near the priest's community and invited two men to live with him: Raphael and Phillipe. The pair had no family, and living in a horrible asylum had filled them with anger and hopelessness. Jean named his new home L'Arche (the Ark) and, in August 1964, a new movement to serve the disabled was born.

Needless to say, Jean's decision came as a shock to his prominent family. How could he give up a promising teaching career at a university to live in a cottage in a French village with two men from a mental institution? It would be years before they would understand the meaning of Jean's calling to a life of smallness and poverty in order to reflect the love of Jesus to people who had been outcasts.

## L'Arche

Jean's first year with the two men had its difficulties: trying to keep the house in good repair, raising enough money for necessities, and at the same time dealing with some of the neighbors who looked askance at this "strange" group in their midst. Jean's cooking skills were not very good, and he says that his inexperience led him to often treat the two men like children and not listen "to the light hidden in their hearts."[4]

Jean candidly admits that at first he felt like he was a savior to the two men, and as such had the power to tell them what to do and how they were to fit into his project. Gradually he learned that the two men were not interested in a "project," but needed friendship, security and care.

Jean soon learned that the people he had taken in were wounded in their self-image and blamed themselves for all the rejection they experienced. They said to themselves: "If I am not loved, it is because I am not lovable, I am no good and I am evil."[5] They needed someone to listen to them and hear their needs and desires. Jean had to learn that L'Arche was as much their concern as his. He writes: "I had much to discover: something about welcome and respect for people, something about liberation of hearts and patience. I had to learn about myself and my faults and defects, my need to dominate and command after spending eight years in the Navy. I had to learn about human growth and suffering, about sharing, and about the ways of God."[6] In short, he had to gain freedom for himself before he could help free the others.

Little by little, the three began to share and laugh and build up a trust for each other. Jean says: "They began to lead me into the world of healing relationships."[7] The three men shopped, cleaned, cooked, did the laundry and other chores together. They went to Mass and said their prayers together. Jean learned more about love from some of the generous women in the neighborhood who brought them hot soup, fruit and vegetables. The threesome began to live more closely together, and Jean began to realize that the two men were actually teaching him. He moved from wanting to help them to listening to them. Jean observed that the qualities of the hearts of these two men could indeed be developed, and that they could indeed grow in freedom of their choices. He gradually came to understand that the more fragile a person's freedom is, the more it has to be respected and protected. Jean was now learning a pedagogy "not of force but of freedom."[8] L'Arche gradually became more of a family, and the cooking improved immensely when some sisters and several more residents joined them.

## Director of a Larger Community

In 1964 Vanier was asked to take over as director of a nearby home for men with special needs. He packed up his little community and joined the larger group, only to find that the place was in chaos and that he was not prepared for such responsibilities. Vanier had to revert to his Navy discipline and organization, and with the help of volunteers and a woman professionally trained in psychiatry, Dr. Richet, the home began to take shape. Workshops were established where the residents could find happiness in making and creating things.

Working with Père Thomas, Jean began to discover that the disabled could speak a language of the heart and often had a deeper understanding of faith than those assisting them. Many maintained a close friendship with Jesus and, because of their own inner anguish, had an intimate, personal connection with his sufferings during his passion and death. Jean was finding his call to gospel living among these people that many consider to be outcasts!

## L'Arche Begins to Spread

The reputation of L'Arche began to spread, especially through its newsletter and Vanier's popular lecture tours. Requests were made to place many with special needs at L'Arche, and a great number of young people volunteered to be "assistants." Many of these youths, moved by the idealism and waves of renewal from Vatican II, no longer felt the need go to seminaries and convents to be of service, and began to sign up to help with L'Arche.

Vanier began buying up other houses in the town and, in spite of some strong resistance from his neighbors, established more homes for his people. Each house would be formed in simplicity and with the Gospels as their inspiration, but at the same time they would be well organized and assisted by volunteers. Often the help of professional medical people and therapists was needed. Nevertheless, the main "therapy" of L'Arche was based on relationships in community, which can bring hope, peace and motivation to the marginal person.[9]

Financial support was acquired through the government and through gifts from donors.

## Joined by His Mother

The passing of Jean's father in 1967 was a milestone for Jean. It meant the loss of a significant role model, but at the same time it freed his mother to join in the work of L'Arche. Jean's father, Georges, had a profound influence on Jean. Georges, a distinguished statesman and war hero, was also a deeply religious man. He was an avid reader of works on spirituality and was dedicated to prayer and contemplation. The simplicity of his spirituality, love of children, deep commitment to others, courage in dealing with losing a leg in the war, and strong leadership abilities provided a role model for Jean and even moved him to write a book about his father, *Be Not Afraid*.[10]

Jean was delighted to have his mother join him, since he had always remained close with her. She had initially disapproved of his work, but gradually came around to see the value of his calling. When her husband died, she left her lovely house in Montreal and eagerly became a "grandmother" to many of the residents and assistants. Pauline Vanier was ninety-three when she passed away. She had known the rich and powerful, but she died with the weak and powerless, always the wise and loving "Mammie" to the many whose lives she touched.[11]

## Père Thomas

Père Thomas continued to serve as spiritual mentor for Jean. Père Thomas, was a popular lecturer, writer and retreat master in his own right, and at the same time served as the spiritual father of the community. He provided them with many extraordinary liturgies, as well as powerful homilies on gospel living. He often put the community members in touch with the suffering of Jesus, the centrality of the Beatitudes, and how God dwells in the heart. Indeed he was instrumental in providing the spiritual framework for L'Arche. He shared with the community his deep love of Jesus and his commitment to prayer, as well as his closeness to Mary, his model for faith and femininity.

## Living With Brokenness

Jean continued to grow in his calling as he learned how to relate to the brokenness of those around him. He came to realize that the weak are often despised and rejected and that this was the story of slavery as well as that of those who are sick or disabled. He came to think that people crushed in their childhood or youth often take revenge on the weak. Living with people who have been crushed led Jean into the depths of his own heart and revealed to him God's plan for humanity—to restore freedom to the weak and the oppressed. We were created for wholeness and communion with God and others. Jean put it this way: "Human persons can freely enter into relationship with God. They can speak together. They can rest in one another. They can celebrate together."[12]

## Learning Our Own Brokenness

Jean learned that the disabled can help us come to love ourselves and others in our brokenness. "They reveal to us the brokenness that we deny in ourselves."[13] Jean had come to this work with the disabled from a background that taught him to compete and be first, to be independent and successful. Being with the disabled freed him from hardness of heart, from the lack of capacity to respond to those crying out to him for friendship. He learned that behind his need to win were fears of being pushed aside, of being vulnerable, of feeling helpless in the face of those in need. He began to get in touch with the darkness and even hatred in his own heart, his capacity to hurt the weak. Jean had to face the elitism and prejudices within himself, and realized that he needed to be freed from these evils in his own heart. Being in community with the disabled helped Jean to know that he too was loved just the way he was and that they could help him heal his inner wounds. Jean puts it this way:

> I do not have to pretend that I am better than others and that I
> have to win in all the competitions. It's O.K. to be myself, just as I
> am, in my uniqueness. That, of course, is a very healing and liber-

ating experience. I am allowed to be myself, with all my psycho-
logical and physical wounds, with all my limitations and with all
my gifts too. And I can trust that I am loved just as I am, and that
I too can love and grow.[14]

Jean's faith also told him that Jesus came to reveal the kingdom to the
poor, and he was now one of the poor. He, like those around him, was
discovering that "God is present in the poverty and wounds of their
hearts."[15]

## Jesus as Model

Jesus served as the central role model for Jean's life with those with special needs. He saw Jesus as the truly free man: free from his culture, from
the corruptions of his own religion, from the fear to criticize those who
abuse, free to talk with and heal outcasts, to rise above the law and heal
on the Sabbath. He writes: "Yes, Jesus is an incredibly free man who cannot be pinned down, labeled or put in a box. He confines himself to no
specific group, whether political or social, national or religious. He is
free to do the work of his Father and to announce to every person, who-
ever he or she may be, that he loves them…. He is free with the freedom
of God."[16] This was the Jesus who became the role model for Jean in his
life and work. Like Jesus, he did not want to have any barriers around
his heart, so that he could feel the vulnerability, anguish and rejection
of his people and could bring healing love and compassion into their
lives. He would live with them in their brokenness, listen to them, learn
from them and together seek God in their weakness and anguish.
Sometimes this meant taking their abuse and even violent outbursts but
showing them forgiveness, rather than the judgment and rejection to
which they were accustomed. The disabled would teach him that to follow Jesus one must give up going up the ladder of success and power
and walk down the ladder to be with the people who are in pain.

Jean's mission was not one of serving the poor, but of gaining the
experience of Jesus from the poor. Jean believed that the poor possess a

unique gift of love and friendship. "We are discovering that the life-giving Jesus is hidden in them. He is truly there. If you become a friend of the poor, you become a friend of Jesus."[17] He came to realize that Christians have been too taken up with "perfection," and that they must be more in touch with their brokenness and vulnerability. In his communities the broken and depressed are welcomed and loved. Only then will there be a "resurrection," as their tense, fearful bodies relax into peace and trust.

One of Vanier's goals was to help people understand how to transform violence and hatred into tenderness and forgiveness, how to stop abusing the weak and to break down the barriers of prejudice and fear. He sees peacemaking as beginning when we accept differences, carry each others' wounds and become open to healing and forgiveness. Jean Vanier offers the world a paradigm for nations and families to live peacefully together.

### Jean's Message to the Young

Jean began to write, hoping especially to reach so many of the young people in the 1960s and 1970s who were leaving the establishment and looking for community and service. He believed that many in that time were looking for freedom, not just from external coercion, but internal freedom where "the forces of love, intelligence and life can flower."[18] At the same time, he was concerned that the culture was in danger of losing the values of family life and moral integrity and thus entering into an era of violence, tension and even despair. He believed that we must once again meet each other as persons, not just as members of society. We must once again open our lives to love, which is "the source and end all things." Jean reminds his readers of Holocaust survivor Viktor Frankl, who came to realize during his days in a concentration camp that the love of his wife gave him a "why" to live and that *"[t]he salvation of man is through love and in love."*[19] Without love, we lose self-value and confidence. We harden our hearts and become depressed and aggressive. Jean became even more committed to his mission: to bring life and freedom to himself and his people by being a loving person. He wrote: "Our hope is to become freer each day in order to accept others, to be fully present to them."[20]

The love experienced with those with special needs is not to be identified with sentimentality. Rather, it is recognition of a covenant, of mutual belonging. It implies listening, feeling empathy, rejoicing as well as suffering with others. It is a "moving toward" as well as a "moving along with." This love shares ideals and visions with others. It wants others to be fulfilled within God's plan. This love brings along with it death to our own comforts, and tears out the roots of egotism that causes self-defense, aggression and gratification. This love entails purifying one's heart and feelings. For the Christian this takes a lifetime of effort, along with an openness to the spirit.

A L'Arche chaplain gave an example of how love transforms the community members. Just before he started a prayer service, Janet, a person with special needs, asked for his blessing. He traced a blessing on her head, but she told him that that didn't work and she wanted a real blessing. After the service she made it clear what she wanted as she put her arms around him and put her head on his chest. He covered her with the long sleeves of his robe and said: "Janet, I want you to know that you are God's Beloved Daughter. You are precious in God's eyes.... I want you to remember who you are: a very special person, deeply loved by God and all the people who are here with you." Janet had received the blessing that she wanted![21]

### L'Arche Goes International

L'Arche continued to grow into the surrounding villages and gradually became worldwide. Within twenty years L'Arche had grown into twenty-five local living situations housing two hundred people with special needs and an equal number of assistants. By 1982 communities were established in India, England, Belgium, Scotland, Ireland, Denmark, Spain, Canada, the United States, Honduras, Haiti, Africa, Australia and Mexico. In all the countries serious efforts were made to keep the communities small, with disabled people living with their assistants. Efforts were also made to adapt to the customs of each area.

As they moved to various countries, the leaders of L'Arche were appalled by some of the attitudes toward the disabled. In Africa, disabled people were abandoned because they were believed to have brought bad luck and contamination. Often they were left in the bush to die. In Haiti, they were mocked and jeered at as though they were fools. In Honduras, great efforts had to be made to help the people see their disabled children as gifts rather than liabilities. Some of the mental institutions in India are infamous for their harsh conditions, where patients are kept in cages, with no toilet or bed.[22]

Struggling against these attitudes, Jean and his people brought respect and love to the disabled and demonstrated to parents what a joy and blessing such children can bring into their lives.

## Gandhi's Vision

Jean's travels broadened his view of his mission. On one trip to establish a house in India, he was struck by the beauty and simplicity of the culture. He became deeply moved by the work of Gandhi, especially with the untouchables. Gandhi's identification with the poor and his dedication to a nonviolent struggle for justice deeply moved Vanier and gave him new insights into the mission of Jesus and the Beatitudes. The world of Gandhi's India taught Vanier a great deal about the striking contrasts between the haves and the have-nots, the wealthy and powerful and the destitute. He observed how technology has put the "empty stomachs of the world" in touch with each other and over and against those who live in luxury and wastefulness. He saw the inequalities and oppression and observed how all this leads to hatred and violence. On the one hand, the powerful charge the poor with laziness and stupidity, and on the other, the poor accuse the rich of arrogance and indifference. Vanier sees all this as a recipe for disaster. He identifies with Gandhi's vision of the power of love and nonviolence as the way to bring peace to this divided world. His prayer is: "May the Spirit of God teach each one of us that the greatness of life comes not in acquiring, but in dispossessing, and in sharing; not in stifling life, but in giving life."[23] Gandhi's notion of "soul force" struck Jean as exemplified in how special needs people can become beacons of hope and love.

## Ecumenism

There is a uniqueness to Vanier's Christian communities in that they are ecumenical, open to people from other Christian communities. In India both Hindus and Muslims are welcome. The chapel in India has shocked some visitors when they see pictures of Jesus along with those of Hindu deities. In the community in England, a Dutch woman assistant remarked that the teachings of Jesus and Buddha are very similar and that she was able to fit in well at L'Arche.[24] In the same community the prayers were adjusted so as not to offend Anglican sensibilities. As Jean puts it, "We do not offer a home to someone because he has a particular religion, but because he is in need."[25] This can present some challenges, especially when it comes to worship services, but the diversity also brings a richness to the communities.

## Structures Emerge

More communities continued to be formed, where helpers and disabled persons could live together, sharing their lives, their joys and setbacks, wounded people from all faiths and backgrounds. Some communities created their own schools and workshops, and all the communities were committed to those with special needs in the areas where they were founded. Each area community has a board of directors, and all the communities belong to the Federation of the Communities of L'Arche. While each community is independent, the leaders in the same region meet frequently for sharing and help. Celebrations and training for both assistants and the disabled are provided on both regional and international levels. Efforts have also been made to stay in contact with the parents of the residents, to support them, try to understand their feelings and urge them to stay connected with their children. L'Arche has done much education with parents of the disabled to help them realize the special gifts of their children. The parents have been organized into hundreds of Faith and Light communities around the world. The finances often come from the state, but some communities are self-supporting from the work they do or live off donations.

## Daily Life

The daily life in L'Arche communities is very simple and normal. Each "family" numbers between six and twenty, half with disabilities. They rise, share breakfast and then work until noon, gather for lunch and then return to work. Meals are important for L'Arche, for they offer valuable times to be together and share. The meals are well-prepared, the food ample, and the fellowship lively. Dinner is a special time for the family, and after dinner if Jean is there he can be found playfully "fighting" his way through the group to get to the head of line to do the dishes. After dinner there is also time for prayer and relaxation, and then to bed. The communities celebrate often with song and dance, food and fun together.

Jean continually uses the family model to describe his communities. He does not want it to be two groups, the assistants and those with special needs living together, but all living as one family. Though the assistants work as a team, they also relate closely with the disabled. The disabled are the center of the community and give it its meaning, and the assistants not only give to them, but they also receive from them. Communion and friendship among all the members of the family is the goal.

The "families" often travel together on visits to other communities or fun trips and pilgrimages. Pilgrimages to such exciting places as Rome, Assisi and Lourdes provide excitement and inspiration for the communities. There are often inspiring events along the way, as these broken folk travel together, dependent on each other. There can be some humorous incidents, as these pilgrims with the hearts of children go out into the larger world. On one pilgrimage the group attended

Mass celebrated by a cardinal who sat on a throne surrounded by bishops. During communion the cardinal left his seat to distribute the hosts, and one of the disabled men went up and sat on the throne. There was some agitation among the bishops, but when the cardinal returned he simply put a stool next to the throne and engaged the man on the throne in conversation.[26]

Everyone gets into a regular routine, and slowly, almost imperceptibly, there is personal growth in all the family members. Here is how one visitor described his experience:

> [T]he extraordinariness of life at L'Arche lies in doing very ordinary things with love and care. It lies in being able to see the miraculous in the most simple events of the daily round of human existence: rising, dressing, working, eating, doing chores, sharing stories, helping each other, praying together, sleeping and dreaming.[27]

So often the members' prayers tell the community what is in their hearts. There is Annie, who stood next to Frank as he lay dying. She prayed: "Oh God, look after Frankie. I don't want him to die. But look after him for me because he is my big honey and I don't want him to die." There also was Charlie, now thirty-five, who was abandoned by his mother at age five. One night he prayed: "Oh God…help me to find my mother. You know that I am her only son. I'm no good because I can't read or write, but if you help me to find my mother, she'll recognize me as her only son and she'll take me back and she'll say she's sorry she left me!"[28]

### The Role of Assistants

Assistants come from all over the world to help at the various L'Arche communities, and they all have different reasons. Some seek living simply in a welcoming and sharing community. Others want to leave the demands of today's hectic life and experience a slower pace. Many come idealistically wanting to help out people who need them. For all, there are lessons to be learned. Joining L'Arche means accepting certain disciplines and structures. It means coming out of one's shell of egoism, taking off masks and pretenses and being one's true self. They find that they are not so much following a way of life as they are entering into relationships with the disabled and taking on the responsibility to free those with special needs from fear and depression. It is living in solidarity that brings about much spiritual conversion.

At first many of the assistants find the experience exhilarating. They are surrounded by loving people who need them, and they are ready to be of service. Then comes a period of letdown, a time when tiredness, loneliness, homesickness and possibly even rebellion set in. The faults of others begin to stick out, people get on their nerves, and they begin to disdain the structures and rules as unreasonable. If the volunteers survive this disillusionment, a more realistic period follows and they begin to enter the community. They can accept the good with the bad, the light with the darkness; they form bonds with the members of the community and begin to walk with the group in the daily routine.

At first there can be fear of getting close to the mentally disabled. Often the wounded person has to lead them and help them enter the community. Some come with a project in mind, and they soon discover that they have to put their project aside and plunge into living with the community. They need to work along with the community, be open to others, listen and take part in the daily routine. They come to see that they are not "helpers," but are instead "partners" who walk with the needy and share their powerlessness. The assistants have to enter into a covenant with the other members, see them as brothers and sisters, especially those who are disabled. They have to put aside their own hurts and desires and give themselves to those who are suffering. Jean believes that then the assistants will begin to discover the presence of God among the wounded. They will now see the disabled as "their people." Jean writes: "Those who came to help me, discovered, like me, the grace at the heart of the poor. We are now 'a people,' a large family, a community. And I cannot imagine the possibility of breaking the bonds of that covenant. That would be the greatest infidelity of all."[29]

Vanier's experience with those coming to assist has put him in touch with the suffering of young people. He observes that many young adults today have a difficult time making commitments. Many have had unstable childhoods, come from broken marriages, have sexual experiences too early, question everything and challenge authority. He believes that when they find someone who is faithful to them, this experience can turn them around. Jean believes that once they are able to make a commitment, they experience a liberation. But the young need space to make this decision, should not be pressured and should be free to leave the community if they so choose. Once they have made their decision freely, they are prepared to put down their roots and stay.

Jean sees joining his communities as answering a call, not joining a party or union. The call is "by God to live together, love each other, pray and work together in response to the cry of the poor."[30] This first and foremost is a call "to be," to be in covenant with the members of the community. Then the call is extended "to do," to serve the needs of the community.

This can be a frightening experience for some when they realize that they must give up some of their own freedom to serve the community. Assistants speak about the difficulties of removing masks, illusions and the desire for success. It takes a while to realize that they are there to share their lives with the disabled, and the latter will be their "teachers" in the art of accepting our human condition and what is essential to human life. Penetrating into the lives of the disabled can provide contact with the wounds and injustices of society and offer a broader vision of the conditions of the world.

Jean has observed that many of those who come "to help" at L'Arche are themselves less mature than those whom they come to help. Often they are not sure of the meaning of their lives and are not capable of making good choices. Living with the disabled teaches them about their own brokenness, and living in community reveals to them how to live with their own weaknesses and frees them to mature and grow.

The assistants find that the disabled help put them in touch with their own limitations and selfishness. The disabled help the assistants face the dark sides of themselves, the truth of themselves. Assistants are gradually brought down from any feelings of superiority and power. Humbled, they see that they too are wounded and impoverished. Facing their own needs, they are drawn into compassion and communion with their disabled sisters and brothers. In the process, many discover new meaning in Jesus' statement: "Whatever you do to the least of my brothers and sisters, you do to me" (Matthew 25:40).

Perhaps the most well-known person who came to work at L'Arche was Henri Nouwen, the popular spiritual writer. Nouwen had come from Holland to be a professor at Yale and, eventually, Harvard. He was a searcher, constantly trying to find his true calling, which brought him to a Trappist monastery, to missionary work in Central America and ultimately to Daybreak, the L'Arche community in Toronto, where he lived for years. Nouwen arrived in deep depression and feeling completely inadequate for dealing with the disabled. He was disarmed and challenged, a man who lived by language with people who could not speak, a man of action with people who could do very little, a renowned scholar with individuals with little mental capacity. Eventually, these very same people taught him about his own vulnerabilities, revealed to him his true self and his authentic calling from God—to love and be loved by the little ones of the world.[31] Nouwen died at L'Arche, and at his funeral many of his special friends danced around his pine coffin, pointing to their hearts that he had so deeply touched.

Nouwen's life at Daybreak reveals the power of the community, and that as friendships grow deeper, all the members become more aware that it is the power of God which binds them together and that they are bonded in a life-giving covenant. One of the early assistants writes about the experience:

> We were incompetent in many ways. We were young and we threw ourselves into this new idea of "living together" without any regard for how late we went to bed, conserving our energies or having a private life of any kind, but in a way that madness, that incompetence was justified by the fact that we were possibly the first to say to handicapped people, "You are loved just as you are."[32]

Jean tells of Peter, who has known a great deal of rejection and suffering due to Down's syndrome, but now has taught some of the assistants to pray. Once, when someone asked Peter how he prayed, he answered: "I listen." When he was asked what God says to him, Peter answered: "He just says, 'You are my beloved son.'"[33] Wisdom from the "little ones!"

Vanier sees those who lead his communities as shepherds. They are people willing to commit to the disabled and to sacrifice themselves for them. He looks for assistants deeply concerned about those with special needs, open and welcoming to them, and ready to listen to their needs and what is in their hearts. They are committed to all the members of the community, not just a few. They must be present to their flock, know their language and be creative in dealing with their needs.

Vanier looks for assistants who want to come and live in community with the disabled. They must be willing to be elder brothers and sisters who care for, understand and relate to the people with special needs. They have to be willing to create family with those who are rejected and hurt. They have to be capable of seeing beauty and value in the disabled, and they need to be competent enough to relate to them and contribute to their healing. The assistants have to be able to live, eat, work, pray and laugh with their housemates, and to see them as family members, not as "residents" or "cases."

Assistants are required to live in communion and friendship with the disabled. They soon discover the richness that comes from this. As they see eyes, hands and hearts reaching out to them in need and trust, the assistants find that their hearts are touched. This gives them the courage and endurance to be able to deal with the tremendous challenges and obstacles that arise in such living conditions.

Jean gives a great deal of credit to the assistants for the role they have played over the years. He writes that L'Arche is the story of many coming out of the rejection and abandonment of asylums to communities where they passed from death to life, anguish to trust and loneliness to hope. He says that this has all happened because of the many assistants who were there to accompany them. By the same token, many assistants were transformed by walking with the wounded and the weak.[34]

In addition to assistants, the L'Arche communities are assisted by those with professional training in psychiatry, medicine, nursing and related fields. Usually these professionals are not members of the community, but they come to help with full knowledge of the dynamics of the households.

### Setbacks

Of course, assistants experience in their work crises, bouts of depression, even outbursts of violence, but there are other setbacks. Assistants at times feel insecurities, inadequacies and discouragement, and they withdraw. For some, the life gets too tedious and boring and they lose their enthusiasm and motivation. Either they have to pass through the struggle to learn to accept the weakness of others and love them or they move on. But even for those who do leave, many have learned a great deal about themselves and about the value of communities of healing and hope in our violent and chaotic world.

### Jean Passes the Torch

As the years passed, Vanier began to fade into the background as the visible leader. In 1975, he stepped down as the international coordinator and soon after became seriously ill from hepatitis and exhaustion. His life of selflessness had caught up with him and it took some time for him to heal. In 1980 Jean resigned as director of the community in France. He now would spend his time giving lectures, conducting retreats, raising money for the communities, and publishing more books on his work. In 1987 the federation met in Rome with a gathering of 350 delegates, and there was a visit from Mother Teresa and a meeting with Pope John Paul II. L'Arche was now an international phenomenon.

## Jean's Reflections on the Disabled

Jean often reflects in his writing on the nature of mental disabilites and the role that people with such disabilities should play in society. He observed that tragically they are so often gathered in crowded institutions or are let loose on the streets, where they live as homeless wanderers unable to fend for themselves. It is not a new problem. In the days of the ancient Greeks, both Plato and Aristotle taught that such people should be killed at an early age, since they cannot reason or work effectively.

By way of contrast, some cultures seem to be more in touch with the spiritual and even blessed aspects of the disabled. In Western culture, they are neither condemned to die nor looked upon as special in the eyes of God. They are viewed as being incomplete, deficient, infirm. We tend to treat them as objects, "poor things" or "half persons," who can be useful, but not really productive. As a result, many disabled persons have experienced rejection and despair. Jean tells of Eric, who is deaf and blind and has a severe mental disablility. He lived in an institution since he was four, and could not walk when he came to L'Arche. He had never known the loving relationship of a parent! Love gave Eric a new sense of self-worth and security and he began to trust himself and others.

Someone must walk with such a person as Eric for a long period and be willing to bear rejection, as the disabled person puts love to a test out of fear of being rejected again. Only slowly does the crushed person open and trust. It is then that positive growth begins to happen, as hope lights up the eyes. Jean tells the touching story of giving a bath to Eric. Eric would relax in the hot water and allow his body to be refreshed and cleansed. As he washed Eric, Jean says that he felt a deep communion with him as the young man abandoned himself in trust. This trust called forth in Jean all that is good in him, his love and tenderness. He writes: "I gave him life; he also gave me life."[35]

Vanier is willing to grant that the mentally disabled have certain deficiencies in the area of reason and responsibility. They are often not good with their head or with their hands. They cannot be fully autonomous because of inherent weakness in the rational and willful self. Many are incapable of understanding or expressing emotion. In contrast, he points to "normal" people who are quite intelligent and are quite independent, but whose hearts are atrophied and without compassion. They too are disabled or deficient.

The mentally disabled often seem to be stronger in the heart area and have a deep capacity to love, trust and make friends. They often have a profound intuition when it comes to the goodness or evil of people or the truthfulness of a situation. Vanier sees how the very weakness of the disabled can lead to a flowering of love.

In their simplicity, the disabled also become a sign that peace and joy do not come from work alone or from wealth. Jean writes how he and his assistants "marvel at their ability to give of themselves in purity and innocence, simply and with great joy. They appreciate their capacity for work but above all the friendly atmosphere of their workshops."[36]

Their joy and peace can attract us to them, and they can teach us many deep lessons about human living. Vanier writes: "The mentally handicapped seen in this light, with their very attractive qualities are a constant reminder of the poverty and receptivity required by love, but also of the wonderment, joy and peace which radiate from those who know how to receive and how to give."[37]

## The Hearts of the Disabled

For Vanier the heart is the core of the human person. It is the place within us where our radical impulse toward the good and love emerges. Influenced by Thomas Aquinas, who sees the gifts of the Spirit dwelling within the heart, he writes: "Behind all the barriers built up since childhood, there is the pure and innocent heart of a child where the gift of God resides. This heart is capable of receiving and giving love, of living in communion with another person and with God, capable of being a source of life for others."[38]

The disabled have often been abandoned and rejected and thus desperately reach out for communion and love. Their capacity to receive and also to give in this area is at times astounding. Childlike, they have a deep hunger for love and closeness. Moreover, the more they receive from others, the more they are able to give. Therein lies their ability to grow. L'Arche hopes to provide the environment and community where such an exchange of love and growth can flourish.

Vanier has learned that those with special needs are challenged in their very being. At the same time, their weakness and simplicity can call forth goodness from those who hold wealth and power. The disabled have a unique capacity to attract the strong to themselves and can draw a certain generosity from them. Perhaps this is the role they have to play in evolution and history: "restoring the balance of the virtues of sensibility and love."[39] The disabled can teach us that the value of human beings lies not in how strong or powerful they are, but in the love they have in their hearts. They can free us from our instincts to recoil from those who are not "normal," and open us to relate to them and learn from them. The disabled can free us from our attachment to power, violence and competition and turn us instead to friendship and peace.

These special ones have amazing qualities of heart and a deep faith and can teach us how God can dwell in our weaknesses. They can draw from us depths of compassion, mercy and forgiveness that we did not know were there. They teach us our own vulnerabilities and how God can come to us in those with love and healing. They teach us to open our hearts much wider than they have been before.

Henri Nouwen has written of an outstanding example of how a person with special needs can be an instrument of God's presence. He writes of Adam, a young man who lived in Nouwen's Daybreak community. Adam was severely disabled: He couldn't speak and needed help to get dressed, be fed, be bathed and to move from place to place. Nouwen noted that Adam was so "empty" of self, so vulnerable, that God seemed to fill him and radiate from him. Many who visited Daybreak in need of healing were profoundly moved by merely sitting with Adam. When Adam died, Nouwen was moved to write a whole book on how Adam's hidden and deserted life of suffering paralleled the life of Jesus and somehow gave him the gift of bringing the presence of Jesus into the lives of those who met him.[40]

From the point of faith, Vanier has learned from his protégés how to live the simple, humble gospel life. He has learned what Jesus meant when he said that the poor are blessed, and he has been able to discover Jesus in them. Jean tells the story of a visit to Mother Teresa in a slum where lepers lived. He reported: "The people there had light in their eyes…. The expressions and smiles of the people seemed to reach right into me and renew me. When I left, I felt an inexplicable joy."[41] In his own work he feels that he is transformed and given fresh energy and a new freedom by the smiles of the fragile and weak. He writes: "My heart is transformed by the smile of the poor person, the expression of the person in despair. They bring new energy flowing from me. They seem to break down barriers and so bring me a new freedom."[42]

Jean has learned to give special attention to the marginal members of the community who have particular needs. They often lack self-confidence and are locked in such despair that they try to harm themselves and others. They can at one point seem to have no desires at all and then suddenly be overwhelmed with desires. Jean believes that if such people are to rediscover hope they must somehow be made to feel loved and accepted. Patience and much listening are needed. The disabled must sense that they are understood and not judged. They need guidance, security, help in discovering their abilities.

At the same time, those with special needs must be made aware of the rules and what is expected of them. At least minimal conformity is expected if they are to live in community. Firmness, with the availability of encouragement and forgiveness, is the order of the day. Growth is understood to be gradual, but growth there should be. The ultimate goal is freedom. He writes:

> The liberation of marginal people from their darkness may mean a long struggle. The reference people [those who set the boundaries] and the community have to know how to accept the violence in themselves, so that they can transform it into tenderness and gradually liberate the marginal people from their anguish. The role of the community of reconciliation is to break the cycle of violence and so lead people to peace.[43]

### Experiencing God in the Disabled

In addition, the handicapped can teach us that God can communicate directly with the human heart and that such people can live intimate relationships with God. New experiences of Jesus' goodness, purity, humility and even suffering and agony have come to Jean through living in L'Arche communities. Like Thomas Merton and other spiritual writers, Jean has learned that God dwells within the true self. In those with special needs this true self is not hidden behind masks, pretenses, false egos or social conventions. In a happy atmosphere the disabled are saved from fears of being themselves and can openly be their true selves. Perhaps this is the reason why God can so easily be experienced in their eyes, their hearts and their spontaneous affection! At the same time, the faith of the disabled person can be more pure, and less encumbered by beliefs, and thus they can be freer to go directly to the divine and receive God's presence.

Being poor and weak, those with special needs have nothing to lose in extending themselves to the other and to God. Power, wealth or glory are simply not part of their agenda, so they relate in true friendship. Vanier puts it in a touching way: "[T]he Kingdom of Heaven is theirs. They have often wept and thus they will be comforted; they have been persecuted and despised and so they will find love. Give them proper living conditions which are humane, harmonious, and they will flower, and God willing, grace will blossom within them."[44] Rather than being made to feel useless and different, they need a loving community where their spiritual lives can flourish and they can come to know Jesus, love, peace and prayer. Vanier's goal, therefore, has been to create small communities where the disabled might be free to be themselves, to share themselves with others and to meet God in everyday life.

### Vanier as Teacher

Vanier is an educator whose pedagogical approach differs from what he finds in mental institutions, where the disabled are made to conform either through fear of punishment or promise of privileges. His fundamental principle of education is "to open the heart and the mind to the needs of others."[45] It is an education in respect and regard for others: It is formation of the head, the heart and the will in loving concern for others. He writes: "The essence of education is to lead a person into relationships with others; in openness and sensitivity to their limitations and in response to their needs. Maturity is growth in responsibility for oneself and for others."[46] At L'Arche, Vanier sees education as helping each person welcome others as they are, appreciate them and respond to their needs of growth and liberation.

### Sex Education

As for sex education, Jean believes that the mentally disabled need to be taught that sex belongs in the context of love and commitment. Their sexuality needs to be integrated into their experience of friendship and love. They need to know that sex cannot be reduced to a physical urge, but to be genuine it must be in the context of tenderness and care. Otherwise, it is reduced to seduction, manipulation, or power over another. Overall, he is pleased with the peace that exists with regard to sexuality within his communities. Admittedly, there is suffering and disturbance in this area, but on the whole he finds that "those with mental handicaps seem to enjoy a liberty of heart that few other people in the world attain."[47] There are cases when the residents discover love and marry. Jean opposes those who encourage sex between residents for self-expression or even for therapeutic value. It is his conviction that such an approach to sex can only lead the disabled to disappointment and further isolation. He writes of what he considers unique in the position of L'Arche: "We esteem genital sexuality as a beautiful and powerful reality which calls forth the person in the depths of his or her being. It is a means of exceptional fruitfulness, a unique means of expression: it is not something superficial."[48]

**The Disabled as Teachers**

The disabled, one leader has pointed out, can fill us with joy and wonder, help us to appreciate simplicity. They can be affectionate, open, welcoming, trusting. What they lack in efficiency they can make up for in prophetic, artistic and even mystical gifts. Their disfigured faces and injured bodies can help us understand that it is the "withinness" that matters and not the appearance. The disabled can also provide leadership to the community and provide the cement that holds the community together. They can teach us how to forgive and how to celebrate and have fun.

In many ways, the disabled are among the most oppressed people in the world, but at L'Arche they can gain the interior freedom to express themselves and make choices. Here they can be themselves and be accepted and loved as they are. They can teach us how to rise above oppression. Jean tells the story of Bernard, who was severely disabled and for many years lived lost in a crowd of other patients in a psychiatric hospital. After only a few months in a L'Arche community, where he received loving attention and had demands put on him, he began to learn how to walk again and take care of himself and others. Bernard now had meaning in his life and could extend himself to others.[49] There is also Patrick, who seems to have within him a deep goodness and yet is often quite anxious. At a pilgrimage to Lourdes, he said: "It makes me so happy when people no longer think of me as handicapped." He now was free to relate to others in normal ways and to share himself with others.[50]

**Building Free Communities**

Jean has spent many years building communities where those with special needs, as well as their assistants, can be freed from rejection, can enjoy the acceptance of their true selves and can receive the love and care that they deserve. Jean holds that each person coming into his communities, whether they are among the disabled or the assistants, has a history of being accepted or rejected, as well as personal experience of difficulties with relationships with parents, family and others. At the same time, there is a yearning in all of us for communion and belonging. Love is what we want most. And yet we fear love because it can threaten our freedom and also make us vulnerable to hurt, rejection and separation. We want community, but at the same time we know that this implies commitment, a certain dependence and a vulnerability to being used, manipulated or stifled.

Jean believes that life in community can reveal a great deal about ourselves. We can say to ourselves that we think we can love everyone, but once we live in community we discover the limits to our love. We find out that we have our weaknesses, our mental and emotional blocks, possibly our destructiveness. We learn of our dark sides. If we give ourselves to community, there can be what Jean calls "growth toward liberation," where we can face ourselves and truly grow.[51] Here community becomes a place of liberation in that we are free to be ourselves yet know that we are accepted with our limitations.

To gain a sense of belonging means to get beyond years of rejection and come to trust in others. It means accepting the limitations of ourselves and others and not expecting perfection in either. Jean writes: "We will never win the Olympics of humanity, racing for perfection, but we can walk together in hope, celebrating that we are loved in our brokenness."[52]

## Beyond Individualism

Jean has observed that the Western world lacks the sense of community that he observed in places such as Africa and India. Westerners are so individualistic that often they don't know their neighbors or even the members of their own families. He questions whether we can ever hope to have any sense of communion with those in our city, nation or world if we cannot be in communion with those living closest to us. Jean senses that this strong drive for individualism in our culture has brought many of us to a deep loneliness. As a result, we often feel separated and armed against each other. It is his conviction that we need to disarm externally as well as internally and rediscover community. He believes that in community we are called to love people just as they are with their wounds and their gifts and that we should not try to make them the way we want them to be. Community should give people space to grow—that is true freedom. In community we give people the gift of their dignity; we help them to trust in themselves.

Jean believes that in an authentic community the members should be moving from "the community for myself" to "myself for the community."[53] The movement must be toward the other, from egotism to love, from selfishness to true freedom. Community for Jean can be a place of purification of our fears, our immaturity, our aggression. Community can "lead us to a deeper love and liberation, a place where cleansed of our egocentric attitudes we will be able to give new life to others."[54] That is the one reason why Jean tries to get all the members of his community to strive for common goals of work, prayer, visits and trips.

Even when communities are established, Vanier maintains that they are strengthened if they have purposes outside themselves, goals to which all the members are committed. L'Arche communities, according to Jean, are not to be closed or ends in themselves, but have a mission outside themselves—to show others how to be healed and how to grow. He wants his homes to be symbols to the world at large of Jesus' call to oneness and freedom. He writes:

> To have a mission means to give life, to heal, and to liberate. It is to permit people to grow to freedom. When Jesus sends people off, he sends them to liberate and heal others. That is the good news. And we can become people of liberation and of healing because we ourselves are walking along that road toward inner healing and inner liberation.[55]

### Not Hierarchical

Vanier's communities are not based on hierarchy, rivalry or competition. Jean believes that true humanity should not be based on hierarchy, with the best on the top and the worst on the bottom. Authentic humanity is experienced in community, where we belong to each other and can call each other to growth and wholeness. A notion that Jean often stresses is the great secret of Jesus that to be his disciple does not mean to climb the ladder of success and power. It is his conviction that if we enter into close relationship with the poor, we will meet Jesus and be led to the heart of gospel life. He once said to the students at Harvard Divinity School: "L'Arche is founded on love for people with mental disabilities. If we keep our eyes fixed on them, if we are faithful to them, we will always find our path. We are constantly called to draw this love from the heart of God and from God's mysterious presence at the heart of the poor people."[56]

### The Acceptance That Brings Freedom

Jean believes that to be in communion with his people means that together they discover that they really belong together. It means accepting people as they are with their limits, their pain, their capacity to grow. Loving them means more than simply doing things for them, but revealing to them their inner beauty and worth. It entails walking with them in their distress and inner pain, often knowing that you cannot take away their anguish but that you can be there for them. Such love lets them know that you accept them with their pain, and you free them to be who they are so they don't have to conform to whom they "should be." Here you are giving them the freedom to grow as they are, and you are neither possessing them nor controlling them. Instead, you are listening to them and helping them become fully themselves. Vanier gives the example of Jane, who came to L'Arche from a psychiatric hospital filled with anger and pain, hitting herself in the head with her fist. She has now been there for ten years, and though she cannot speak or walk, her eyes are bright with life and she has been transformed as a person.

As another example of the power of community, Jean writes about a young Muslim girl, Ghadir, who was taken in at L'Arche, her body exhausted, twisted and battered. She was a little flower that had been crushed by military and political power, but at L'Arche she was nursed back to health. "While all around us there are troops causing both fear and violence...the smile of Ghadir flowing from the weakness of her body is a light in the world. You too are called to meet in the face of Ghadir and others like her, the gentle presence of God."[57]

**Not the Perfect Life**

L'Arche communities are not communities seeking perfection, idealism or superiority. These are families where differences are treasured and where wounds are carried as a source of wisdom. These are communities where the weakest and poorest can be a sign of the presence of Jesus. These are communities where people nourish each other with respect and love; where they try to understand each other rather than judge; where the vulnerable can feel secure; where people are free to love and be loved. These are communities where the members need each other; where the members learn to bear each other's sufferings and mourn the deaths of those who pass on. Suffering becomes a basis for unity in the community. It can bring people together in their anguish, their woundedness, as they reach to try to be there for each other.

Somehow, strangely, dealing with one another's sufferings can bring joy and even laughter.

## The Importance of Forgiveness

In Jean's communities people are allowed to have their flaws and know that they are forgiven. He writes: "Forgiveness is letting go of unrealistic expectations of others and of the desire that they be other than they are. Forgiveness is the liberation of others to be themselves; not making them feel guilty for what they may have been. Forgiveness is to help people flower, bear fruit, and discover their own beauty…."[58]

Vanier teaches that forgiveness is essential for authentic community. First, we must forgive ourselves for our blocks, jealousies, prejudices and hatreds and allow God and others to love us with our flaws. Second, we must be able to forgive the wounds and clashes that arise in community. We have to be able to look to the positive attributes of our enemies and be able to pray for them.

Jean tells the story of Chantal, a middle-aged resident who had been deeply hurt by the rejection of her mother. Occasionally her mother would bring gifts to the household but paid no attention to her daughter while she was there. Yet each evening Chantal would say a special prayer for her mother. She was a living example of what forgiveness is![59]

## Places of Pain

For Jean, community can also be a place of pain, a place where the darkness in our hearts is revealed: the anger, jealousy and pettiness. Community exposes us to conflict, loss and death of loved ones. Conflicts arise from the tensions between the values of togetherness and independence, between the need for space to grow and feeling the pressures of competition and domination. Conflicts arise out of being torn between caring for self and caring for others, between being open to others and being closed. On one hand, a strong sense of belonging can stifle personal development. On the other, rivalry and aggressiveness in the group can take away the freedom to serve others. Yet, Jean believes that in the midst of all this Jesus calls us to friendship with himself and with others. Jesus calls us "to liberate people from the demons of fear, of loneliness, of hatred and of egoism that shackle them. To liberate people so that they also can love, heal and liberate others."[60]

## Places for Growth

For Vanier the main purpose of his communities is personal growth. These are places where people can move toward wholeness and can find their true selves through a sense of belonging. This, of course, is achieved only after much struggle, inner pain, intense listening, fervent prayer. His communities consider those whom society devalues to be valuable and in community are "capable of awakening what is most precious in a human being—the heart, generosity, the dynamism of love."[61]

## A Place to Love the Enemy

Jean is realistic about community. He knows that we are often drawn to those who flatter us or who attract us. For him that is too easy and often does not offer growth. He takes his cue from Jesus, who told us to love our enemies. We grow by coming closer to people who are different from us, are threatening to us and who remind us of our vulnerabilities. People who disagree with us, outshine us, intimidate us, even endanger us, can challenge us. Enemies can frighten us, stifle us. Community should help us get in touch with why we have alienated this enemy and be prepared to forgive their offenses against us. Authentic community occurs when we are able to break down these barriers and can stretch out our hand to our enemies.

## Mutual Trust

Mutual trust is one of the foundations of Jean's communities. This, of course, takes time; for tests have to be passed and breakdowns need to be patched up. Trust only grows after long endurance of suffering together, after many trials have been endured and fidelity has passed the test of time. The third party in this partnership of trust, according to

Jean, is God: "As we discover gradually that God and the others trust us, it becomes a little easier for us to trust ourselves, and in turn to trust others."[62] Community should be the place where all feel free to be themselves and have the confidence to share themselves with others.

### Accepting Diversity

Community for Vanier is not uniformity. Rather, authentic community should allow each person to be unique. At L'Arche even the littlest and weakest person is seen as a gift to the community. Difference is viewed as a treasure rather than a threat. Leadership is service, not domination. The members are present to each other, work together while caring for each other and regularly celebrate their differences and blessings together.

True community should encourage individual freedom and individuality. According to Jean, community should foster individual conscience and the capacity to grow. He warns that some communities, in order to promote unity, suppress conscience and try to prevent people from thinking. Such communities use brainwashing, fear and strong authority to make the members conform. They demand blind obedience. All of this prevents personal growth and weakens personal freedom.

Vanier wants his communities to be authentic, where people can keep their own secrets and make their own conscience decisions. Of course, this risks mistakes and even betrayal, but at the same time it provides a free environment where strong and loving individuals can develop. Jean puts it this way: "There is nothing stronger than a heart which loves and is freely given to God and to others."[63]

### Model Communities

Jean wants his communities to be models for other families and communities. He is convinced that fear and prejudices are causes of hatred and wars. He wants his communities to model the Christian community, where people can be healed in their deepest weaknesses, where they can live in dignity. He writes: "The response to war is to live like brothers and sisters. The response to injustice is to share. The response to despair is a limitless trust and hope. The response to prejudice and hatred is forgiveness. To work for community is to work for humanity."[64]

**Authentic Families**

Jean has been dedicated to recreating true Christian community, genuine families. His are communities of love, forgiveness; places without judgment. They are places where people are vulnerable as Jesus was, but who are open to resurrection. They are communities of thanksgiving for God's blessings, communities where there is concern for people outside their walls, who are lonely and in pain. Jean writes: "We are small and weak, but we are gathered together to signify the power of God who transforms death into life."[65]

Jean says that his people are beginning to understand the hidden years of Jesus, who lived simply yet radically among Jewish neighbors. Jesus' hidden years have taught those in the L'Arche communities that it is not necessary to do big things and be a success, and that there is a value in doing little things for their families out of love. He writes:

> ...our handicapped people, discover the joy of belonging to a family of which they are the center and which is geared to their well-being and to their growth. And they discover what is essential: that they are loved by the Father; and that they are called to live the Beatitudes in communities of love and mutual trust, communities of welcome and of celebration.[66]

**Celebrations**

The central family celebration for the communities is Eucharist. Here all the members seem to rise above their pain and suffering and enjoy Communion with each other. It is not always calm. There might be an argument in the corner, someone wiggling his wheelchair in place, some laughter or a moan. The server might pour the water for the priest and then go water a plant! But they are all there together, in the presence of God and each other. They are blessed, and at the kiss of peace there is always much commotion.

There are other times to celebrate and experience the closeness of the community. There are birthdays, special meals, weekend breakfasts, feast days. There are times for laughter, times for tears. There are times when there are serious accidents, illness or even the death of a brother or sister. "They are times of grace and wonder, when we are all brought back to the essential in deep silence."[67]

### A Sign to the Church

Vanier wants his worldwide organization to be a clear sign to the church and to the world that they must reach out to the marginal. He writes:

> L'Arche is a sign that love is possible, that the weak, whatever their weaknesses, have gifts and a message to give. L'Arche is a sign that faith and competence can embrace and work together for the human and spiritual growth and development of each person. It is a sign that institutions can become communities when people work together in a spirit of love and unity.[68]

In fact, Vanier has been successful in reproducing authentic "domestic churches," where Jesus is an empowering presence and the gospel is lived and celebrated amidst the outcast and suffering.

C H A P T E R    S E V E N

## Corrie ten Boom: Freedom From Hatred

It was December 1944, a gray, freezing day in Ravensbrück, an extermination camp in Germany. A frail, thin fifty-four-year-old woman was being released from the camp due to an atypical clerical error on the part of her Nazi captors. She had endured the unspeakable horrors of the camp and witnessed tens of thousands of women put to death and burned in ovens. She had lost her father in the camps and watched her own sister wither and die beside her. Now, by some fluke of fate, she was free to sadly return home and struggle to begin a new life. Somehow, amidst the suffering and death of the camp, this woman had learned that the power of Jesus Christ can help people overcome any suffering and loss and sustain love and forgiveness in their hearts. She had promised her sister that if she lived through this she would spend the rest of her life dedicated to freeing people from the hatred and evil she had experienced in the camps. And that is what this woman did for the next thirty-three years: Corrie ten Boom traveled the world preaching about love and forgiveness to everyone she encountered and declaring: "Jesus is victor!"

### Family Background

Corrie (short for Cornelia) was born in 1892 in the old city of Haarlem in the heart of Holland, about twenty miles east of Amsterdam and ten miles from the shores of the North Sea. She was born in a three-story row dwelling called Beje (BAY-ya), which housed the family watch shop on the first floor. Corrie was the youngest of four children. Her two older sisters were Nollie and Betsie, and her brother was Willem. Corrie always felt that her sisters were the pretty ones and that she was plain, and that caused her to be shy around the boys to whom she was attracted. She looked up to her brother for his brilliance and goodness and she admired his calling to be a minister. The entire family would suffer in the horrors of the future Holocaust.

Corrie's grandfather, Willem, died the year she was born, but had left the family a legacy of watchmaking and closeness to Jews. Willem bought the Beje in 1837 and opened his watch shop there. The house was in the Jewish area, and Willem established close relations with his Jewish neighbors that would deeply affect the family. Early on, he organized a prayer group in his home to pray for peace in Israel and for the Jewish people. From that time on, the family tradition was one of deep respect for the Jews and gratitude toward them for bringing forth the Hebrew Scriptures and Jesus of Nazareth. The Ten Boom family was in the Dutch Reform evangelical tradition, but unlike some other evangelicals, they did not see Jews under a curse that deserved punishment, nor did they make attempts to convert Jews. It was simply their hope that one day Jews would be gathered into Jesus' embrace. It was the family goal to serve Jews rather than convert them.

Corrie's father, Casper, had moved to Amsterdam when he was eighteen and opened his own jewelry store in the Jewish section of the city. The Ten Booms lived in a tiny house in the poor section of town and barely sustained themselves with the store. Because of his background, Casper had no problem feeling at home in the neighborhood, and he was close to his Jewish neighbors. He participated in their Sabbaths and other holy days, studied the Old Testament and Talmud, and was able to discuss such delicate topics as the fulfillment of the prophecies of the Old Testament in the New Testament. Corrie's father passed on to his children the family love for the Jewish people. Casper once told his children: "Love for the Jews was spoon-fed to me from my very youngest years." "As a result," said Corrie, "deep respect and love for the Jews became a part of our home life."[1]

When Casper's father died, he moved back to Haarlem, took over his father's watch shop and continued to open the home to people of all faiths. "When he met anyone interested in the Bible," commented Corrie, "he did not hesitate to invite him or her to his Bible-study groups. He once told us about the extraordinary combination in his group studying the book of Romans. There were agnostics, atheists, fundamentalists, a Calvinist, a liberal, and a Roman Catholic."[2] True to the family tradition, Casper had a special regard for Jews. Corrie also remembered trips to Amsterdam, when Casper would visit wholesalers:

> Many of these were Jews, and these were the visits we both liked best. After the briefest possible discussion of business, Father would draw a small Bible from his traveling case; the wholesaler, whose beard would be even longer and fuller than Father's, would snatch a book or a scroll out of a drawer, clap a prayer cap onto his head; and the two of them would be off, arguing, comparing, interrupting, contradicting—reveling in each other's company.[3]

One of Casper's chief competitors in Haarlem was a Jewish watch-maker, yet he harbored no resentment toward the man. As he told his nephew once, "Mr. Kan is not my competitor. He is my colleague. And do not forget, he belongs to God's chosen people."[4]

Corrie's father was a gentle and loving watchmaker, a man of strong principles. He was more dedicated to his craft of watchmaking than to his business, and at times he would even forgot to charge his customers or would encourage simple repairs rather than the purchase of a new watch from his shop. Casper was a self-educated man of high culture and read literature in many languages. He was also a deeply religious man and he rode around town on his bicycle to adjust the clocks of the wealthy. He would at the same time instruct the servants in the Scriptures. Amazingly, he would sometimes gather his family with Bibles in six different languages, including Greek and Latin, and they would discuss various passages.

Evenings at home were also spent with classical music played by the family, each member knowing how to play some instrument. Often the family entertainment would be singing Bach's chorales in three parts. When they could, they would also attend concerts, and once heard the famous Albert Schweitzer play the organ in the cathedral.

Corrie tells many stories of her father's wisdom in guiding her. When she came to him with questions about "sex-sin," he told her she was too young to bear such burdens. Once when she panicked at the thought that her father would one day die, he told her to live in the present and not get ahead of herself. And when she was jilted by a young man she dearly loved for a girl with money, her father told her not to lose her precious gift of love but to direct it another way. His advice would prove to be prophetic indeed! Corrie would never marry and would give herself entirely to free others from misery and hatred.

Corrie's "Mama," in spite of her frail health, cooked meals for elderly shut-ins and young single mothers. Even when she was confined to a sickbed, she would busy herself knitting caps and dresses for the neighborhood babies and composing cheerful notes for the neighborhood shut-ins. She and her husband also took in a number of foster children: first, starving German urchins after World War I, and then the children of missionaries who were out of the country preaching the gospel. At any one time, the family might have four to eight extra children and several live-in aunts in the house. This extraordinary family had little money, but much love, faith and laughter to share with all.

After secondary school Corrie stayed home and took care of an elderly aunt and her mother. She later kept the books for her father's business, learned the watchmaking trade herself, becoming the first licensed woman in that trade in Holland. When Corrie was in her twenties, her mother had a massive stroke and became disabled. She was moved to the front room where she could look out on the busy life in the street, where she had been so active in her service of others. She lasted three more years and was able to teach Corrie many lessons about love. She writes:

> Mama's love had always been the kind that acted itself out with soup pot and sewing basket. But now that these things were taken away, the love seemed as whole as before. She sat in her chair at the window and loved us. She loved the people she saw in the street—and beyond: her love took in the city, the land of Holland, the world. And so I learned that love is larger than the walls which shut it in.[5]

This would be a valuable lesson for Corrie when she was confined to prison camps.

Surprisingly, Mama was able to go to her daughter Nollie's wedding, though she could speak only a few words, Mama amazed everyone when she sang out clearly "Fairest Lord Jesus," her favorite hymn. Several weeks later, Mama slipped away.

Corrie's older sister, Betsie, was an extraordinary woman and throughout her life provided much inspiration to the family. She was a deeply spiritual person, a profoundly joyful spirit who always counted the blessings of life. Betsie and Corrie were very close and would end up helping each other get through many sufferings in the camps.

Corrie's brother, Willem, was a brilliant student and was dedicated to his religion. He was the only family member who went to college and was eventually ordained a minister in his church. As early as 1927, when he was writing his doctoral thesis in Germany, he commented on the terrible evil that was taking root in that country, where there was growing contempt for human life. He wrote to his wife, "I expect that in a few years' time, there will be worse pogroms than ever before. Countless Jews from the east will come across the border to seek refuge in our country. We must prepare for that situation."[6] Not long after Willem's prophetic statement, Adolf Hitler came into power and began his brutal persecution of the Jewish people.

When Willem returned to Holland to begin his ministry, he saw the signs of repression, such as many of the Jewish clock companies and other businesses closing in Germany. Willem headed up his church's program to reach out to Jews, and as the Jewish refugees began to pour out of Germany, he scrimped enough money to build a home for elderly Jews. As the numbers of refugees grew, Willem and his family gave up their own living quarters to house the frightened and homeless refugees fleeing from Nazi repression.

Even though the family heard stories of the atrocities in Germany, where Jewish stores were broken into, people were beaten and killed, and elderly men had their beards set afire, all this seemed remote. They believed that Germany was a cultured country and would soon get rid of Adolf Hitler and his hoodlums. Little did they know that this madness would take over, would engulf their own country, and that they too would become victims of it.

### Corrie's Many Activities

Corrie always juggled many balls in the air. Besides working in the watch shop, she went to mission camp to learn what other faiths had to say about the Bible, attended a theological school (rather unsuccessfully), took care of the foster children and organized clubs for girls. She began this work for younger girls in conjunction with the YMCA, and soon it grew to the point where she had to rent a house for the meetings and a gymnasium for the exercise activities. Eventually, she opened coed clubs, which were unique for the times, and gave young people an opportunity to meet one another, sing, play music, study languages, pray and discuss the Bible. The clubs got so popular that Corrie was out every evening. Later on, in the camps and after the war, she met a number of "alums" from the clubs, who expressed gratitude for all that the gatherings had done for them personally and spiritually.[7]

Corrie was also deeply involved in working with "exceptional children." She was often amazed at the depth of their spirituality as she taught them the Bible stories and about nature. Some of them were confined to hospitals or even prisons, and Corrie would visit them and bring care and hope. This work further convinced her that everyone is a child of God and prepared her to reject the Nazi position that such disabled people were useless to society and should be eliminated.[8]

## Holland Is Invaded

The year 1940 was a milestone for the Ten Booms. The foster children had all moved on, Nollie and Willem were married and on their own, and only Corrie, Betsie, Casper and one aunt were at the Beje. Suddenly, the Germans began to bomb Rotterdam and demanded that the Dutch surrender. While negotiations were still going on, bombers wiped out the center of Rotterdam, killing eight hundred and wounding thousands. Holland surrendered after five days of valiant effort to stop the Blitzkrieg, and German tanks and troops moved in to occupy the country. Betsie amazed the family when she actually prayed for the German pilots dropping the bombs because she felt that they were caught up in the horribly evil movement that had been let loose in their homeland.[9]

At first the Nazi occupation was rather calm. Yet German armament and soldiers were everywhere and the occupiers talked down to the Dutch people. Ration cards and ID cards were issued and there was a 10:00 PM curfew, but there was not much violent repression. In fact, the watch shop did very well, selling watches and clocks to the soldiers for their mothers, wives and sweethearts. The newspapers carried only propaganda, and when the radios were confiscated the Ten Booms held onto one of theirs and were able to keep up on the news.

The repression came on gradually as the Nazis began to test the populace. There were minor attacks on Jews: rocks were thrown through some of their store windows and foul words were scrawled on synagogue walls. Signs gradually went up forbidding Jews from entering shops and public places. The Nazi party members began to be a stronger presence, and they were pleased to see that some Dutch were drawn to them out of need for more food and better clothing, jobs and housing. Those who were anti-Semitic joined because they shared the Nazi hatred of the Jews. Then synagogues were burned and Jews were seen being packed into trucks and driven off to unknown destinations. Many young men were dragged from their homes and their families and sent off to labor camps. It soon became apparent that the Nazis had no use for the elderly, weak or infirm. They seemed driven to have power over those whom they considered to be inferior. At one point, Corrie's sister Nollie, who had married, confessed that she was hiding a Jewess in her home and was imprisoned. Corrie had to go to great lengths to gain Nollie's freedom through the help of a kind doctor who diagnosed her as permanently disabled and a burden to society and had her released.

As the persecution of Jews in Holland accelerated, Casper, though quite old by then, devoted himself to the rescue effort. He even attempted to get his own yellow Star of David to wear, so he could identify with the Jews in their time of trouble. Although Corrie kept him from doing this, he compensated by taking off his hat to every Jew he would meet. He once stunned Corrie by his comment when he saw the soldiers packing Jews into the back of a truck: "Those poor people" (Corrie thought he meant the Jews), but then he continued, "I pity the poor Germans, Corrie. They have touched the apple of God's eye."[10]

The rabbi of Haarlem came to the Ten Boom residence early in the occupation and asked Casper to watch over his precious books. The two had often prayed and read the Hebrew Scriptures together and often exchanged books. "[O]ld friend," the rabbi said, "books do not age as you and I do. They will speak still when we are gone, to generations we will never see. Yes, the books must survive." The rabbi left and the family never saw him again.[11]

The family now began the risky business of taking Jewish refugees into their home and inviting them to feel as much at home as possible.

Casper had always read a portion of Scripture to the family before retiring for the night, and one evening, when he was preparing to read from the prophet Jeremiah, he halted and then passed the Bible over to one of the Jewish men, saying, "I would consider it an honor if you would read for us tonight." For Christmas 1943 the family decided to celebrate Hanukkah as well as Christmas. Corrie remembered: "We were all very Jewish those evenings."[12]

At one point Corrie asked one of the Dutch Reformed pastors if he would protect a Jewish mother and baby in his home. The minister refused and warned her not to get involved. Even when Corrie showed him the child, he refused and said, "No. Definitely not. We could lose our lives for that Jewish child." Casper, overhearing the conversation, took the baby in his arms, and said, "You say we could lose our lives for this child. I would consider that the greatest honor that could come to my family."[13] When warned that taking in Jews could mean imprisonment or worse, Casper replied: "I am too old for prison life, but if that should happen, then it would be, for me, an honor to give my life for God's ancient people, the Jews."[14]

The Ten Boom house became known as the "happiest underground address in all of the Netherlands."[15] Jews of all ages were taken in: the frightened, depressed and distraught were lovingly cared for. Some needed medical care. Others needed help having their babies; some died and needed to be buried secretly. False identities had to be established and "Smit" seemed to be the favorite name to assume. Seven or eight people at a time lived in the "hiding place" and then were moved on to more remote areas of Holland and to other countries by coworkers in the underground. Hundreds of Jews passed through the Ten Boom house on their way to freedom, as the "Beje" became the center of what came to be known as "God's underground."[16]

Corrie's brother, Willem, was most dedicated to this work. He had hiding places in his own home and knew farms in the remote rural areas where Jews could be hidden. The Jews staying with Corrie's family would gather in the parlor for songs, language lessons, prayer services and parties and would hide at night in the secret room that had been ingeniously built on the third floor. Regular safety drills were conducted during the day, wherein the whole group could take their things and hide in about seven seconds in case the Gestapo, Nazi secret police, showed up. The Ten Boom women had to be trained in how to lie, since they had been truthful all their lives.

Corrie grew more and more active in the underground movement. Now fifty years old, she looked rather awkward riding her bike on the metal rims (the rubber had been confiscated) and collecting stolen ration books for their guests. After a year and a half, Corrie began to realize that their house was becoming known as more than a watch shop where an old man and two spinster sisters lived. Too many people were gathering there and the network had grown so large that she knew sooner or later they would have trouble with the authorities. At one point she was called in for questioning, thinking the end had come, but managed to feign innocence. Now people were getting arrested in the city, and it was only a matter of time before someone would break down and turn them in.

One morning when Corrie was down with a severe case of the flu, a man came to the shop door and insisted on talking with her. She dragged herself downstairs, passing many Jewish refugees holding a prayer service with her brother Willem and encountered the stranger. He said that his wife had been arrested for hiding Jews and that he needed money to bribe a guard for her release. She sent someone to get the money and hand it to the man, and went back to her sickbed. Soon she awoke to hear the door buzzer ringing repeatedly, and saw the residents were scrambling for the hiding space. It was the Gestapo! The family had been betrayed by the man wanting money. The Gestapo shouted charges at her for hiding Jews and they began beating Corrie, Betsie and some of the others. The whole family was arrested and taken to the police station. That night they gathered around their Father for prayer: "Thou art my hiding place and my shield: I hope in thy word...Hold thou me up, and I shall be safe." The next morning they were all herded into a bus and driven to the Hague to be interviewed. When the Gestapo officer saw how elderly Corrie's father was, he offered to release him if he would promise not to cause any more trouble. The old watchmaker stood erect and startled the officer with his answer: "If I go home today...tomorrow I will open my door again to any man in need who knocks."[17] Casper was immediately told to get back in line with the prisoners. They were all loaded on a truck that drove off into the night. The family was taken first to a prison at Scheveningen. The stressful and jolting trip had taken a horrible toll on the elderly father. He lived only ten more days, died separated from his family and was buried in a pauper's grave. Betsie later wrote that her father was indeed a Christian martyr.

### Prison Life

Corrie was placed in a filthy cell with four other women and limited to a diet of bread and water. She soon grew ill and after some kind treatment in the Hague by a doctor and nurse, Corrie was returned to the prison and put in solitary confinement so as to not spread her illness. Her bedding was foul smelling and filled with a choking dust. She lay alone, sick, and her only comfort was looking out her small window as she hungered for sunshine, freedom, her family and home. Corrie discovered that she could find peace by asking comfort from Jesus.

After seven weeks, she was allowed outside for the first time to walk in a dilapidated garden that smelled of burned bones and from where she could here the rattle of machine guns executing prisoners. It was a short and bitter taste of the freedom for which she longed. Returning to her cell, Corrie's heart ached when small children were brought to the prison, wailing for their parents.

A number of times she had to survive intense examinations concerning the activities of her family. She cleverly never gave into the false offers of favors from her inquisitors. At times she even made inroads toward the faith of these hardened officers. Eventually, Corrie was told of her father's death and the release of her family members with the exception of Betsie. She also learned that the Jews who had been staying in her house were not discovered and had been spirited off to safety.

Suddenly, Corrie and the other prisoners were ordered to gather their things and were crowded into vans and buses and driven to a woods, where they had to march, surrounded by armed soldiers who screamed at them and kicked them as they moved along. They were eventually crowded into the barracks of a concentration camp at Vught.

In the camp the prisoners were at times allowed to work outdoors and enjoy the fresh air and sunshine, but all the while they realized that they were surrounded by guards who were brutal murderers, who had beaten and shot prisoners to death. Those who broke the rules were put in "cells" the size of footlockers with their hands tied above their head to hasten the "educational process." The women were crowded into dormitories with over a hundred other prisoners and forced to work long hours, often in filthy workrooms. Amazingly, a merciful German guard helped Corrie smuggle letters written on toilet paper to the family. In the men's camp next to them, the women could see the prisoners marching off to work with their heads shaved, and could hear the shots as they were executed. On one day, seven hundred male prisoners were shot.

It did not take long before Betsie and Corrie began organizing discussion groups where the prisoners were encouraged to share their lives and hope, and to join in songs, prayers and Bible study. Betsie, in her uniquely heroic way, continued to pity the guards as wounded human beings. She remained dedicated to her mission of teaching people how to love rather than hate. Her prayerful presence brought peace and hope to those around her in the barracks. When she heard that the person who had betrayed the family to the Gestapo had been identified, she prayed for him and felt sorry for the suffering he must be experiencing. This amazed Corrie, who fell ill at the thought of the man and wanted to kill him. Betsie's example in time moved Corrie to forgive the man and begin praying for him as well.

Amid all the anguish, there were fortunately times for saving humor. For instance, the women in the barracks had a code phrase ("thick clouds") to warn the group of an approaching guard. On one occasion, a particular guard, who was obese, heard the code words and was furious, thinking that the image referred to her weight. Everyone chuckled and the code was quickly changed to the word *fifteen*.[18]

### Ravensbrück

From Vught, Corrie, Betsie and her fellow prisoners were crammed into filthy boxcars and shipped off for three long days and nights of travel to Ravensbrück, a notorious extermination camp in Germany. There was bread to eat but no water during the trip. When the horrible journey ended, the sick, elderly, children and mentally disabled were separated and sent off in trucks, presumably to be killed.

The surroundings of the camp were ominous: acres of low, gray barracks surrounded by concrete walls with electrified wiring and guard towers. High smokestacks emitted thin gray and ghoulish vapor into the sky. The able women were stripped of all their belongings and their clothes. They were then forced into group showers, their heads were shaved, and they were issued a thin dress, an undershirt and wooden shoes. (Corrie was able to smuggle a Bible into the barracks.)

Fourteen hundred women were crowded into barracks built for four hundred, and the beds were stacked to the ceiling in three tiers. Five women had to sleep on their sides on one bed a little over two feet wide. There were eight overflowing toilets for the women to use. The day started at 4:30 AM, with the women standing for hours in the cold and rain for roll call. The lines—there were thirty-five thousand women—stretched endlessly into the darkness. Some stood motionless, holding the hands of their children or even nursing their babies. Others, who were ill, had to lie on stretchers awaiting their number to be called. Anyone who resisted would be severely beaten. After roll call, the prisoners faced a long day of physical work in nearby factories. Corrie soon discovered that hatred on the part of the guards as well as the prisoners began to be a tangible force in the camp.

Though ill with tuberculosis, Corrie had to join the others for hard labor for twelve hours a day. Often the women had to strip nude and stand in line for medical inspections, while guards watched them with sneers and smiles. Through it all, Betsie and Corrie constantly turned to their faith and to prayer so they could survive these horrors. Both said that during these trials they came to better understand the humiliation and suffering that Jesus endured for them. The image of Jesus being stripped of his clothes and dying on a cross gave them both strength and hope. The hatred and cruelty they witnessed around them also gave them both a taste of what hell was like.

Both sisters also learned about prayer and fasting as they ate their rations of bread and boiled turnip water. Often they were able to share their faith with others during night prayer meetings, as biblical passages were passed through the prisoners in many languages. The presence of lice and fleas kept the guards from coming into the group and disturbing their prayer meetings. (This moved Betsie to actually praise God for the vermin!) A familiar Bible passage now had new meaning for the sisters: "Who shall separate us from the love of Christ? Shall tribulation, or distress, or persecution, or famine, or nakedness, or peril, or sword? Nay, in all these things we were more than conquerors through him who loved us" (see Romans 8:35–39). At night the two sisters would share their dreams of how, when they were freed, they would renovate their house in Holland and would tour America telling how their faith in Jesus had enabled them to conquer the worst possible situations.

Corrie and Betsie also gained strength by reflecting on the bright spots in the camp: like the camp midwife who so tenderly treated the expectant mothers and compassionately helped them give birth, or the old lady who illegally carried stools out to roll call for the sick to sit on. Corrie and Betsie tried to be part of this positive energy and used every opportunity to bring hope and courage to the despairing prisoners.

The rigors of prison life gradually wore Betsie down; she fell seriously ill and was sent to the hospital. Corrie was not allowed to see her, but was able to sneak in a window for a short visit before she was discovered and driven out. Betsie was soon sent back to the work camp, but her condition continued to deteriorate. As she and Betsie were driven to work, Corrie thought:

> I yearned for freedom! Someday we shall be freed; some day the time will come when we shall no longer be surrounded by electrified barbed wire and prison walls.... We shall walk freely wherever we will. Trees, flowers, grass and meadows will again surround us. We shall sing and hear music. We shall not be driven alone with whips.[19]

Betsie now became extremely ill and weak. As the two sisters lay in their crowded bed, shivering under their coats, Betsie asked something of Corrie that she did not want to hear. She asked Corrie to return with her to Germany and bring the love of Jesus back to those people who were filled with such bitterness. She asked Corrie, who simply wanted to return to being a Dutch watchmaker, to go back among the guards and show them how to love once more. Then Betsie said that they must travel the whole world with the same message—the good news of Jesus' love and forgiveness. As Betsie was carried to the hospital barracks, her last words to Corrie were: "We must tell people what we learned here. We must tell them that there is no pit so deep that He is not deeper still. They will listen to us, Corrie, because we have been here."[20]

The next day Corrie peeked through the hospital window and saw her sister's lifeless body. Amazingly, the grief lines were gone; the deep hollows of hunger and disease were not there. Her face was full and young, filled with happiness and peace![21] Later Corrie led a memorial service in the barracks, and that very night gave her sister's place in bed to a desperate Russian woman, who was an outcast among the prisoners.

Soon after Betsie's death, Corrie was summoned after roll call and expected the worst. Much to her surprise, she was told that she was to be released, but first she must stand naked for another physical, only to be told that she was not well enough to be discharged. She was then put in a clinic filled with diseased and deranged German women, many of whom had been put in prison for having sex with non-Germans. Corrie was beginning to see that her release was due to an error, and she hoped that she would be free before it was discovered.

After a week, it was decided that Corrie was well enough to be released. She was given her clothes and belongings back and had to sign an agreement that she had never been ill or had an accident in the camp and that the treatment had been good. After a lecture was given to her group to never again give their bodies to foreigners and to be available to German soldiers, Corrie walked through the gate a free woman. The Germans for all their order and precision had released Corrie by mistake! Though her sister had died, she knew that Betsie would not have been able to be freed, and the separation would have been unbearable for both of them.

The small amount of money and food that was given to Corrie on her release was soon stolen, and she spent her first three days of freedom journeying without food and encountering cruel treatment from most of the Germans she met. National Socialists had been taught to have no regard for the weak and the old, and she qualified on both counts. Fortunately, she did meet up with some Germans who had compassion on her and gave her food and shelter. On the way home she witnessed the destruction and suffering that Hitler had brought upon his people.

Once Corrie reached Holland, she realized that the war was coming to an end, and she began to enjoy the friendliness and helpfulness of her homeland. It slowly dawned on her that she was once again a free woman! It was not surprising that those who knew Corrie did not recognize her, for she was thin and pale, her eyes were hollow and her hair fell wildly about her face. At a local hospital she received good food, tender care and new clothes and was nursed back to health.

Corrie visited Willem, who was in bad condition, but still serving the many sick in his home. She returned to her hometown, had a wonderful reunion with her sister and her family and visited the local cathedral for peaceful prayer. Although she realized that she was at last free, when walking down the street Corrie would instinctively feel that she should be marching five by five as she had done so often in the camp. When she returned to her old house, she found it had been ransacked and then used as a homeless shelter before it was boarded up. She was able to find some of the family treasures, and as she thanked God for giving her back her life, she resolved to spend the rest of it loving others and extending hospitality. She met once again with the women from her old scout group, and they exchanged stories of their difficulties during the war well into the night. Corrie assured them: "If you belong to the Savior you need fear nothing. I have learned that from experience."[22] Together the women resolved to help rebuild their country and to share their faith in Jesus with others.

**A Mission to Free Others**

Corrie began her work of healing in her own country of Holland. Working out of an old mansion, she welcomed hundreds returning from the concentration camps or from years of hiding in attics and closets. Some were silent; others couldn't stop talking about their loss. Some were withdrawn; others were very offensive. Most were scarred and broken, looking for healing, needing to root out the hatred in their hearts for those who had oppressed them and killed their loved ones. Corrie, who had spent years "standing in front of a crematorium, knowing that any day could be your day," found that she had a different perspective than most who were still concerned about material things. Slowly, Corrie and many others were able to help their fellow Dutch heal and return to normal, peaceful life.[23] At the same time, she wrote a book, *A Prisoner, and Yet,* telling of her experience in the camps. It became a best-seller in Holland.

## America

After her work among her own people in Holland, Corrie decided to travel to the United States and tell her story there. At first, she received few welcomes and quickly discovered that everyone was very busy and not really interested in what a middle-aged spinster had to say. Some told her that they had real ministers to preach to them and that she should go back from where she came. As her money ran out, she felt embarrassed and humiliated, and one night fell across her bed, discouraged, crying and asking God for guidance. The next day she came across a church that many Dutch people attended, and they helped her find speaking engagements. For the next year Corrie traveled across the country with some success, telling her story and encouraging people to seek Jesus for support and guidance. As the year ended, however, she felt that she had to face up to a calling that was quite distasteful: return to Germany, the one place she dreaded most, and bring her message there.

## Germany

When Corrie arrived in Germany, she found that the war had left many Germans sitting in the ruins of their country, humiliated and in despair. She rented a former concentration camp at Darmstadt and began taking in refugees. Corrie had the barbed wire taken down, painted the barracks with light colors and planted many flowers. Homes were built and many church people pitched in to help the refugees find their way back to normal life. Corrie raised money for the project and spent much time walking through the camp, teaching people how she had survived her ordeals by turning to her faith. She tells one touching story of a new arrival who was crouched in a corner like a whipped child. Corrie welcomed and comforted her and discovered that she had been a professor of music in Dresden. When Corrie told the woman that she was a lover of Bach, the woman invited her to walk to a minister's house several miles away, where she would be allowed to play. Off they went, and soon Corrie was listening to a beautiful Bach piece played on a battered old piano without ivory on the keys. Corrie saw a light in the professor's eyes and a new bounce in her step as they returned to the camp.[24]

In the camp Corrie met another refugee, a man who had been a lawyer, but who now sat without legs in a wheelchair, filled with bitterness and self-pity. When she tried to comfort him, he said: "What do you know about bitterness? You still have your legs." Corrie proceeded to tell him about the man who had betrayed her family to the Gestapo, caused three of them to die in the camps, and how she had hated that man. She said that she confessed her hatred to Jesus and that he took it away and filled her heart with love. She told how she was able to forgive the man and actually wrote to him as he sat on death row after the war. Her letter said: "The harm you planned was turned into good for me by God. I came nearer to Him.... I have forgiven you everything. God will also forgive you everything, if you ask Him."[25]

A year later the disabled man surprised Corrie when he picked her up at the train station in a car specially outfitted for his needs and announced that he had surrendered his hatred and bitterness to God.[26] Corrie tells many such stories, in which she was able to share her own sufferings during the war with these refugees and show them how she was able to cope and remain strong through her faith.

One of the most difficult tasks Corrie undertook in Germany was to visit the prison camps, where former concentration camp guards (including some her own former guards from Ravensbrück) were imprisoned. Ironically, the roles were now reversed: She was free and they were locked up. Yet she wanted to somehow bring freedom to these women in the midst of their bitterness. At first, Corrie found that when she tried to talk with them, they looked at her with stone faces and gave no response. When she asked the woman in charge, Corrie was told that these German women felt that they were too educated and too advanced in their religious thinking to pay any attention to a simple old Dutch woman. That night, it came to her—she had a box of chocolates, which was a rare treat at that time anywhere in Germany. The next day she announced that she had brought the women prisoners a treat. The women's faces lit up at the sight of the candy, and they now saw Corrie as a generous friend. Suddenly, they were willing to listen to her messages of hope.[27]

At one point, Corrie had an occasion to return to her former prison in Vught in Holland. There she met one of her former guards and stood trembling at the memory of the suffering that she and Betsie had endured there. Corrie saw that the young man was truly repentant for what he had done, and she found herself able to forgive him. In fact, Corrie actually wrote to the Queen and asked for amnesty for the prisoner.

Her most powerful story of her own need to forgive is set in Munich, where Corrie went to speak in a church basement after the war. Her reflection that night was on her experience at Ravensbrück and the power of forgiveness. Afterward the Germans, who tend to be stolid, filed out with little to say. It was then that a man worked his way toward her. It was a former guard from Ravensbrück; Corrie remembered having to walk naked with her sister Betsie past this man in the camp. The man congratulated her on her talk and, though he did not recognize her, acknowledged that he had been a guard at Ravensbrück. He said that he had asked God's forgiveness and now wanted her forgiveness. Corrie's blood ran cold. She reached for her purse rather than taking his hand. She had so glibly talked of forgiveness and now, thinking of what had happened to her and Betsie, could not move herself to forgive this man and shake his hand. She stood there for what seemed to be an endless time, praying to Jesus for the help to forgive this man. Slowly she reached out with a "wooden handshake," and then something incredible took place. She writes:

The current started in my shoulder, raced down my arm, sprang into our joined hands. And then this healing warmth seemed to flood my whole being, bringing tears to my eyes.

"I forgive you, brother!" I cried. "With all my heart."

For a long moment we grasped each other's hands, the former guard and the former prisoner. I had never known God's love so intensely as I did then.[28]

Corrie's work in a large German factory, which housed hundreds of refugees, was also challenging. Men, women and children had been crowded here for a several years and most had to sleep on mattresses on the floor. When Corrie first came, she was invited to speak to the refugees, but she said that she wouldn't feel comfortable addressing them and then going back to her comfortable apartment. She would have to live with them. So in two months Corrie returned and prepared to move into the factory. She went to the overcrowded kitchen and prepared her simple meal, and then sat down at a cardboard box to have her first meal as a refugee. Corrie started by quietly moving from one family to the next, listening to their tales of horror, losing everything, fleeing from bombs, moving from one camp to another. She walked quietly around, surrounded by the sounds of arguments, babies crying, the shouts of playing children and many other sounds from the two hundred people there. They asked her if there was any hope for themselves and the other nine million German refugees who lived in bombed-out ruins, had no jobs and were barely subsisting day by day. Corrie could only tell them what she had been through in the camps, and her stories seemed to evoke respect and interest. She told them of the horrors of the camps and how she was able to survive by casting all her care and burden on the Lord. She told them how Betsie had taught to always count one's blessings, to pray often and to hand one's hatred and bitterness over to the Lord. It was his presence that kept them going through the hell of life in a concentration camp!

It was certainly not lost on the German refugees that Corrie held no resentment toward the very people who had oppressed her and her family, and that she had actually come to live in solidarity with them. Corrie lived for ten months in the factory, a time that she said was exhausting but also most gratifying in terms of the hope she was able to bring to so many. She now felt a call to go back to America.

**Return to America**

Corrie had no money to go to America, so she applied to work as a stewardess on a freighter. As luck would have it, one of the officials in the shipping office had read her book about her life in the camps and agreed to give her free passage aboard a freighter. The trip was rough, and she had to share her cabin with the gyrocompass, which constantly whistled.

At times the seas were rough, and she had to hold onto a rope to stay in bed. On Sunday Corrie asked if there could be a church service. The captain agreed, but when she arrived no one else appeared except the cabin boy to bring coffee. She asked him if he was going to stay, but he snapped, "I will not have anything to do with that Bible and God business."[29] Corrie went away discouraged and went back to her cabin seasick, wondering if she really was cut out to be a missionary. The next Sunday she tried again and asked the captain to encourage the men to come to the service. Ten men showed up, including the cabin boy. The men were riveted while Corrie told her story and how her faith had saved her. The cabin boy was heard to comment, "It was not boring at all."[30]

In the United States Corrie began to tour campuses, telling her story to young people who had no idea of such suffering. But she soon realized that many of them were in prisons of their own. She befriended the students as any grandmother would, and told them: "Not all prisoners are behind bars. There are prisoners of self, lust, money, ambition, or pride. You can be liberated today."[31] She reminded them that smoking, alcohol and drugs can also be a prison. She taught them what she had learned when she faced death daily in the camps: The power of Jesus is stronger than the power of evil! She reminded them of Jesus' love for sinners and invited them to turn to him. Corrie brought many students up short with her message that their world was on fire and they were wasting their time on frivolous matters. She reminded them that they are the salt of the earth and the light of the world. Many students turned their lives around as a result of these unusual visits from an old lady from Holland. She could speak with authority about suffering and misery—she had been there! She could encourage others to service—her whole life was dedicated to it.

Corrie even went to Hollywood and evangelized film stars in their extravagant homes. Those who were Christians complained that they often received derision from their colleagues. They told her how difficult it was living the gospel life amidst such emphasis on wealth, beauty and sex. She tried to give them her encouraging message of faith, but left realizing how difficult it must be to live a life of commitment in such an environment.

### A Missionary to the World

Corrie next set out on a mission tour that would last for the next thirty years and would bring her to sixty countries. She would spend much time in bus stations and airports. She would ride in planes, cars, trains and rickshaws. She would sleep in comfortable beds, on rubber mattresses and straw mats. Her bathrooms ranged from ones with exotic sunken Roman baths to mud huts with a bucket of water. When most people her age were retired, Corrie took her Bible in hand and traveled from place to place, bringing the good news of Jesus to anyone who would listen (and even to some who didn't want to hear). She spoke before tens of thousands in stadiums, thousands in universities, hundreds in town halls and churches, and to small groups in prisons. She shared her life story with crowds in theaters in India and South America and with small groups of girls in summer camps. She called herself "a tramp for the Lord." Corrie's message was one of love and light, of healing and forgiveness, and she carried it forth like a modern-day apostle Paul.[32]

In her many books Corrie tells striking stories from her travels. In London she encountered a Palestinian woman in a mental institution, who was filled with hatred for the Jews who had bombed her home and killed her husband. The woman told Corrie that the chaplain had told her to pray and banish the hatred from her heart. Corrie sympathized that this is easier said than done, and told the woman of the hatred that was in her own heart toward the guard who beat her sister Betsie because she was too weak to shovel. She told the woman how hard it was for her to root that hatred out of her heart and that she was able to do that only after much prayer that Jesus would fill her heart with love. Together the two women knelt down and prayed. A week later the woman was discharged from the mental institution with peace in her heart.

### Stories From Africa

Corrie shared anecdotes of her visits to African prisons, where she tried to bring words of hope to those locked up in horrible conditions. At one prison she was refused permission to speak to the men, but just stood looking at the warden until he relented and allowed her to speak to those sentenced to death. She went down the long hall and was allowed into the tiny cell of one of the men on death row. He told her that he was filled with hatred for the men responsible for taking away his family and his life for his political views. Corrie told him of the hatred she had had in her heart for the guards who brought so much suffering and death to her family. She told him that only through the power of Jesus was she able to forgive these people and encouraged the condemned man not to face his God with bitterness in his heart. The man listened and agreed to pray with her. The next day she heard that before the man was executed he sent his wife a message: "Don't hate the people who brought me here and who will cause my death. Love them. Forgive them. I cannot, and neither can you, but Jesus in us can do it."[33]

In Rwanda Corrie visited a desolate prison where the men had to sit and sleep in the mud outside because there was not room for them in the building. She saw in their eyes the same looks she had seen in Ravensbrück—misery, hopelessness and anger. Corrie did not know what to say to these men and prayed for guidance. She read in her Bible that the fruit of the Spirit is joy, and suddenly felt herself filled with joy and prepared to bring that to the prisoners. She met their grim faces and began to speak of the joy that Jesus can bring us in the midst of suffering. She could tell that they were thinking that she was some do-gooder who would give them this message and then return home, leaving them in this hellhole. Then Corrie told them her story about the crowding in the camp, the icy roll call each morning, the beatings and shootings. She told how one morning in the midst of their horrible three-hour roll call, a skylark appeared with its song and then came every morning at the same time. For many it seemed to come as a reminder that God's love was still in the world, even in the midst of this horror. Gradually, she saw joy coming to the faces of the men, and the prisoners, along with the guards, were allowed to accompany Corrie to her car. The prisoners began shouting at her, and when she asked an interpreter what they were saying, he told her they were chanting: "Old woman, come back. Old woman, come back and tell us more of Jesus."[34]

Corrie visited one country in Africa where each day the government was arresting and executing Christians. Even though this was a dangerous situation for her, Corrie spoke in the local church on Sunday. Fear and tension filled the air as each one wondered: "Will I be next?"

Corrie read them a passage from the Bible (1 Peter 4:12–14) that speaks about the fiery ordeals that test faith, how Christians are called to share in Christ's suffering, and that God's glory rests upon people who are reproached for being Christ's followers. She told them how her father taught her that if she were called to be a martyr, she would be given the strength from Jesus. She shared how Jesus' power had saved her in the camps. She told them how she had to face punishment by death if she taught the Bible, and how she continued to do this, even converting some of the guards. Corrie tells of how the fear and anxiety lifted from the faces in the congregation. They softly sang an old gospel song and left. More than half of them were killed that week!

## India

Corrie went to India several times and spoke to the many poor and desolate there about how her faith had helped her survive the horrors of the concentration camps. On one occasion she met a woman missionary, who was very ill and wanted Corrie to pray with her. After the prayer the woman revealed that she had leprosy, and Corrie left, filled with doubt that anything could be done for the missionary. Five years later Corrie returned to India and a lovely lady appeared at her door and asked if she recognized her. When Corrie said no, the lady said: "Do you remember a time in Vellore when you laid hands on a leper patient and prayed in Jesus' Name that she be healed?... The Lord wonderfully healed me. The doctors say I am absolutely healed from leprosy."[35]

## Russia

In Russia Corrie often had to visit Christians secretly to avoid their being punished. She writes of visiting an old couple in a one-room walk-up. The elderly wife was propped up on a small sofa, bent and twisted from multiple sclerosis. Her husband spent most of his time caring for her. Corrie embraced the woman and kissed the index finger of her right hand because she knew that was the only part of her body she could control, the finger the woman used to translate Christian books into Russian and Latvian for secret distribution. Corrie had heard about these books and praised the woman for her amazing efforts and filled her in on the news from around the world. The husband said that even though his wife was severely crippled, she was in part blessed because her condition prevented the secret police from having any clue about her publishing work. When Corrie returned to Holland, she sent the woman a new typewriter to replace the old broken-down one on which she had been working over the years. Later, she received a letter from the woman's husband that his beloved wife had passed away, but had worked on her books until midnight the night she died.[36]

Corrie felt quite frustrated in Russia because most people avoided her, not wanting to be seen with "the old woman with a Bible."[37] When she invited people to her hotel room to speak about the Gospels, they refused, telling her that all the rooms were bugged and monitored by Communist officials. Undaunted by this, and always having a sense of humor, Corrie began giving her sermons into the not-so-well hidden microphones in her hotel rooms. On one occasion, some secret service men sat down next to her table, seemingly knowing about her hotel room messages and wanting to check on her firsthand. Corrie was delighted to know that her messages were being detected, and she talked loudly to a friend about Jesus, knowing that the secret police would get her message. No harm in trying was this courageous old woman's thought.

**Japan**

Corrie was terrified about visiting Japan. She didn't know the language, didn't know if anyone would assist her, and was not sure how she would be received in a nation where there were so few Christians.

She made her visit soon after the war and spoke at a small church in Tokyo. At the time, Tokyo was in ruins. The Japanese people had been humiliated and defeated and two atomic bombs had been dropped on two other cities, killing hundreds of thousands and leaving many more maimed for life. She told them that she felt anguish and related how when things had been hopeless for her, she turned her burdens over to the Lord. As she spoke, Corrie could see some light coming back into the eyes of these people, some smiles appearing on their faces, and she knew that she had helped rekindle their faith.

On another visit to Japan, no one met Corrie at the airport, and when she asked the cab driver to take her to a hotel where English or German was spoken, she ended up at a small dirty hotel. She felt lost, lonely and afraid to go outdoors, lest she get lost. The noise, mosquitoes, roaches and predominant fish for food depressed Corrie. Wondering if all this was a big mistake, she turned to her Scriptures and prayer and soon became convinced that this trip was part of God's plan. Then the name of a missionary she knew in Japan came to her and she was able to find his number in the phone book. Her friend was able to come meet her and secure a room for her at a Christian fellowship house. She spent the next several weeks giving talks to missionaries, many of whom had become discouraged with lack of results in Japan and needed her inspiring message on how to find hope in the midst of despair.

Corrie spent a great deal of time in the Japanese prisons. At one point she visited political prisoners, and when asked to get amnesty for one prisoner held for war crimes against the Dutch, she requested that her Queen release all 260 prisoners in the same situation. Two years later they were all freed. Her travels to prisons brought her all over Japan, sometimes in police wagons or jeeps over rough roads. Her message to the long rows of prisoners sitting on their heels was always of how God's love and light can enter their grim world. The prisoners often applauded her message of hope and some of them became Christians. She established small Christian communities in the prisons and sent them materials for Bible study.

**Vietnam**

Now in her seventies, Corrie traveled to Vietnam to be with the young American soldiers. She knew that they were experiencing the same violence, death and hopelessness she had known in the camps, and she wanted to bring them the Good News of the Gospels. Wading through the rice paddies and the jungle, she was welcomed by the boys in the front lines—"an old lady who had come from a country where there was peace."[38] Corrie told the young men that they faced two possibilities: either to come home alive or to fall in action. She asked them to reflect on whether they were ready should the latter happen. She asked them to come to the Lord who is willing to prepare them. Years later she met a mother whose son had written after Corrie's visit to Vietnam. He wrote: "Now I know what it means to receive Jesus Christ as my Savior. I did it and what peace there is in my heart." Three weeks later, the young soldier was killed in action.[39]

Corrie also visited the hospitals in Vietnam, bringing them the love and care that only a grandmother can give. She visited the wounded and reminded them that they were beloved children of God. One young soldier took her aside and said that he had done many wrong things in his life and was not able to go to the Lord for forgiveness. Corrie told him that the only ones who can't be forgiven are those who think they are so good that they don't need it. She assured him that Jesus loves sinners and freely offers them forgiveness. Suddenly, she looked around and she realized that many others in the ward were listening and were eager to embrace her message of forgiveness.

**The End of Her Mission**

Corrie ended her long journey in 1977, when she moved to a house called Shalom in Placentia, California. She felt a new freedom now, a freedom to enjoy life, welcome friends and to continue to write books and make films. For over three decades she had traveled the world in flowery, below-the-knee dresses, granny shoes and her hair in a roll. She rode camels, carried babies on her back papoose style, bowed in oriental fashion, waded in swamps and sat in dank prison cells. Now Corrie was free to enjoy the natural beauty of California and sleep in the same bed each night!

Corrie's comfortable retirement did not last long. First she began to have heart trouble, and a pacemaker was inserted. The next year she suffered a severe stroke that rendered her mute, and then more strokes paralyzed her. Still, her indomitable spirit persevered and with peace and patience she lived for five more years. On her ninety-first birthday, Corrie died peacefully. Her journey was over, and as she often wrote when she autographed her books: "Jesus is victor."

## CHAPTER EIGHT

## Susan B. Anthony: Freedom for Women

The year was 1895, and the women's suffrage movement was celebrating the seventy-fifth birthday of its beloved leader. There had been tumultuous gatherings in four Western states, and now thousands packed the Golden Gate Hall in San Francisco to pay tribute and listen to the words of this stately elderly woman dressed in a velvet gown and surrounded by flowers. The newspaper wrote that she was seated on a throne like a princess, and that many speeches were given to praise her for her life's work for the freedom of women.

It was not always like this for Susan B. Anthony. Just twenty-five years earlier in the same city, she had been condemned as a heretic for taking on the cause of a prostitute convicted of murder. Often during her countless speeches on the circuit, she had been threatened, booed and shouted at. Yet her style was always self-possessed, sensible and fearless.[1] For half a century she had endured severe hardship, crisscrossing the country and challenging audiences. She spent many months lobbying, harassing and charming the members of Congress on behalf of women's rights, and in person put pressure on a number of presidents, such as Chester A. Arthur, James Garfield and Theodore Roosevelt, to give women the vote.

## Family Background

Susan was born in 1820 in Adams, a rural town in the beautiful Berkshire Mountains of Massachusetts. Her father, Daniel, was a Quaker and fell in love with Lucy Read while in school. Their marriage, which was considered to be "out of meeting," was deeply frowned upon by Quaker society. Had it not been for Daniel's high standing in the community, he probably would have been asked to leave the Quakers. Throughout his life he was always a bit of a maverick, holding strong positions against the use of alcohol and slavery. Eventually he was asked to leave the Quakers. It would seem that Susan was deeply influenced by her father's activism, and he supported her in all her causes throughout her life.[2] Daniel was industrious and liberal in his views, and firmly but gently guided Susan in self-discipline and earnestly convinced her of her self-worth. His Quaker beliefs encouraged the development of her own "inner light," and she was allowed to have her own quiet time to reflect, wander the mountains and fields and enjoy the pleasures of nature in the various seasons.

Susan's mother was raised on a farm in the Baptist faith. Once she decided to marry Daniel, she had to give up the singing and dancing she loved so much and adopt the austere, somber lifestyle and the drab gray clothing of the Quakers. All this because the husband's ways at the time had to dominate the life of his obedient wife. Her life had been incorporated into the life of her husband, and she was now without her own legal rights and was completely dependent on him. This was the Jacksonian period of "the rise of the common man," but such thoughts were not applied to the common woman.[3] Early lessons indeed for Susan!

Susan's mother was expected to have a large family, since the Quakers were dwindling in numbers, but prevailing values did not permit her to speak about sexuality or reproduction. She quietly had eight children, but lost one in childbirth and one in infancy. Lucy was devoted to her children and even tried to help them break out of Quaker austerity by dressing them in occasional plaids and allowing them to attend the occasional party. Susan observed and had to participate in the drudgery of her mother's homemaking: cooking, sewing, hauling water and endless laundry. She learned early on that in marriage the wife endured many burdens for which she seldom received recognition.

Lucy, though shy and reserved, attended an early conference on women's rights with her husband and supported his work on behalf of temperance and abolition. She also supported her daughter's choice to remain single and work for women's rights, and the two remained close until Lucy's death at the age of eighty-six.

Susan was also influenced by her grandparents. On the maternal side, she received wonderful hospitality and loved to listen to her grandfather's stories of his days in the Revolutionary War. Her Quaker grandparents gave her careful instructions in her religion.[4]

Education was important to the Quakers, and Susan was expected to do her lessons in the small school set up by Grandfather Anthony. (She worked such long hours at her studies that her eyes crossed, and one eye remained so and was always of source of embarrassment to Susan.) Another important value she learned from her Quaker religion was that women were, atypically for the times, allowed to speak up at meetings and express their own inner light.

Susan's father early on was a farmer and shopkeeper but soon got caught up in the growing industrialization in the East and decided to open a small mill to manufacture cotton cloth. The growth of this industry opened work opportunities for farm girls and many were hired in the mills. They worked six days a week, twelve hours a day for $1.45 per week. Although this was a pittance, it offered the young women a chance to move off the farm, be more independent and actually be paid for their work. When Susan's father took into his house eleven such workers, she saw how much more work of cooking, laundry, endless chores and difficult needlework fell upon her mother and her daughters. Observing the mill girls, Susan learned the price that women would have to pay for some meager independence.

## The Move to Battenville

The mill was a great success, and soon Susan's father was funded to open a factory and some small mills in the Battenville area, just north of Albany, New York. Here Susan first met slaves, and as a Quaker simply could not understand the practice of one person owning another. Her father now built a fifteen-room house for his family, where he could provide simple housing for his workers as well as homeschooling for his children and workers. Daniel even hired as a teacher, Mary Perkins, a graduate of one of the new seminaries for the education of women. Mary provided Susan with a new model for a young woman: independent, well-educated and professional, but severely underpaid. Even though Daniel was prospering, he continued to pay his mill girls the same, usually less than half what the men were paid. Once Susan asked that an exceptional young woman be made overseer in the mill, but her father told her that this would never do in his mill. Another lesson learned!

Susan succeeded in her studies and at fifteen began to teach summer sessions in her father's school. One winter she boarded with a Quaker family and taught their children for the grand sum of one dollar per week. From there she moved up to the district school, where she received an extra fifty cents per week. It did not take Susan long to notice that the women received only a fraction of what the male teachers made![5]

## Off to a Female Seminary

When Daniel saw how Susan loved school, he began to search for a place of higher education for her. Even though his business was beginning to fail during the depression of 1837, he decided to enroll two of his daughters, Guelma and Susan, at Deborah Moulson's Quaker Female Seminary near Philadelphia. The trip there with her father on wagons, trains and boats was a thrilling experience of the travel that would become so much of Susan's future.

The experience at the seminary was not a happy one for Susan. She became quite homesick, was deeply depressed, and the moralism and perfectionism of the school filled her with constant guilt for the smallest wrongdoing. Although Susan was able to study math, science and philosophy, the focus of the school was strict formation in humility and virtue. If Susan was to be a "modern" woman, she must learn to be a pious pleaser. She was thus expected to suppress her feelings and throw herself into her work, always guided by a strict and unbending moralism. She was to seek moral perfection and was constantly reminded of her imperfections. Diaries were maintained to keep track of personal defects, and letters home had to be read and corrected by the headmistress before they could be sent out. Susan was under constant pressure to be perfect, and the school caused her to have a poor self-image and lose confidence in her abilities. She became plagued with self-doubts and feelings of inferiority. The headmistress even led Susan to believe that her defects were partially responsible for the older woman's poor health. After this experience, it would take years before Susan would regain her self-confidence.

Fortunately, Susan had the opportunity at the school to have exposure to outstanding women like Lucretia Mott, who though modest, was a strong and independent woman who had moved beyond personal piety to strong commitment to civic responsibility. Lucretia was an organizer for the abolitionist movement, which reinforced the antislavery position Susan had learned from her father.

**Called Back From School**

The depression in 1837 caused Daniel's business to fail, so his daughters were called home from school. On returning they found that all the mills were closed and their home was gone, and all their personal belongings were on the auction block. Susan learned the lesson that by law her father owned everything and that the few things her mother did have could be taken away to pay his debts.[6] Fortunately, Lucy's brother stepped in and allowed the family to bid for the things they wished to keep. Nevertheless, the family was forced to move into an abandoned hotel in a broken-down hamlet with the appropriate name of

Hardscrabble. Susan had to once again face the drudgery of cooking, baking, washing and weaving.

## A Teaching Job

Susan soon was told that she would have to go to work and help support her family. She took a teaching job at a Quaker boarding school in New Rochelle, New York, where she was paid thirty dollars for a semester's work. At the school Susan became fast friends with Eunice Kenyon, who ran the school. Once again she had to suppress her feelings of homesickness and her distress over losing her sister Guelma to marriage. Would she ever marry? So far she had never met a man that measured up. Her emotional attachments had been much stronger with her sisters and with women friends. She was firm by this time that she would not marry to simply adorn some man's household with her feminine charms and with a brood of children.

Teaching in Eunice's school offered Susan the opportunity to grow in autonomy and self-determination. Now she was responsible only to herself and her students and could develop her own way of teaching, which at that time was quite strict and authoritarian. She was beginning to have her own views on temperance, politics and slavery. Trips to New York City exposed her to diverse views on many issues. And in New Rochelle she met vehement anti-abolitionists as well as young black women who socialized freely with white people. Susan's world was expanding, but she was still quite lonely, and after a short teaching stint she decided to move back with her family.

## Headmistress

In 1845 Susan's father was able to move to a farm in Rochester, New York. The farm was shrewdly purchased by Susan's brother Joshua, who both secured Lucy's inheritance for her (she could not legally inherit) and also protected the money from Daniel's creditors. Susan moved with the family and soon was offered a job as headmistress at the Canajoharie Academy in the lovely Mohawk Valley. At first, Susan felt quite inadequate for the position, but eventually during her three years there she gained independence and self-confidence. She could now keep her salary of ninety-five dollars per year for herself, and took on a new image as a lady of fashion, with pretty dresses, fancy hats and shoes, and even occasionally wore her hair in braids. She began to lighten up with her students and became more relaxed and personal with them. She even accepted some date invitations and ventured out to a few dances, at first discovering dancing to be fun, although awkward. Quite soon, however, she became completely turned off by the excessive drinking at the dances and stopped going.

Susan had become a secure individual. She no longer needed to go home often and felt that she was now emotionally and financially independent. A good feeling for a young woman in the mid-nineteenth century! Still she was fully aware that she was earning half of what male teachers were making.

**An Interest in Reform**

In time Susan began to lose interest in teaching. He social life was minimal, few things stimulated her, and she was beginning to wonder what to do with her new independence. Visits from her Quaker father encouraged her toward his reform notions, and she decided to turn to one of his causes, the Temperance Movement. She joined the Canajoharie Daughters of Temperance and in 1849 gave her first public speech on how drunkenness destroys morality and exposes women to seduction. She was appalled how men would marry women for their money and then throw away the money on "riotous living." She decried situations in which women supported lazy husbands and then had to watch these same men drink up the income.[7]

Susan decided to leave teaching and return home to Rochester when she realized that a cousin, Margaret, was about to give birth and needed her. She came to her cousin's aid, attended her every need, and kept her house, all the while having to put up with the husband who did little but complain. Margaret died, leaving Susan distraught, discouraged about marriage, and fearful that she would be left an "old maid." She returned home, disheartened and confused about what she should do with her life. She knew she would never marry unless she would be able to live on the level of equality with her husband. Ultimately, Susan decided that for her to marry would mean giving up all her special work for "the cause."[8] Throughout her life she experienced a deep feeling of loss when her associates would give up "the cause" to get married and raise a family.

The family farm was flourishing when Susan arrived, and her father had also undertaken a new position selling life insurance. Susan set aside her fancy clothes, put on calico and started to work in the garden. It soon became clear that Susan was no good at farmwork, and she began to spend more time at antislavery and temperance meetings. She became a student of the abolitionist movement, attending the lectures of the Quaker abolitionists, Stephen and Abby Foster, in Rochester. She also traveled to Syracuse to hear the great William Lloyd Garrison, the radical founder of the abolitionist movement in Boston. The abolitionist movement was gaining momentum with the passing of the Fugitive Slave Act in 1850, which allowed slave owners to recapture escaped slaves and even freed slaves in the North and return them to the South. Frederick Douglass, an escaped slave, had become a strong abolitionist, and the Underground Railroad was now flourishing. Susan was encountering escaped slaves moving through Rochester on their way to freedom in Canada.

### Encounter With the Women's Movement
In 1848, while Susan was working in her school in Canajoharie, a meeting was held in Seneca Falls, New York, that would change her life forever. Susan read about the meeting in the papers and was fascinated with the accounts of the controversial Elizabeth Cady Stanton, who had called the meeting to initiate the Women's Rights Movement. A second meeting was soon called in Rochester, which stirred Susan's family and friends, but at that time Susan was vaguely aware of the movement

through the newspapers. In conservative Canajoharie, she had to be satisfied with her temperance work. It was only on visits home to Rochester that she had the opportunity to meet active abolitionists like William Lloyd Garrison and Frederick Douglass.

## A Meeting With Stanton

Susan was later invited to Seneca Falls to hear more lectures on abolition, and while there she met Elizabeth Cady Stanton. The two liked each other immediately. When Stanton invited Susan to her home, they became close friends and would become the moving forces behind the women's movement for the next fifty years. They were hardly a matched pair. Stanton was from a wealthy background, was married to a prominent political figure and was busy having babies and raising children. Susan was from a common background, was unmarried and was a former schoolmarm, hoping to become a reformist. Somehow they clicked. Susan the keen analyst; Stanton the synthesizer; Susan the critic; Stanton the writer. At first, Susan needed to be mentored on the women's movement and speechwriting. (Initially, Stanton wrote Susan's speeches for her.) Anthony said that her friend made the bullets and she fired them.[9] But eventually each woman became a force in her own right, and together they would help forge a movement that would make a profound difference for women all over the world.

## The Temperance Movement

Susan continued her work in the temperance movement. She had observed how drunkenness had led to so much financial, emotional and even physical abuse of wives. Ironically, at the time the temperance movement was led by male clergymen, since women were forbidden to speak in public. When Susan did attempt to speak at one of the meetings, she was silenced. She walked out of the meeting and immediately started her own organization, The Woman's State Temperance Society. She persuaded Stanton to address the first convention, and she showed up in her "Bloomers" with her hair in a short bob. She gave a rousing

speech on temperance, but made many of the other women uncom-
fortable by wading into other issues, such as women's right to divorce
and their rights over the children. The movement's rejection of
Stanton and her radical views ultimately led to her leaving the temperance movement.

## Joining the Women's Movement

Susan was gradually learning that for women there were even more
serious issues than those addressed by the temperance movement, and
unless women were able to gain financial independence and the right to
vote, neither temperance nor any of the other women's issues would
ever be resolved. Women had to be paid salaries equal to men; married
women had to have rights to their own money and rights over their
own children in divorce. Suffrage would be a statement that women's
judgment is sound and worthy to be counted, and would give women
access to what is due them in justice.

Susan's resolve and commitment began to increase, and she became
a strong force on the women's rights speaking circuit. Along the way,
she would be joined by other women speakers. At one point she shared
the stage with the famous former slave, Sojourner Truth, who was a formidable opponent to both slavery and the oppression of women.

At the gatherings, Susan often had to endure what she called "sex
hatred" from wild mobs of male opponents. Here is her account of one
incident:

> At the evening session, I placed myself...to take the door fee.
> Some thirty passed up quietly, when there came, with heavy
> tramp, a compact gang of forty or fifty rowdies.... There they
> stamped, and howled, and whistled, and sang "the star spangled
> banner"—marched on to the platform, seated themselves at the
> table, pulled out a pack of cards, and then took the table and
> threw it to the floor with a crash. Under the circumstances, we
> made no attempt to speak, and soon left the hall.[10]

Susan spoke in schoolhouses, barns, sawmills, any space where people could gather. Traveling by sleigh or wagon on muddy roads, often crossing dangerously swollen streams, she had to stay in run-down inns and sleep on mattresses infested with bed bugs. For food, Susan often had to be satisfied with soda bread, canned meat and vegetables and dried fish.

Susan would take breaks by visiting Stanton's home, where Susan would help with the cooking and the children, as the two formulated plans for their movement. Elizabeth once observed: "[W]henever I saw that stately Quaker girl coming across my lawn, I knew that some happy convocation of the sons of Adam were to be set by the ears, by one of our appeals or resolutions."[11] The two were now convinced that political rights were the answer for the freedom of women.

**A Statewide Campaign**
Susan decided to launch a statewide campaign in New York for married women's property rights. Stanton gave a brilliant speech at a women's convention in Albany, the state capitol, and ten thousand petitions were presented to the state assembly. The women were turned down, but they had entered the political arena and the feminist fires were beginning to spread. A new ideal of the true "new woman" was beginning to emerge: The woman who is equal, her own person, and free to develop her own powers and gifts. Most importantly, the new woman was not to lose her identity or her legal rights by entering into a marriage in which she would be inferior.[12]

For Susan, marriage should be an equal partnership. She rejected the view that women were inferior in body and mind, and held that they were completely equal to men and should be just as free to seek their own individual happiness. Neither did she want women to be placed on a pedestal; from a perch they would have no access to power. Susan said: "You may pet us and worship us, and all that; but if you don't recognize our womanhood, you have done nothing."[13] She pointed out to men that they had the right to wives who were "full-fledge women," who were intelligent and well-educated. She doubted whether many men really wanted to spend the rest of their lives with wives who were pets, canary birds or hothouse plants. She firmly rejected the traditional stereotypes of woman and man. She said: "The old idea that man was made for himself and the woman for him, that he is the oak, she the vine, he the head, she the heart—he the great conservator of wisdom principle, she of love, will be reverently laid aside with other long since exploded philosophies of the ignorant past."[14]

Susan held a vision for the woman of the future and gave herself to this vision, knowing full well that she would not live to see it accomplished. Prophetically she said:

> I look for the day when the woman who has a political or judicial brain will have as much right to sit on the Supreme Bench or in the Senate as you men have now; when women all over this country will have equal property rights, equal business rights, and equal political rights with men; when the only criterions of excellence or position will be the ability, honor and character of the individual without regard to whether he or she be male or female. And this time will come.[15]

In 1854 Susan decided to broaden her influences beyond the state of New York, and she headed south to Baltimore and Alexandria with a friend, Ernestine Rose. On a visit to Washington, D.C., Susan again met slavery face-to-face and was stunned by its deep oppression of the human spirit. The maid in her hotel was a slave hired out by her master, who took her whole pay of eight dollars a month. Susan returned to New York even more determined to continue her work for the freedom of women.

Back in New York, Susan set out to canvass the whole state on her own. She sent out notices, secured town halls or churches to give her speeches, and arrived in a city or village where she would have to find her own accommodations. In the afternoon she would speak to the women and then invite them to bring their husbands at night. The harsh winters of upstate New York made the travel by sleigh and the work difficult, but Susan plodded on from place to place. Though normally quite healthy, Susan had a severe cold that began to affect her lower back, and once she had to be wrapped in blankets and carried to her sleigh. Susan conducted fifty-four meetings in all and was self-supporting, charging a twenty-five-cent entry fee for the evening sessions (knowing that the husbands held the purse strings). Her supporters described her as "good-looking" and "strong-minded," while enemies wrote that she was a "strident spinster" with a "'lean and cadaverous' look."[16] She had become an articulate and powerful advocate for the rights of women.

## Abolition

After her New York campaign, Susan visited Boston and was inspired by her meetings with abolitionist leaders like William Lloyd Garrison and Theodore Parker. Now recognized to be an effective speaker, she was engaged by the movement and given a small salary of ten dollars a week plus expenses to speak against slavery and racial discrimination. She once denounced slavery as follows:

> What is American Slavery? It is the Legalized Systemized robbery of the bodies and souls of nearly four millions of men, women and children. It is the Legalized traffic in God's Image; It is the buying and selling of Jesus Christ himself on the auction block, as Merchandise, as chattel property, in the person of the outraged slave.[17]

For Susan, slavery was depriving four million people in this country of their freedom; it was a wholesale system of wrongful outrage on millions of God's children. It was "legalized prostitution" of millions of young black women.

At a teachers' convention she dropped a bombshell by denouncing the exclusion of colored children from the public schools and then returned to women's rights by advocating coeducation throughout the school system. Meanwhile, she continued trudging across New York

giving poorly attended and often hostilely received speeches on abolition. When John Brown was executed after his raid on Harper's Ferry,
Virginia—an attempt to start an uprising against slavery—Susan faced
the fierce hostility of the anti-abolitionists and organized a rally in
Rochester to honor Brown. Before three hundred people she gave a
marvelous speech in support of Brown and then sent the proceeds from
the meeting to Brown's widow and children.

Susan soon grew weary on the abolition trail, where slavery began
to overshadow the women's issues. Susan had taken the radical position
of Garrison that no compromises should be given to either the North
or South on slavery. She met tremendous opposition by New
Englanders, whose economies and industries thrived on the backs of
the southern slave. In Syracuse, she saw benches broken and knives
flashing, and was pelted with rotten eggs. In Rochester, a brave mayor
had to protect her by sitting on the stage with a gun across his lap.

By 1860, with the country near civil war, Susan joined Stanton in
Albany to push for property rights for married women. Victory came at
last, as legislation was passed giving women rights over property, business, contracts and joint rights over their children. Both Susan and
Stanton now turned their efforts to gain these same rights as well as
broaden the divorce laws in other states.

## Civil War

Once the Civil War broke out and the southern states left the Union, the
whole reform picture shifted. The Anti-Slavery Society now backed off
and allowed the war to do its work, and the women's movement had to
cancel its national convention. New York repealed the legislation giving
women property rights! For a time, Susan returned home to Rochester
and stayed busy with farmwork, housekeeping and reading. The period
was difficult for her and she began to have doubts about her mission
and her own abilities to carry it out.

Susan's time off did not last long and once again she took up her
abolition work and went on a lecture tour of western New York. Besides

advocating the abolition of slavery, she encouraged women to recognize that their efforts for the war were just as valuable as those of the soldiers. She sternly opposed Lincoln's plan for gradual emancipation, which started with border states and then proposed the export of freed slaves to Africa. Susan called for complete emancipation now. To the question of what to do with freed slaves, she firmly said: "Welcome them to all the blessing of our free institutions; to our schools and churches, to every department of industry, trade and art."[18] Along the way, in 1862, Susan suffered the loss of her father, Daniel, who had so strongly supported her causes and campaigns for so many years.

By 1862 it became clear to Lincoln that the border states would not accept his plan to emancipate their slaves. He accepted that the war was not only to preserve the Union but was also over emancipation. Lincoln issued his Emancipation Proclamation, freeing all slaves in the South, yet allowing slavery in the border states because they had stayed in the Union.

Susan called a new women's convention, where the participants commended the president for his proclamation but called for freedom for all slaves and all women as well. During the war Susan was somewhat of a "person without a cause," but she continued to speak for abolition and gathered hundreds of thousands of signatures, which ultimately would help in the passing of the Thirteenth Amendment to abolish slavery.

As the war was coming to an end, Susan was at loose ends and decided to visit her brother in Leavenworth, Kansas. During the last days of the war, she saw the huge supply trains, Northern troops everywhere, and thousands of freed slaves pouring into the city, where they still faced severe racial prejudice. Susan set herself to help these former slaves get the supplies they needed, have access to education and gain employment.

After the end of the war and the assassination of Lincoln, Susan continued her opposition to the plans for Reconstruction. She was utterly shocked by the Thirteenth Amendment, which allowed all male citizens, including former slaves to vote. She was outraged that all "persons" were allowed to vote, but that only males were considered to be persons. Susan was distraught to see that the abolitionists for whom she worked so hard were not supporting the women's vote, not wanting to divert attention from black rights. Even her longtime friend, Frederick Douglass, who had been a staunch supporter of the women's movement, refused to take a stand on women's suffrage, lest it detract attention from his own cause.[19] Susan could be caustic on the matter. When the famous publisher Horace Greeley challenged her by saying that bullets and ballots go together and asked if she would be ready to fight, she quipped: "Certainly, Mr. Greeley, just as you fought in the late war—at the point of a goose quill."[20] When politicians said that the vote would bring women into politics, which was too filthy for women, she answered that maybe the filth comes from not having women present. She also pointed out the irony of hiring women to clean the legislative halls and empty the spittoons, but then saying that it would be "degrading" for women to pass legislation with the men.

### The George Train Affair

After the war, Anthony and Stanton needed to get their movement for the women's vote rolling again, and they were desperate for support and financial assistance. They turned to George Train, a wealthy entrepreneur, who supplied them with money and traveled with them on their campaigns. Unfortunately, Train was also an outspoken racist, and their association with him drew a great deal of fire from many quarters. The years with him became chaotic and miserable for Susan. He funded her establishment of a feminist newspaper, *The Revolution*, in which Stanton and Anthony could continue their crusade for women's rights, especially suffrage, and deal with the problems women had in the workforce.[21]

## Working Women

Susan had been aware of the plight of working women from the time she worked for her father and observed the low pay and long hours of the "mill girls." Industrialization had given young women a way toward independence, but it also opened opportunities for exploiting them. Difficult and often dangerous work in the factories, overcrowded living in tenements and low pay characterized the experience of many women, especially the growing number of immigrant women who had come to America to work. Susan observed that in the United States there were three million women working for a pittance. In New York City over fifty thousand women were working for less than fifty cents a day. In this same city over twenty-five hundred babies were left at one foundling home run by nuns. Many women were being forced into prostitution and, even there, the money earned went largely to the men running the operation. In her newspaper Susan often turned her attention to this oppression of women and maintained that giving women the vote would do much to eradicate these abuses. To establish justice in this country, Susan believed that we "must put into the hands of all women...the ballot, the symbol of perfect equality, that right protection of all other rights."[22]

In 1868 Susan began organizing women's groups to teach them to gain political power, express their grievances and press for their rights. She wanted to gain access to the National Labor Union, which advocated for women workers but at the same time denied them membership. Susan began to organize working women's associations, and at the local meetings she was appalled by the stories of what the women were subjected to in the factories. Women told of situations in which they spent long hours making ladies' cloaks for two dollars apiece. One reported how she made two dozen men's shirts and was paid only $1.20 for the lot. Another made one dollar a day making men's hats. Susan encouraged them to organize and go to the press. She also encouraged women with money to leave their lives of luxury and dependence on their husbands, and to open businesses where they could hire women and treat them fairly. She succeeded in getting some representation for women in the Union, but was excluded herself because of her position on gaining the vote for women.

Susan had now become a lightning rod, beloved by many women as a liberator, and hated by many others as an unsexed witch.[23] She took on all comers: the Protestants who feared that giving women the vote would bring many Catholic women in and thus give more power to the church; the free-thinkers who feared that suffrage for women church members would put God in the Constitution; the free-whiskey men who feared that if women could vote that would be the end for liquor sales; and both the Democrats and Republicans who feared that a plank in their platform for women's suffrage would create a backlash. Susan had answers for them all. Women must receive the justice that is their due! To those who said women were not physically strong enough, she pointed to the rigors that she had endured on her speaking tours. (At one point she had delivered nearly one hundred speeches during a seven-month period to forty-two thousand people.)[24]

After two exciting years, Susan's newspaper, *The Revolution,* began to fail. George Train, the financial backer who had talked her into starting the paper, walked away and left her with a mountain of debt. To pay off this debt and continue her mission, Susan set out on another one of her lecture tours advocating women's rights, especially their right to vote. She worked and saved for years until she paid every penny of her debt.

### Continuing Opposition

Susan was convinced that it was necessary for women to gain political clout before they could gain economic and social independence. Opposition to her struggle for women's right to vote continued to build from many different quarters. Many women's clubs kept their distance. They had been organized for mutual support, and did not want to wade into controversial issues. Some women wanted to think that from the pedestal of beauty, modesty and motherhood they wielded enormous power over their husbands. Many cherished their "place" and did not want to be associated with "aggressive" women. As an article in a Philadelphia newspaper put it in 1848: "The ladies of Philadelphia, therefore,...are resolved to maintain their rights as Wives, Belles, Virgins, and Mothers, and not as women."[25] Many new female immigrants from Europe had been used to patriarchal societies and were opposed to the women's movement. Those women who had been able to gain education and jobs were beginning to once again readjust to male domination in order to protect what they had gained. There had been some progress for women's suffrage on a state level, as in Wyoming and Colorado, but there was still much resistance on a national level.

Those opposed to the women's movement portrayed its advocates with severity, as women "entirely devoid of personal attraction." They were portrayed as women who couldn't get a man, so they set out to avenge themselves on the men who slighted them. Or they were women who had been dethroned by their husbands, and they now go as vagabonds across the country giving boring talks and violating the rules of good taste and decency. They were described as: "old maids" or "badly mated" women, "mannish women" or "hens that crow." One reporter scorned women for wanting to be in the men's professions of law, medicine, legislature or even the military, when there would be the likelihood of them giving birth in the midst of a trial, during surgery, in Congress or even in the midst of battle.[26]

**Illegal Women Voters**

After years of considering the act of voting illegally, Susan decided to take the step in 1872. She and about seven other women decided to register to vote in a local barbershop in Rochester. At first, the officials refused to allow the women to register, but when Susan threatened to bring charges against them in court, the officials were intimidated and allowed the women to register. On November 5, she and fourteen other women showed up at the polls and cast their ballots. The press called for the arrest of these women, and several weeks later an embarrassed deputy marshal showed up at Susan's house and placed her under arrest. At the hearing she refused bail, but ultimately her lawyer paid it so that she would not be imprisoned. She was indicted by a grand jury and went to trial. While awaiting trial, Susan traveled throughout the area defending her right to vote. She remained completely convinced that denying the right to vote to women in our republic was outrageous and degrading on many levels.

The trial turned out to be a clear dramatization of the kind of male domination Susan had been opposing for so many years. The judge, Justice Ward Hunt, was described by Stanton as "a small-brained, pale-faced, prim-looking man, enveloped in a faultless suit."[27] He heard the arguments and declared Susan to be an incompetent witness to testify on her own behalf because she was a woman. He then instructed the jury to render a verdict of guilty! Susan was stunned, and when the judge asked if she had anything to say, she gave the judge more than he had bargained for. Launching into a powerful speech against the trampling of her rights, she said:

> Yes, your Honor, I have many things to say; for in your ordered verdict of guilty, you have trampled under foot every vital principle of our government. My natural rights, my civil rights, my political rights are all alike ignored. Robbed of the fundamental privilege of citizenship, I am degraded from the status of a citizen to that of a subject; and not only myself individually but all of my sex are, by your Honor's verdict, doomed to political subjection under this so-called Republican government.[28]

The judge realized he had made a mistake by asking Susan if she had anything to say and tried to silence her. But on she went at great length about her manifold loss of rights. The judge told her to be seated, but

Susan continued, pointing out that the jury of men were not her "peers," because all are held up to be legally her superior. Again Susan was ordered to sit, but she continued to use this opportunity to rail against the fact that women were disenfranchised and could not therefore receive fair trials. Seeing that he was losing control of his own courtroom, the judge boomed out that she would have to pay a one-hundred-dollar fine and courts costs. To this judgment, she defiantly answered: "May it please your honor, I will never pay a dollar of your unjust penalty."[29] Susan never did pay her fine, and the publicity she had gained for her cause was priceless.

**Going International**

In 1883 Susan decided it was time to broaden her scope. She had just finished a campaign going from state to state and had spent much time lobbying in Washington. She and Stanton had also finished the arduous work of writing the first volume of their *History of Woman Suffrage*. She decided to go to Europe where she would meet Stanton who had gone there earlier. Beginning in London, Susan soon learned that women there were engaged in the same fight for their legal rights as were American women. Moving on to Italy, she found extreme poverty among women and a strong movement for suffrage and educational opportunities. In Ireland she visited many broken-down shacks, where impoverished women struggled to raise large families. In France she found that the code established by Napoleon had given husbands complete legal rights over their wives, and provided for wives to be imprisoned for adultery, with no such sanctions for husbands. She found a strong movement for women's rights in France, though one that was looked at with deep suspicion by the government. Susan began to discuss with other women organizing an International Council of Women.

The first meeting of the international women's movement was held in Washington, D.C., in 1888. Women from England, France, Ireland, Norway, Denmark, Finland, India, Canada and the United States gathered to discuss and advocate women's unity in their diversity and to promote their rights as human beings and citizens. Subsequent meetings were held in Chicago and then London.

## The Religious Issue

Anthony and Stanton had clashed on many issues; one of them was the issue of religion. Stanton had come to believe that the Christian churches, with their theology of patriarchy, were in large part responsible for the oppression of women. She also grew concerned over the increasing power of Roman Catholicism in the United States, due to the high rate of immigration. Catholicism represented to many the epitome of patriarchy, male dominance, the exclusion of women and an emphasis on their submission. The church's control over its people was also perceived by many to be a danger to the American separation of church and state. Stanton had come to believe that an all-out attack on the Christian churches would help the women's cause. To do this, Stanton organized the *Woman's Bible*, which was largely a series of essays by Stanton and other scholars that demonstrated how the Scriptures had been used to justify the oppression of women.

Susan, on the other hand, did not see the churches as such a danger to the women's movement, and she tended to keep her distance from organized religion. She remained only loosely associated with the Quakers, attending meetings when back in Rochester, and she had little interest in theological issues. Susan firmly believed in religious freedom and was tolerant of all beliefs and even lack of belief among her suffragettes. It was her position that the women's movement should have no theological bias so that any woman could be part of it.

At the same time, Susan observed that there was great deal of hypocrisy in religion. She was often confronted by ministers who barred her from speaking in their churches and denounced her as an infidel from the pulpit. Some ministers had held mandatory prayer meetings at the same hour as Susan's speech and told the women in their congregations that their salvation depended on their attending these services.[30] Susan pointed out that these very same ministers approved of the evils of slavery and condemned abolitionists!

As for her own beliefs, Susan did not think that God was responsible for human ills; humans bring these sufferings upon themselves. She believed that the essence of all religions was equal rights for all and that the emancipation of women would help women bring redemption to the world. Susan was a common-sense pragmatist who maintained that sentiment gave no guarantee for justice. Susan had become quite secular in her approach to spirituality and looked upon her work as her prayer. She once commented: "I pray every single second of my life; not on my knees but with my work…. Work and worship are one with me."[31] Her driving force seemed to be the improvement of society rather than adherence to or the promotion of religion.

Susan stayed clear of the *Woman's Bible* and Stanton's campaign against the churches mainly because she believed that the focus should always be on the vote and women's rights. With regard to opposition to women's rights, Susan always held that the voices in the saloons had more force than the voices of the churches. For her, it was human barbarity that brought oppression to women, and not the Hebrew Scriptures. If women could get the vote and their civil rights sorted out, the religious questions would be addressed in due time.

When the national women's convention censored Stanton for the *Woman's Bible*, Susan was put on the spot. Her loyalty to Stanton and her belief in freedom of discussion in the movement put her in a dilemma. She held that women had just as much right to "interpret and twist the Bible to their own advantage as men have always twisted and turned it to theirs," but she did not want her people to lose focus on the right to vote.[32] For a time Susan thought of resigning her presidency over the issue, but she decided to stay on for the benefit of the group and had to accept the censoring of Stanton.

### Fresh Troops
It was evident that a new stage of the feminist movement had arrived. Younger and well-educated women had their own views on how to be

liberated and were not necessarily listening to the "old guard." They were more satisfied with the degree of equality they had, and they resisted the strident, confrontational and controversial tone of the founders of the women's movement. Many women, perhaps as they are today, were adapting to the more moderate forms of male domination and were no longer wanting to be confrontational or in a "bashing" posture.

## Defending Black Women

Susan also took up the cause of women of color. As in the case of the recent Civil Rights Movement, black women were also left behind during emancipation. Susan pointed out that after being freed, black women now were under the control of their husbands rather than their owners. Moreover, they did not receive the right to vote as did the black men. In addition, segregation had deprived them of their rights, as it had black men.

Susan insisted that black women have membership in the women's associations. (They had been excluded from most women's clubs). Susan condemned the deceitful exaggeration of black men raping white women, as well as the barbarity of lynching many blacks for this crime. She pointed out how the emphasis on this rape issue had resulted in the ignoring of abuses to black women. Susan also pointed out that black women were treated as poorly in the North as they were in the South. On one occasion, she had to dismiss one of her own secretaries because she refused to take dictation from a black woman friend of Susan's. Unfortunately, Susan often got distracted from these abuses because of her complete dedication to women's suffrage.

## The Turn of the Century

As the nineteenth century came to an end, the United States had extended its influence by acquiring other territories: Hawaii, the Philippines, Puerto Rico and Guam. Susan was appalled by such imperialism and the promotion of a male-dominated culture to other lands. She believed that war was a masculine endeavor and wrote: "All of our wars today are the result of a government *wholly masculine....* Man is the fighting half of the human family, and woman is the peace-making half."[33]

As a new century approached, Susan decided it was time to look back and leave a record of her historical work. It was time to write her own story. In 1896 Susan engaged a reporter from Indiana, Ida Harper, to write her biography. Trunks, boxes and bags of documents and letters were assembled in Susan's attic and a whole team of women set to work organizing, dictating and writing. Susan was seventy-seven and still full of energy as she went back through the memories of her campaigns and battles of half a century.

### Passing the Torch

Susan decided that when she turned eighty she would pass the torch of leadership to a younger woman. At the women's convention in 1900, it was announced that Carrie Chapman Catt, who had spearheaded women's suffrage in Colorado and was on the organization's planning committee, would take over the post. It was the end of an era! Susan was hosted at a reception at the White House and later gave her farewell speech, saying: "Once I was the most hated and reviled of women, now, it seems as if everybody loves me."[34]

Passing the torch of leadership did not mean that Susan was finished with her crusade, as is evident in the dispute she carried on with former President Grover Cleveland. In an article in the *Ladies' Home Journal*, Cleveland took on the suffragettes. He declared his faith in "simple and unadulterated womanhood" and claimed that those women who are discontented with their "ordained lot" and their "appointed ministrations" are in fact perverting a gift of God to the human race. Cleveland pointed to the old and natural order of things, in which Adam was put in the garden to care for it and Eve was his "helpmate." The restlessness and discontent on the part of these aggressive women's clubs was therefore to be viewed as incorrigible. Cleveland described the good wife as "a woman who loves her husband and her country with no desire to run either." He concluded with enunciating the "everlasting truth": "the hand that rocks the cradle is the hand that rules the world."[35]

The press was eager for Susan's response, and she did not disappoint them. "Ridiculous! Pure fol-de-rol," she said. She dismissed Cleveland's writing as "gush" and questioned what he knew about the woman's sphere. Aren't women themselves the best judge of that? Furthermore, she pointed out, if men were carrying out their responsibilities to enforce the laws about saloons, gambling and prostitution, women wouldn't be so insistent on voting. As for the "cradle" notion, Susan commented that that would be fine if you could keep the boys in the cradle. But they soon get out and get involved in all kinds of corruption. And why shouldn't women be just as able to join clubs of resistance rather than just settle down to the humdrum of housework? After all, she observed, men hang out in clubs and are free to spend their money in saloons. Then these very men return home to abuse their wives, some of whom are actually working to support their husband's bad habits. She closed with a final volley: "I think that Mr. Cleveland is a very poor one to attempt to point out the proper conduct of the women."[36]

Back home, Susan took up one of her final missions: She set out to have women admitted to the University of Rochester. In the East more progress had been made in this regard. Vassar had opened in 1860, followed by Hunter in New York and then Wellesley, Smith and Bryn Mawr. Yet by 1900 only a fourth as many women as men were gaining higher education. Susan persuaded the president of the University of Rochester to admit women and paid the way of the first, who was greeted with boos and shouts. The young woman was forced to leave in two years for health reasons and no more were admitted for the time being. Susan was told that to add more women one hundred thousand dollars would have to be raised for expanded facilities. The figure was eventually lowered to fifty thousand, and Susan raised the money herself, asking money from her sister and a local minister and donating the last two thousand from her own life insurance. The women were in!

## Toward the End

Soon after the victory at the university, Susan was found unconscious in bed. She had had a stroke and it temporarily left her partially paralyzed. Susan was told to rest, but soon rallied and went to a fundraising event in Madison Square Garden. Meanwhile, Ida Harper had finished her two-volume biography of Anthony and had begun to finish the other volumes of the *History of Woman Suffrage*.

Susan at last no longer had to worry about money. Her women's organization set aside an endowment whereby she would receive a regular income of eight hundred dollars per year. But after her stroke she had lost a lot of energy. She still paid visits to her close friend Stanton, who was now well into her eighties, and when it was announced that Stanton had died, Susan was crushed and set out for New York for the funeral. At the wake, she was moved that Stanton had asked that her friend Susan's picture be placed on the coffin.

Susan now began preparing for her own death by disposing of her possessions and making arrangements for her papers. Gaining some new energy, she visited Booker T. Washington at his Tuskegee Institute for black students and spoke to the student body. Then she set out for another trip to Europe where she attended an International Council meeting in Berlin, and proudly watched Carrie Chapman Catt unveil a plan for an international suffrage movement. The leaders were wined and dined at the palace and then traveled through Germany and England before returning home. Though exhausted, she went to Kansas to see her ailing brother and then returned there for his funeral a month later.

Susan continued her travels until the end. Off to a convention in Oregon, then a tour of the West Coast. On to Washington for a celebration of her eighty-fourth birthday in the White House, where she continued to try in vain to persuade Teddy Roosevelt to support women's suffrage. Then to a convention in Baltimore, where she encouraged the women to carry on with the cause, concluding with her famous motto: "Failure is impossible." Her vision was still hopeful, and she saw the dawning of a new day for "women at the editor's desk, women teaching in the colleges, women healing the sick, women practicing in the courts, women preaching from the pulpit and lecturing from the platform—call them the new women or what you please— they are the women the world welcomes today."[37] She believed that women would some day work side by side on an equal level with men in the workplace as well as in the home. She even believed that one day women were likely to become governors and presidents.

The seemingly indefatigable Susan returned to her home in Rochester for the last time. After fifty years of working for women's rights, all told Susan had $2,308 in the bank, two five-hundred-dollar government bonds, five small shares of stock and some land in Kansas that her brother had left her. She made out her will, leaving everything she had to "the cause." Susan once said: "I have had but one object before me all my life. As soon as my mind began to unfold I saw the injustice of the system which deprives woman of the natural rights of the human being. I did not shrink from this…I consecrated myself to the work of reforming this system."[38] Her only regret was that she could not live to see women get the right to vote.

# BIBLIOGRAPHY

Anderson, Floyd, ed. *Council Daybook: Vatican II*, sessions 1, 2. Washington D.C.: National Catholic Welfare Conference, 2005.

Anthony, Katherine. *Susan B. Anthony: Her Personal History and Her Era.* New York: Doubleday, 1954.

Barry, Kathleen. *Susan B. Anthony: A Biography of a Singular Feminist.* New York: New York University Press, 1988.

Blockson, Charles L. *The Underground Railroad.* New York: Prentice-Hall, 1987.

Bowman, Thea. "The Non-Catholic in the Catholic School." Washington, DC: NCEA, 1984.

———. "The Gift of African American Sacred Song," in James Abbington, *Readings in African American Church Music and Worship.* Chicago: GIA, 2001.

———. "Justice, Power and Praise," in Edward Grosz, ed., *Liturgy and Social Justice.* Collegeville, Minn.: Liturgical, 1989.

———, ed. *Families: Black and Catholic, Catholic and Black: Readings, Resources and Family Activities.* Washington, DC: USCCB, 1985.

Bradford, Sarah. *Harriet Tubman: The Moses of Her People.* Butler A. Jones, intro. Gloucester, Mass.: Peter Smith, 1981.

Bredhoff, Stacey. *American Originals.* Seattle, Wash.: National Archives Trust Fund Board and University of Washington Press, 2001.

Buckmaster, Henrietta. *Let My People Go: The Story of the Underground Railroad and the Growth of the Abolition Movement.* Darlene Clark Hine, intro. Columbia, S.C.: University of South Carolina Press, 1992.

Cepress, Celestine. *Sister Thea Bowman: Shooting Star.* Winona, Minn.: St. Mary's, 1993.

Clinton, Catherine. *Harriet Tubman: The Road to Freedom.* New York: Little, Brown, 2004.

Dalton, Frederick John. *The Moral Vision of Cesar Chavez.* Maryknoll, N.Y.: Orbis, 2003.

Downey, John. *A Blessed Weakness: The Spirit of Jean Vanier and L'Arche.* San Francisco: Harper and Row, 1986.

Feister, John Bookser. "We Are All Children of God." *Extension,* April/May, 1989.

Finkelman, Paul, ed. *His Soul Goes Marching On: Responses to John Brown and the Harpers Ferry Raid.* Charlottesville, Va.: Unversity Press of Virginia, 1995.

Franklin, John Hope and Alfred A. Moss, Jr. *From Slavery to Freedom: A History of African Americans.* New York: Knopf, 2000.

Gaughan, Sister Benedict, O.S.B., ed. *Jean Vanier: Selections from His Writings.* Springfield, Ill: Templegate, 1989.

Häring, Bernard. *Free and Faithful in Christ, volume 1: General Moral Theology: Moral Theology for Clergy and Laity.* New York: Seabury, 1978.

———. *My Hope for the Church: Critical Encouragement for the 21st Century.* Peter Heinegg, trans. Liguori, Mo.: Liguori/Triumph, 1999.

———. *The Johannine Council: Witness to Unity.* Edwin G. Kaiser, trans. New York: Herder and Herder, 1963.

———. *The Law of Christ: Moral Theology for Priests and Laity,* volume one. Edwin G. Kaiser, trans. Westminster, Md.: Newman, 1961.

———. *Priesthood Imperiled: A Critical Examination of Ministry in the Catholic Church.* Liguori, Mo.: Triumph, 1996.

Harper, Ida Husted. *The Life and Work of Susan B. Anthony.* New York: Arno and The New York Times, 1969.

Harper, Judith. *Susan B. Anthony: A Biographical Companion.* Santa Barbara, Calif.: ABC-CLIO, 1998, p. 333.

Jones, Arthur. "She Sings a Ululu Story that Began in Africa. *NCR,* September 9, 1988.

Koontz, Christian. *Thea Bowman: Handing on Her Legacy.* Kansas City, Mo.: Sheed and Ward, 1991.

Larson, Kate Clifford. *Harriet Tubman: Portrait of an American Hero.* New York: Ballantine, 2004.

———.*Bound for the Promised Land.* New York: Ballantine, 2004.

Levy, Jacques. *Cesar Chavez: Autobiography of La Causa.* New York: Norton, 1975.

Mandela, Nelson. *Long Walk to Freedom.* New York: Little, Brown, 1995

————. *The Struggle Is My Life.* New York: Pathfinder, 1986.

Marie, Victoria. "Sister Thea Bowman, FSPA: Franciscan, Educator, Prophet, Poet." *Proceedings of the 8th Annual African American Adult Education Research Pre-Conference* (of the 2000 Adult Education Research Conference at The University of British Columbia). Athens, Ga.: University of Georgia, 2000.

Matthiessen, Peter. *Sal Si Puedes: Cesar Chavez and the New American Revolution.* New York: Random House, 1969.

McGowan, James A. *Station Master on the Underground Railroad: Life and Letters of Thomas Garrett.* Moylan, Pa.: Whimsie, 1977.

Meer, Fatima. *Higher Than Hope: The Authorized Biography of Nelson Mandela.* New York: Harper and Row, 1988.

Njemanze, Beatrice. "Sister Bowman Touches Her African Roots," *Mississippi Today,* September 13, 1985.

Nouwen, Henri. *Jesus: A Gospel.* Maryknoll, N.Y.: Orbis, 2001.

————. *Adam: God's Beloved.* Maryknoll, N.Y.: Orbis, 1997.

Pitrone, Jean M. *Chavez: Man of the Immigrants.* Staten Island, N.Y.: Alba House, 1971.

Ruchames, Louis, ed. *John Brown: The Making of a Revolutionary.* New York: Grosset and Dunlap, 1969.

Rynne, Xavier. *The Third Session.* New York: Farrar, Strauss and Giroux, 1965.

Sampson, Anthony. *Mandela: The Authorized Biography.* New York: Knopf, 1999.

Sherr, Lynn. *Failure is Impossible: Susan B. Anthony in Her Own Words.* New York: Three Rivers, 1996.

Spink, Kathryn. *Jean Vanier and L'Arche: A Communion of Love.* New York: Crossroad, 1991.

Taylor, Fabvienen. "Praying." *NCR,* November–December, 1989.

Taylor, Ronald B. *Chavez and the Farm Workers.* Boston, Mass.: Beacon, 1975.

Telford, Emma. "Harriet: The Modern Moses of Heroism and Visions," as dictated to Emma Telford, 1911, on deposit at Cayuga County Historical Society, Auburn, New York.

Ten Boom, Corrie. *Amazing Love.* New York: Pillar, 1976.

————. *Clippings from My Notebook.* Nashville, Tenn.: Thomas Nelson, 1982.

———. *Corrie ten Boom's Prison Letters.* Old Tappan, N.J.: Fleming H. Revell, 1975.

———. *This Day Is the Lord's.* Old Tappan, N.J.: Fleming H. Revell, 1975.

———. *In My Father's House: The Years Before "The Hiding Place."* Old Tappan, N.J.: Fleming H. Revell, 1976.

———. *Father ten Boom: God's Man.* Old Tappan, N.J.: Fleming H. Revell, 1978.

———. *Not Good if Detached.* Fort Washington, Pa.: Christian Literature Crusade, 1959.

———. *A Prisoner and Yet.* Grand Rapids, Mich.: Zondervan, 1947.

———. *Her Story.* New York: Inspirational, 1995.

Corrie ten Boom, with John and Elizabeth Sherrill. *The Hiding Place.* Washington Depot, Conn.: Chosen Books, 1971.

Vanier, Jean. *An Ark for the Poor: The Story of L'Arche.* Ottawa: Novalis, 1995.

———. *The Broken Body: Journey to Wholeness.* New York: Paulist, 1988.

———. *The Challenge of L'Arche.* Ottawa: Novalis, 1981.

———. *Community & Growth: Our Pilgrimage Together.* New York: Paulist, 1979.

———. *Eruption to Hope.* New York: Paulist, 1971.

———. *From Brokenness to Community.* New York: Paulist, 1992.

———. *Man and Woman He Made Them.* Mahwah, N.J.: Paulist, 1985.

Wilkins, John, ed. *Considering Veritatis Splendor.* Cleveland, Ohio: Pilgrim, 1994.

# N O T E S

## Chapter One: Bernard Häring

1. Bernard Häring, *My Witness for the Church* (New York: Paulist, 1992), p. 11.
2. Häring, *My Witness*, p. 11.
3. Häring, *My Witness*, p. 12.
4. Häring, *My Witness*, p. 15.
5. Häring, *My Witness*, p. 15.
6. Häring, *My Witness*, p. 27.
7. Häring, *My Witness*, p. 101.
8. Häring, *My Witness*, p. 67.
9. Häring, *My Witness*, p. 24.
10. Häring, *My Witness*, p. 18.
11. Bernard Häring, *My Hope for the Church: Critical Encouragement for the 21st Century*, Peter Heinegg, trans. (Liguori, Mo.: Liguori/Triumph, 1999), p. 15.
12. Bernard Häring, *Free and Faithful in Christ, volume 1: General Moral Theology: Moral Theology for Clergy and Laity* (New York: Seabury, 1978), p. 63.
13. Bernard Häring, *The Law of Christ: Moral Theology for Priests and Laity*, volume one, Edwin G. Kaiser, trans. (Westminster, Md.: Newman, 1961), p. 99.
14. Häring, *Free and Faithful in Christ*, p. 66.
15. Häring, *The Law of Christ*, p. 100.
16. Häring, *Free and Faithful in Christ*, p. 62.
17. Häring, *Free and Faithful in Christ*, p. 127.
18. Häring, *Free and Faithful in Christ*, p. 131.
19. Häring, *Free and Faithful in Christ*, p. 223.
20. Häring, *Free and Faithful in Christ*, p. 235.
21. Häring, *Free and Faithful in Christ*, p. 253.

22. Reading the "signs of the times" was a core task of the Council. See Edward P. Hahnenberg, "Treasures of Vatican II: Our Compass for the Future," *Catholic Update*, September 2005.

23. Häring, *My Witness*, p. 46.

24. Häring, *My Witness*, p. 53.

25. Floyd Anderson, ed., *Council Daybook: Vatican II*, sessions 1, 2 (Washington, D.C.: National Catholic Welfare Conference, 2005), p. 295.

26. Bernard Häring, *The Johannine Council: Witness to Unity*, Edwin G. Kaiser, trans. (New York: Herder and Herder, 1963), p. 57.

27. Pastoral Constitution on the Church in the Modern World, 1.

28. Häring, *The Johannine Council*, p. 101.

29. Anderson, *Council Daybook*, session 3, p. 174

30. Häring, *The Johannine Council*, pp. 102–103.

31. *Xavier Rynne, The Third Session* (New York: Farrar, Strauss and Giroux, 1965), p. 125.

32. Häring, *My Witness*, p. 60.

33. Häring, *My Witness*, p. 16.

34. Häring, *My Witness*, p. 74.

35. Häring, *My Witness*, p. 78.

36. Häring, *My Witness*, p. 82.

37. Häring, *My Witness*, p. 94.

38. Häring, *My Witness*, p. 93.

39. Häring, *My Witness*, p. 226.

40. John Wilkins, ed., *Considering Veritatis Splendor* (Cleveland, Ohio: Pilgrim, 1994), p. xi.

41. Wilkins, p. 9.

42. Wilkins, p. 11.

43. Wilkins, p. 13.

44. Quoted in Häring, *My Hope*, p. ix.

45. Häring, *My Hope*, p. 13.

46. Häring, *My Hope*, p. 104.

47. Häring, *My Hope*, p. 112.

48. Häring, *My Hope*, p. 112.

49. Bernard Häring, *Priesthood Imperiled: A Critical Examination of Ministry in the Catholic Church* (Liguori, Mo.: Triumph, 1996), pp. 129–130.

50. Häring, *Priesthood Imperiled*, pp. 129–130.

51. Häring, *My Hope*, p. 121.

52. Häring, *My Hope*, p. 129.
53. Häring, *My Hope*, p. 52.
54. Häring, *My Hope*, p. 62.
55. Häring, *My Hope*, p. 63.
56. Häring, *My Hope*, p. ix.

**Chapter Two: Cesar Chavez**

1. Jacques Levy, *Cesar Chavez: Autobiography of La Causa* (New York: Norton, 1975), p. 9.
2. Levy, p. 42.
3. Jean M. Pitrone, *Chavez: Man of the Immigrants* (Staten Island, N.Y.: Alba House, 1971), p. 158.
4. Ronald B. Taylor, *Chavez and the Farm Workers* (Boston, Mass.: Beacon, 1975), p. 61.
5. Taylor, pp. 62–63.
6. Peter Matthiessen, *Sal Si Puedes: Cesar Chavez and the New American Revolution* (New York: Random House, 1969), p. 224.
7. Taylor, p. 64.
8. Levy, p. 85.
9. Pitrone, p. 27.
10. Taylor, p. 83.
11. Matthiessen, p. 321.
12. Pitrone, p. 38.
13. Levy, p. 109.
14. Matthiessen, p. 52.
15. Levy, p. 5.
16. Levy, p. 163.
17. Matthiessen, p. 57.
18. See www.chavezfoundation.org/cesarechavez.html.
19. See http://www.ufw.org/_page.php?menu=research&inc=history/09.html.
20. See www.ufw.org/_page.php?menu=research&inc=history/09.html.
21. Matthiessen, p. 115.
22. Matthiessen, p. 59.
23. Matthiessen, p. 84.
24. Matthiessen, p. 88.
25. Matthiessen, p. 178.
26. Matthiessen, p. 367.

27. Frederick John Dalton, *The Moral Vision of Cesar Chavez* (Maryknoll, N.Y.: Orbis, 2003), p. 120.

28. Taylor, p. 83.

29. Levy, p. 194.

30. Levy, p. 196.

31. Levy, p. 270.

32. Levy, p. 109.

33. Levy, p. 246.

34. Matthiessen, p. 196.

35. Pitrone, p. 162.

36. Taylor, p. 45.

37. Dalton, p. 45.

38. Dalton, p. 155.

39. Dalton, p. 163.

40. Matthiessen, p. 147.

41. Dalton, p. 109.

42. Dalton, p. 108.

43. Dalton, p. 111.

44. Dalton, p. 155.

**Chapter Three: Harriet Tubman**

1. Kate Clifford Larson, *Harriet Tubman: Portrait of an American Hero* (New York: Ballantine, 2004), pp. 213–224.

2. Henrietta Buckmaster, *Let My People Go: The Story of the Underground Railroad and the Growth of the Abolition Movement*, Darlene Clark Hine, intro. (Columbia, S.C.: University of South Carolina Press, 1992), p. 7.

3. Catherine Clinton, *Harriet Tubman: The Road to Freedom* (New York: Little, Brown, 2004), p. 16.

4. Sarah Bradford, *Harriet Tubman: The Moses of Her People*, Butler A. Jones, intro. (Gloucester, Mass.: Peter Smith, 1981), p. 23.

5. Larson, p. 79.

6. Bradford, p. 29.

7. Clinton, p. 36.

8. John Hope Franklin and Alfred A. Moss, Jr., *From Slavery to Freedom: A History of African Americans* (New York: Knopf, 2000), pp. 164–165.

9. Clinton, p. 235.

10. Bradford, p. 30.

11. Larson, p. 88.
12. Clinton, pp. 50ff.
13. Buckmaster, p. 47.
14. Clinton, p. 83, quoting Charles L. Blockson, *The Underground Railroad* (New York: Prentice-Hall, 1987), p. 119.
15. The numbers of trips and people rescued have been exaggerated in the past. See Kate Clifford Larson, *Bound for the Promised Land* (New York: Ballantine, 2004), p. xvii.
16. Clinton, p. 91, quoting James A. McGowan, *Station Master on the Underground Railroad: Life and Letters of Thomas Garrett* (Moylan, Pa.: Whimsie, 1977), pp. 130–131, 135.
17. Bradford, p. 76.
18. Larson, p. 102.
19. Bradford, p. 91.
20. Larson, p. 110.
21. Larson, p. 113.
22. Clinton, p. 126, quoting Louis Ruchames, ed., *John Brown: The Making of a Revolutionary* (New York: Grosset and Dunlap, 1969), p. 188.
23. Clinton, p. 135, quoting Paul Finkelman, ed., *His Soul Goes Marching On: Responses to John Brown and the Harpers Ferry Raid* (Charlottesville, Va.: University Press of Virginia, 1995), p. 218.
24. Larson, pp. 182–183.
25. Buckmaster, p. 292.
26. Clinton, p. 162.
27. Bradford, p. 95.
28. Bradford, pp. 105–106.
29. Stacey Bredhoff, *American Originals* (Seattle, Wash.: National Archives Trust Fund Board and University of Washington Press, 2001), p. 55.
30. Clinton, *Harriet Tubman: The Road to Freedom*, 203, quoting from Emma Telford, "Harriet: The Modern Moses of Heroism and Visions," as dictated to Emma Telford, 1911, on deposit at Cayuga County Historical Society, Auburn, New York, p. 3.
31. Clinton, p. 192, quoting "Harriet Tubman Is Dead," *Auburn Citizen*, March 11, 1913.
32. Clinton, p. 209.
33. Clinton, p. 214.
34. Bradford, p. 77.

## Chapter Four: Thea Bowman

1. Celestine Cepress, *Sister Thea Bowman: Shooting Star* (Winona, Minn.: St. Mary's Press, 1993), p. 36.
2. *Thea Bowman: Her Own Story* (Video), Oblate Media.
3. Cepress, p. 17.
4. Arthur Jones, "She Sings a Ululu Story that Began in Africa," *NCR* (September 9, 1988), p. 4.
5. Thea Bowman, "The Non-Catholic in the Catholic School" (Washington, D.C.: NCEA, 1984).
6. Cepress, p. 97.
7. Cepress, p. 23.
8. Victoria Marie, O.S.F., "A Final Farewell to Sister Thea Bowman," *Viterbo Strides* (Fall 1990), pp. 6–7.
9. John Bookser Feister, "We Are All Children of God," *Extension* (Apr/May, 1989), pp. 24–27.
10. Cepress, p. 100.
11. *Thea Bowman: Her Own Story.*
12. Christian Koontz, *Theo Bowman: Handing on Her Legacy* (Kansas City, Mo.: Sheed and Ward, 1991), p. 36.
13. Jones, p. 4.
14. Cepress, p. 36.
15. Cepress, p. 260.
16. Cepress, p. 10.
17. Cepress, p. 30.
18. Cepress, p. 30.
19. Beatrice Njemanze, "Sister Bowman Touches Her African Roots," *Mississippi Today* (September 13, 1985), p. 7.
20. Cepress, p. 87.
21. Cepress, p. 89.
22. Koontz, pp. 5–6.
23. Cepress, p. 31.
24. Lyn Hartmann, *Milwaukee Journal* (January 17, 1988).
25. Hartmann.
26. Fabvienen Taylor, "Praying," *NCR* (November–December, 1989), p. 20.
27. Thea Bowman, ed. *Families: Black and Catholic, Catholic and Black: Readings, Resources and Family Activities* (Washington, D.C.: USCCB, 1985), p. 11.

28. Koontz, p. 47.

29. Koontz, p. 47.

30. Koontz, p. 80.

31. Cepress, p. 35.

32. Cepress, p. 33.

33. Cepress, p. 32.

34. Cepress, p. 32.

35. Cepress, p. 36.

36. Cepress, p. 34.

37. Cepress, p. 35.

38. Thea Bowman, "The Non-Catholic in the Catholic School" (Washington, D.C.: NCEA, 1984), p. 21.

39. Bowman, "The Non-Catholic in the Catholic School," p. 22.

40. Sister Thea Bowman, "The Gift of African American Sacred Song," in James Abbington, *Readings in African American Church Music and Worship* (Chicago: GIA, 2001), pp. 209ff.

41. Cepress, p. 44.

42. Thea Bowman, *Prayer and Action* (Video), Louisiana Conference, 1987.

43. Thea Bowman, "Justice, Power and Praise," in Edward Grosz, ed., *Liturgy and Social Justice* (Collegeville, Minn.: Liturgical Press, 1989), p. 27.

44. Bowman, "Justice, Power and Praise," p. 27.

45. Bowman, "Justice, Power and Praise," p. 28.

46. Bowman, "Justice, Power and Praise," p. 34.

47. Bowman, "Justice, Power and Praise," p. 37.

48. Cepress, p. 107.

49. Cepress, p. 109.

50. Cepress, p. 110.

51. Cepress, p. 113.

52. Cepress, p. 120.

53. Thea Bowman, *Almost Home* (Video), Liguori Publications, 1989.

54. Cepress, p. 11.

55. Koontz, p. 74.

**Chapter Five: Nelson Mandela**

1. Nelson Mandela, *Long Walk to Freedom* (New York: Little, Brown, 1995), p. 493.

2. Fatima Meer, *Higher Than Hope: The Authorized Biography of Nelson Mandela* (New York: Harper and Row, 1988), pp. 11–12.

3. Mandela, *Long Walk to Freedom*, p. 19.
4. Meer, p. 8.
5. Mandela, *Long Walk to Freedom*, p. 36.
6. Meer, pp. 20–21.
7. Mandela, *Long Walk to Freedom*, p. 77.
8. Mandela, *The Struggle Is My Life*, (New York: Pathfinder, 1986), p. 2.
9. Mandela, *The Struggle Is My Life*, p. 13.
10. Mandela, *The Struggle Is My Life*, pp. 17ff.
11. Mandela, *Long Walk to Freedom*, p. 104.
12. Mandela, *Long Walk to Freedom*, p. 122.
13. Mandela, *The Struggle Is My Life*, p. 34.
14. Mandela, *The Struggle Is My Life*, p. 38.
15. Mandela, *The Struggle Is My Life*, p. 39.
16. Mandela, *Long Walk to Freedom*, p. 136.
17. Mandela, *Long Walk to Freedom*, p. 139.
18. Mandela, *The Struggle Is My Life*, pp. 72–76.
19. Meer, p. 68.
20. Meer, p. 153.
21. Meer, p. 162.
22. Anthony Sampson, *Mandela: The Authorized Biography* (New York: Knopf, 1999), p. 151.
23. Mandela, *Long Walk to Freedom*, p. 241.
24. Mandela, *The Struggle Is My Life*, p. 125.
25. Mandela, *The Struggle Is My Life*, p. 132.
26. Mandela, *Long Walk to Freedom*, p. 252.
27. Mandela, *The Struggle Is My Life*, p. 135.
28. Mandela, *The Struggle Is My Life*, p. 137.
29. Sampson, p. 174.
30. Mandela, *Long Walk to Freedom*, p. 318.
31. Mandela, *Long Walk to Freedom*, p. 322.
32. Sampson, p. 181.
33. Sampson, p. 204.
34. Mandela, *Long Walk to Freedom*, p. 363.
35. Sampson, p. 218.
36. Sampson, p. 227.
37. Mandela, *The Struggle Is My Life*, p. 192.
38. Mandela, *Long Walk to Freedom*, pp. 453–454.

39. Mandela, *Long Walk to Freedom*, p. 456.
40. Mandela, *Long Walk to Freedom*, p. 459.
41. Mandela, *Long Walk to Freedom*, p. 480.
42. Mandela, *Long Walk to Freedom*, p. 497.
43. Mandela, *Long Walk to Freedom*, p. 504.
44. Mandela, *Long Walk to Freedom*, p. 535.
45. Mandela, *Long Walk to Freedom*, p. 540.
46. Sampson, p. 510.
47. Sampson, p. 515.
48. Sampson, p. 570.
49. Mandela, *The Struggle Is My Life*, p. 1.

**Chapter Six: Jean Vanier**

1.  Sister Benedict Gaughan, O.S.B., ed., *Jean Vanier: Selections from His Writings* (Springfield, Ill: Templegate, 1989), p. 12.
2.  Kathryn Spink, *Jean Vanier and L'Arche: A Communion of Love* (New York: Crossroad, 1991), p. 25.
3.  Jean Vanier, *From Brokenness to Community* (New York: Paulist, 1992), p. 13.
4.  Jean Vanier, *The Broken Body: Journey to Wholeness* (New York: Paulist, 1988), p. 71.
5.  Vanier, *From Brokenness to Community*, p. 14.
6.  Gaughan, pp. 16–17.
7.  Vanier, *Broken Body*, p. 72.
8.  Spink, p. 42.
9.  Jean Vanier, *Community & Growth: Our Pilgrimage Together* (New York, N.Y.: Paulist Press, 1979), p. 174.
10. John Downey, *A Blessed Weakness: The Spirit of Jean Vanier and L'Arche* (San Francisco: Harper and Row, 1986), pp. 31ff.
11. Henri Nouwen, *Life of the Beloved* (New York: Crossroad, 1999), pp. 95–96.
12. Vanier, *Broken Body*, p. 18.
13. Vanier, *Broken Body*, p. 102.
14. Vanier, *From Brokenness to Community*, p. 28.
15. Vanier, *From Brokenness to Community*, p. 20.
16. Vanier, *Broken Body*, p. 42.
17. Vanier, *Broken Body*, p. 73.
18. Jean Vanier, *Eruption to Hope*, (New York: Paulist, 1971), p. 3.
19. Vanier, *Eruption to Hope*, p. 28.

20. Vanier, *Eruption to Hope*, p. 33.

21. Nouwen, *Life of the Beloved*, p. 58.

22. Jean Vanier, *The Challenge of L'Arche* (Ottawa: Novalis, 1981), p. 104.

23. Vanier, *Eruption to Hope*, p. 103.

24. Spink, p. 119.

25. Griff Hogan, ed., *The Church and Disabled Persons* (Springfield, Ill.: Templegate, 1983), p. 58.

26. Spink, *Jean Vanier and L'Arche*, p. 67.

27. Downey, *A Blessed Weakness*, p. 12.

28. Vanier, *The Challenge of L'Arche*, p. 21.

29. Vanier, *Community & Growth*, p. 35.

30. Vanier, *Community & Growth*, p. 28.

31. Henri Nouwen, *Jesus: A Gospel* (Maryknoll, N.Y.: Orbis, 2001), pp. xiff.

32. Spink, p. 64.

33. Vanier, *From Brokenness to Community*, p. 23.

34. Spink, p. 184.

35. Quoted in Spink, p. 102.

36. Vanier, *Eruption to Hope*, p. 43.

37. Vanier, *Eruption to Hope*, p. 43.

38. Jean Vanier, *Man and Woman He Made Them* (Mahwah, N.J.: Paulist, 1985), p. 37.

39. Vanier, *Eruption to Hope*, p. 44.

40. Henri Nouwen, *Adam: God's Beloved* (Maryknoll, N.Y.: Orbis, 1997).

41. Gaughan, p. 76.

42. Vanier, *Community & Growth*, p. 116.

43. Vanier, *Community & Growth*, pp. 172–370.

44. Vanier, *Eruption to Hope*, p. 48.

45. Vanier, *Man and Woman He Made Them*, p. 35.

46. Vanier, *Community & Growth*, p. 35.

47. Vanier, *Community & Growth*, p. 116.

48. Vanier, *Community & Growth*, p. 122.

49. Vanier, *The Challenge of L'Arche*, p. 72.

50. Vanier, *The Challenge of L'Arche*, p. 150.

51. Vanier, *Community & Growth: Our Pilgrimage Together*, p. 1.

52. Gaughan.

53. Vanier, *Community & Growth: Our Pilgrimage Together*, p. 5.

54. Vanier, *From Brokenness to Community*, p. 5.

55. Vanier, *From Brokenness to Community*, p. 5.

56. Vanier, *From Brokenness to Community*, p. 7.

57. Vanier, *Broken Body*, pp. 144–145.

58. Gaughan, p. 59.

59. Downey, pp. 86–87.

60. Vanier, *From Brokenness to Community*, p. 9.

61. Vanier, *Community & Growth*, p. 172.

62. Vanier, *Community & Growth*, p. 14.

63. Vanier, *Community & Growth*, p. 25.

64. Vanier, *Community & Growth*, p. 26.

65. Vanier, *From Brokenness to Community*, p. 52.

66. Hogan, p. 61.

67. Vanier, *Community & Growth*, p. 106.

68. Jean Vanier, *An Ark for the Poor: The Story of L'Arche* (Ottawa: Novalis, 1995), p. 115.

**Chapter Seven: Corrie ten Boom**

1. Corrie ten Boom, *Father ten Boom: God's Man* (Old Tappan, N.J.: Fleming H. Revell, 1978), p. 33.

2. Corrie ten Boom, *Father ten Boom*, p. 37.

3. Corrie ten Boom, *Father ten Boom*, p. 38.

4. Corrie ten Boom, *Father ten Boom*, p. 39.

5. Corrie ten Boom, with John and Elizabeth Sherrill, *The Hiding Place* (Washington Depot, Conn.: Chosen Books, 1971), p. 50.

6. Corrie ten Boom, *The Hiding Place*, p. 51. See also Ten Boom, *Father ten Boom*, p. 107.

7. Corrie ten Boom, *In My Father's House: The Years Before "The Hiding Place"* (Old Tappan, N.J.: Fleming H. Revell, 1976), pp. 119ff., 183ff.

8. Ten Boom, *In My Father's House*, p. 149.

9. Ten Boom, *The Hiding Place*, p. 63.

10. Ten Boom, *The Hiding Place*, p. 68.

11. Ten Boom, *The Hiding Place*, p. 72.

12. Ten Boom, *The Hiding Place*, p. 113.

13. Ten Boom, *The Hiding Place*, p. 95.

14. Ten Boom, *In My Father's House*, p. 15.

15. Corrie ten Boom, *A Prisoner and Yet* (Grand Rapids, Mich.: Zondervan, 1947), p. 7.

16. Ten Boom, *The Hiding Place*, p. 93.

17. Ten Boom, *The Hiding Place*, p. 128.

18. Ten Boom, *The Hiding Place*, p. 167.

19. Ten Boom, *A Prisoner and Yet*, p. 132.

20. Ten Boom, *A Prisoner and Yet*, p. 132.

21. Ten Boom, *The Hiding Place*, p. 198.

22. Ten Boom, *A Prisoner and Yet*, p. 165.

23. Corrie ten Boom, *Her Story* (New York: Inspirational, 1995), p. 210.

24. Ten Boom, *Her Story*, pp. 213–214.

25. Corrie ten Boom, *Corrie ten Boom's Prison Letters* (Old Tappan, N.J.: Fleming H. Revell, 1975), pp. 81–82.

26. Ten Boom, *Her Story*, pp. 214–216.

27. Corrie ten Boom, *Amazing Love* (New York: Pillar, 1976), p. 30.

28. Corrie ten Boom, *Clippings from My Notebook* (Nashville, Tenn.: Thomas Nelson, 1982), p. 94.

29. Corrie ten Boom, *Not Good If Detached* (Fort Washington, Pa.: Christian Literature Crusade, 1959), p. 31.

30. Ten Boom, *Not Good If Detached*, p. 31.

31. Corrie ten Boom, *This Day Is the Lord's* (Old Tappan, N.J.: Fleming H. Revell, 1975), p. 48.

32. Ten Boom, *Her Story*, pp. 185–186.

33. Ten Boom, *Her Story*, p. 233.

34. Ten Boom, *Her Story*, pp. 225–236.

35. Ten Boom, *Her Story*, p. 274.

36. Ten Boom, *Her Story*, pp. 306–307.

37. Ten Boom, *Her Story*, p. 467.

38. Ten Boom, *Clippings from My Notebook*, p. 123.

39. Ten Boom, *Clippings from My Notebook*, p. 123.

## Chapter Eight: Susan B. Anthony

1. Judith Harper, *Susan B. Anthony: A Biographical Companion* (Santa Barbara, Calif.: ABC-CLIO, 1998), p. 333.

2. Judith Harper, p. 14.

3. Kathleen Barry, *Susan B. Anthony: A Biography of a Singular Feminist* (New York: New York University Press, 1988), p. 14.

4. Judith Harper, p. 21.

5. Judith Harper, p. 22.

6. Katherine Anthony, *Susan B. Anthony: Her Personal History and Her Era* (New York: Doubleday, 1954), p. 57.

7. Lynn Sherr, *Failure Is Impossible: Susan B. Anthony in Her Own Words* (New York: Three Rivers Press, 1996), p. 4.

8. Judith Harper, p. 27.

9. Katherine Anthony, p. 119.

10. Quoted in Judith Harper, pp. 123–124.

11. Barry, p. 74.

12. Ida Husted Harper, *The Life and Work of Susan B. Anthony* (New York: Arno and The New York Times, 1969), volume 1, pp. 170–171.

13. Sherr, p. 9.

14. Sherr, p. 48.

15. Sherr, p. 48.

16. Barry, p. 102.

17. Judith Harper, pp. 276–277.

18. Ida Husted Harper, p. 62.

19. Judith Harper, p. 81.

20. Sherr, p. 10.

21. Katherine Anthony, p. 228.

22. Sherr, p. 29.

23. Barry, p. 219.

24. Sherr, p. 24.

25. Sherr, p. 310.

26. Sherr, p. 33.

27. Katherine Anthony, p. 293.

28. Katherine Anthony, pp. 296–297.

29. Barry, p. 256.

30. Sherr, pp. 36–37.

31. Judith Harper, p. 164.

32. Sherr, p. 41.

33. Barry, p. 328.

34. Barry, p. 332.

35. Sherr, pp. 29–30.

36. Sherr, pp. 29–31.

37. Sherr, p. 49.

38. Sherr, p. 53.

# INDEX

á Kempis, Thomas, 10
abolitionist movement, 77–79
Adam, Karl, 7
Adams, Abigail (first lady), 77
Adams, John (president), 77
African National Congress, 135, 136, 138, 142–143, 145–146, 149, 151, 154, 157, 159
Afrikaans, 150
AIDS. *See* HIV/AIDS.
Alinsky, Saul, 43
Alphonsus, Saint, 19
ANC Youth League Manifesto, 137
ANC. *See* African National Congress.
Anthony, Daniel, 232, 234, 236
Anthony, Guelma, 234
Anthony, Joshua, 236
Anthony, Susan B.
    abolition and, 243–244
    as headmistress, 236–237
    as teacher, 236
    education, 232, 234–235
    Elizabeth Cady Stanton and, 239, 241, 244, 246, 251, 252–253
    family, 232. *See also individual members.*
    *History of Woman Suffrage,* 251, 257
    on marriage, 238, 241–242
    Quakerism and, 232–233, 234, 241
    on "sex hatred," 240
    slavery and, 234, 236, 243, 244
    Stanton, Elizabeth Cady and, 239, 241, 244, 246, 251, 252–253
    temperance, 236, 237, 239–240
    voting, 249–250
    women's movement and, xiii, 240–242, 244, 246, 247–248
Aquinas, Thomas, 10, 187
Arthur, Chester A. (president), 231
Augustine, Saint, 10

Bantu Education, 141
Battenville, New York, 234

Benedict XVI, Pope. *See* Ratzinger, Cardinal Josef.
Bernard of Clairvaux, 10
Biko, Steve, 151
biographical theology, xi–xii
birth control
    Alphonsus on, 19
    Augustinian view, 19
    Crowley on, 19
    Curran on, 22–23
    Häring and, 19–22
    *Humanae Vitae,* 19–20, 22
    Zalba on, 19
Black Codes, 95
Black Consciousness Movement, 152
Black Power Movement, 152
Blitzkrieg, 207
Boff, Leonardo, 21
Botha, P.W. (South African president), 155
Bowman, Mary Esther, 103
Bowman, Thea
    as "Bertha," 102
    birth of, 102
    black culture and, 108–109, 111–113, 117
    black history and, 110, 113
    black spirituality and, 114–115
    conversion, 105
    on death, 127
    education, 104–105, 109–110
    illnesses of, 106
    lecturing, 101
    on liturgy, 124–125
    music and, 101, 102, 119–120, 123
    religious life, 105–106
    *60 Minutes* interview, 113
    teaching career, 106–107, 110
    the "Thea experience," 121–123
    travel to Africa, 112
    U.S. bishops and, 101
    at Viterbo College, 106, 110–111
    writings of, 115

276